His initial career developed in Local Government, to senior management positions in the London Boroughs and to other Boroughs around London, and from Bristol to Southend and Harrow, etc., then emigration with his family of six to New Zealand when he was required to return and face a three-month trial at the Old Bailey – at the end of which, he was cleared. Another setback enabled him to work in the then Soviet Union as a Project Manager, building the world's second largest plant manufacturing Optical Glass Fibre, which was followed by a period in Ceauşescu's Romania. Being one of the few Englishmen in these countries at the time proved to be very much to his advantage in terms of work opportunities and making many good friends.

Dedication

To Jean, who shared the upheavals, the distress and the everlasting worries of the time; and to Julie, Christopher, Jeremy and Carole, my children, who fortunately were too young then to appreciate the seriousness of the events around us.

Brian Edwards

My Career and Times in the London Boroughs, the Soviet Union and Ceaușescu's Romania

AUSTIN MACAULEY PUBLISHERS™
LONDON • CAMBRIDGE • NEW YORK • SHARJAH

Copyright © Brian Edwards (2018)

The right of Brian Edwards to be identified as author of this work has been asserted by him in accordance with section 77 and 78 of the Copyright, Designs and Patents Act 1988.

All rights reserved. No part of this publication may be reproduced, stored in a retrieval system, or transmitted in any form or by any means, electronic, mechanical, photocopying, recording, or otherwise, without the prior permission of the publishers.

Any person who commits any unauthorised act in relation to this publication may be liable to criminal prosecution and civil claims for damages.

A CIP catalogue record for this title is available from the British Library.

ISBN 9781788784580 (Paperback)
ISBN 9781788784597 (Hardback)
ISBN 9781788784603 (E-Book)

www.austinmacauley.com

First Published (2018)
Austin Macauley Publishers Ltd™
25 Canada Square
Canary Wharf
London
E14 5LQ

Acknowledgements

I would like to record my thanks and appreciation to all my colleagues and all the friends that I made whilst serving in the many positions I held, both here in the UK and when in the Soviet Union and Ceauşescu's Romania, not forgetting the time of my National Service in Hong Kong. These friends and colleagues enhanced my life in so many ways and I shall always remember them with affection and regard.

Synopsis

Anybody picking up this book, other than my close friends or colleagues, will have no idea of what they may expect to find. So hopefully this synopsis will highlight events that I hope will entice the reader to take a greater interest.

I have led a most unusual life and career, with most of the major events following on from my holding senior surveying positions in the major London boroughs, when I, as the chief building surveyor for Camden Council, was suddenly arrested and committed for trial at the Old Bailey, just as I was about to emigrate to New Zealand with my family of six. Obtaining High Court's approval, we continued on with the understanding that we would return when sent for. This, in fact, happened just after 6 months there and we returned only to find that a mistake had been made. Then, in spite of seeking an early trial date, it was finally set for two years later, then after a three-month trial, I was completely cleared of all charges.

Returning to local government, I obtained a higher position for the London Borough of Southwark, when, after a short time there, I was suspended, without accusation, whilst the department was investigated and told that it was likely to take two years!

Fortunately, a friend offered me a very good position, as a project manager, building an optical glass fibre plant in a town some 5-hour car drive from Moscow, which I gladly accepted.

In the then Soviet Union, this turned out to be a most unusual time, with weekends usually spent in Moscow, or sometimes in other towns, like Leningrad (now St Petersburg) or Vladimir. As there were few Englishmen around at the time, we found this to be very much to our advantage.

Just after a year in this position, just when Russia was hoping to share joint venture opportunities with the UK, I started up my own company, together with a Russian colleague and we explored a number of exciting possibilities in Russia and Ukraine, again with interesting experiences.

Following on from Russia and through some friends, I explored the same possibilities in Ceauşescu's Romania, again meeting very interesting people and making good friends.

Along the way and during my career, I met with some very special people. Starting off, and whilst in Camden, for the responsibility of the tomb of "Karl Marx" (which stood me in good stead when later working in the USSR). Made close friends with the Countess and Count of Rome (Romanian), met a Napoleon Pope, the Romanian Secretary of State, had taken out to lunch the present day Countess of Tolstoy, met with the chairman of a very large American company called Westinghouse, the British Ambassador to Moscow, and being invited to attend a dinner with Boris Yeltsin, then President of the USSR and many, many others.

I have written three other books, as follows:

1. An Autobiography – Troubles, Trials and Travels (Three London Boroughs, the Old Bailey, the KGB and Me.)
2. A Spy story – To Romania with Love (The Romanian KGB)
3. A Love story – From Romania with Love.

Also had some poems published in a book of 20 authors.

Chapter 1
The Beginning

The beginning of my career was fairly routine. By good fortune, I was able to attend the then Luton Technical College, in Park Square in Luton which dealt mainly with all aspects of the building industry, all the theoretical and also the basic crafts, bricklaying, plumbing, painting etc., and of course, backed with the appropriate academic subjects. The teaching staff were wonderful, committed, very supportive and friendly and we all thoroughly enjoyed our time there.

When I was 16 years old, it was time for me to move on and choose a specific career. By chance, a local builder by the name of Richardson & Bottoms Ltd had contacted the college head, Dr Charlesworth, looking for a management trainee and my name had been put forward.

It was Jim Richardson, the principal partner, who came one day to consider me for the position, to be indentured in Building Management and trained directly by him over a 5-year period. After a very pleasant interview, he quickly agreed to take me on and I started about a week later.

This was possibly one of the luckiest moments in my career, for Jim Richardson was a unique person, both in character and ability. Very personable and pleasing person to meet and one never forgot him, for he was also remarkably good looking. In fact, he was the spitting image of "Errol Flynn", remarkably so. I once found by chance a picture of him dressed in his military uniform of a captain. He had risen in the ranks from a sergeant, which was a remarkable achievement in those days. Later, I was to witness his effect on almost any woman, for when they met him, they were clearly very attracted by his looks and charm. Many a conquest followed.

He was also utterly honest (not something always associated with small builders), also very fair and supportive, and was my guiding mentor for the next five years and also two years after my return from National Service. In all, it gave me a thorough grounding in the building process.

The firm had a fairly large estate on which they built housing. They also carried out repairs and alterations to almost any type of property, commercial, shops, factories etc.

For the housing on the estate, I quickly had been trained in preparing all the plans for submission to Luton Council for Building Regulation and Planning approvals. Today, so many years later, when I drive past the estate it's quite pleasing to see them all and difficult to imagine that I had indeed designed every one of them.

About three years into the training, Jim decided that I would benefit from a period on site and so I started as a carpenter, having natural skills developed via my interest in cabinet-making. Again, I found this very enjoyable, particularly the high spirits of those working on site. Very quickly I made a close friend of a carpenter named George Gibson and on and off we stayed friends for over 60 years. Sadly, he died recently, aged 96. But the thing I remember about him the most was his remarkable singing ability. There, in the shell of the houses, he would break into a song, his fine tenor voice sailing around the empty walls of the house. He usually sang some Italian Neapolitan love song which we all knew. I liked singing and always sang at home when working in my workshop, so I joined in and I am sure that the entire building site rested a while and enjoyed it. It certainly set the atmosphere for the site which was indeed a very happy one and the memory has stayed with me ever since.

The other partner in the firm was Len Bottoms. He was fairly large in size and had one of those cheery-red faces. His main task was to organise and supervise all the building on the housing sites. He was quite a different sort of person from Jim, but I always got on well with him.

In 1956, I was called up for my National Service and so left R & B for two years, returning to them afterwards.

National Service in Hong Kong 1956 to 1958

I was very lucky, indeed, as I had been selected to do my National Service in Hong Kong, then considered to be the best posting in the British Army. However, it was a cultural shock, as I am sure it was for most young fellows so conscripted. First of all, we had to report to a place called Barton Stacy, on the edge of Wales. It was for a six-week period, during which we would receive our basic training, ready to go to our posting in the Royal Engineers.

I do remember our first day, so strange and so new. We were given our uniform and general kit and then sent to bed in a billet of about 20 young men. Being a rather stressful day, we were all off to sleep very quickly, only to be rudely awakened the next morning at 6 am by a young corporal, shouting, 'Get up, wakey wakey, rise and shine.' I quickly washed and shaved, then out onto a square where we began our basic training in marching and all that goes with it. Then breakfast and onto the next part of our training.

After a while, one became somewhat used to it and had made friends, in some ways almost enjoying it. Though it took some time to get used to being shouted at, though eventually, one became somewhat immune. However, I believe that two young men thought otherwise and actually committed suicide!

However, some memories still stay with me. I remember one young fellow from Wales who in the evening used to swing from rafter to rafter over our beds, just like a monkey, amazing.

Then, on another occasion, we had formed up outside a billet to collect our tropical kit, going in one by one.

When I went in I was amazed to see, behind the counter, one of the Devlin brothers (a nephew of Len Bottoms, the firm's other director.)

Of course, we had a laugh, like fancy seeing you here, and you lucky bastard, and going to Hong Kong. When I had got all my kit, I went back into line. The next person who came out, came up to me and said, 'Do you know the chap behind the desk in there?'

'Yes,' I said, 'we used to work for the same building firm, why?'

'Well,' he said, 'he is calling you all the names under the sun and hopes that the sky falls down on you, very nasty!'

This incident was, of course, a shock then for we had often met at the firm and exchanged pleasantries. But until then I had no idea that he despised me so much. It really was a shock for I was always friendly towards everybody. I suppose he was jealous, as no doubt he had hoped for the position that I had obtained at the firm, he being Len's nephew. However, it was one of life's lessons, for no matter how nice another person may be towards you, you do not always know their true feelings. Sometimes this realisation can take years to materialise.

After Barton Stacy, we went to another camp in Surrey for a few more weeks, until our ship came in to take us to Hong Kong, another major event.

The ship was quite large and had docked at Southampton. It was all very exciting, moving into our new billets, or should I say bunks. At last, the food was acceptable and the routine easy and pleasant. It is such a long time ago that now I cannot remember the precise route. Certainly through the Mediterranean and then the Suez Canal, around the Philippians and then to Hong Kong, and overall, it was a pleasant journey. Once in Hong Kong, we were taken on the back of an army truck, from the docks through Kowloon and then about 19 miles to Tai Lam, where the camp was based, right next to the beach.

Hong Kong was a particularly good posting as the army stationed there really had nothing to do. They were there just in case, as a result, life was somewhat relaxed for all. I can say that my almost entire time was spent relaxing, with a lot of time on the beach, or sailing, and waiting for Friday evening when we would all go off by bus to Kowloon or Hong Kong Island, stay in the YMCA, sightseeing during the day and have a great time in the nightclubs. We always returned back to camp quite tired and ready for another relaxing week.

However, during the winter months the Regiment we, that is the 24th Field Squadron of the Royal Engineers, would go on military exercises up in the hills surrounding the camp. We would go with the 48th Brigade of Ghurkhas, with whom the regiment was attached, a wildly enthusiastic lot who took their military life very seriously. It was two weeks of hard work and discomfort and boy were we glad to get back to camp.

My duties in Hong Kong, that is after I had achieved the same rank as Hitler, (no, not as a "field marshal," but corporal), and was to supervise the staff running the officers mess and make sure that the accounts etc., were all OK. I enjoyed this responsibility and for which my army discharge papers gave me credit.

Life in HK had its moments. On one occasion, we were to take all the silver from the officers mess to the Governors' mansion, there on Hong Kong Island up there on the peak! (They were having a ball!) By chance, I met the Governor, a most charming and friendly chap and we stood there, a drink in hand, overlooking the magnificent harbour and talked about life in general. Rank didn't seem to concern him.

The other special event was our occasional visits to the Portuguese island of Macau (It later went back to the Chinese). We got there by a very pleasant five-hour ferry ride then stayed in a hotel famous for gambling. The hotel had balconies surrounding a centre area where the gambling took place and I can recall them now, leaning over the balcony and lowering their bets by very long lines to the tables below.

Eventually, our national service time came to an end, mine had been from the 13th of October, 1955 until the 28 October 1957, two most unusual years which helped set my way of thinking for the future. (No, not to lie on the beach all day, but to see more of the world and do something with my life.)

So back to the UK to be demobbed at a place called Barton Stacey and then to return to civilian life.

Back to the Firm
1957 to 1962

On my return from my National Service, I, of course, went around to see Jim Richardson who was delighted to see me and immediately arranged for me to start work again for the firm, this time as assistant manager. It almost seemed that I had not been away, for I quickly fitted in and life was very pleasant. At that time, I lived with my parents in 8 Rutland Crescent, in Luton, a very wonderful, happy time with my main interest in cabinet-making taking up a lot of my spare time. So happy was that period in my life that now, even after 55 years have passed, I sometimes drive past the house, stop and think back to those happy times.

When I look back now, I am totally amazed by how my parents coped with everyday demands, particularly, my mother. She had a family of six, herself and husband, Gert and Alf Edwards, my sister Pauline, my brothers, David and Roy, and of course, myself. In those days, they didn't have washing machines, vacuum cleaners, refrigerators, or of course, a car. So each day, my mother would have to cook for us all, do all the washing by hand, clean the carpets, sometimes by removing them and beating on the line, but worst of all, was to get the shopping, she had to walk down a steep hill to town, then laden with two large heavy bags she would struggle up the hill back home. This situation lasted for years and on top of that, we had, for a time, three lodgers, usually service people who were based at Vauxhall, making nine. Of course, my father helped the best he could and we did also. But the most amazing thing was that in spite of this immense workload, she remained always full of good spirits, giving us great support. Even visiting the school's head teachers to see how we were getting on. One thing was very apparent, and that was the wonderful relationship my parents had. Nothing but love and respect for each other, never, ever falling out with each other.

Of course, later on, we did get a car and as we grew older, of course, we did more and eventually, the household appliances, that make such a difference.

"How strange it is that life can only be truly understood and appreciated, retrospectively."

Now I was back from the army, I could see my friend George Gibson and his charming wife Desiree, who only lived a little way away in Silsoe, Beds.

However, I suppose I had changed, or matured to some extent as my interests broadened and I started to go to dances, the main venue being the "London Hammersmith Pally", a large dance hall with a well-known band.

It was there that I met my future-wife Jean Deakins, and of course, we met up as often as could be arranged, as our relationship developed.

After a while, I began to think about the future and how things were going, career-wise. Although very happy at the firm, I sought more and wished to widen my potential. So I began to look through various job adverts, particularly in local government, when I spotted one in Bristol for the Bristol City Housing Department. It would be a very big change, but I was up for it and applied. Not long afterwards, I was asked to attend an interview for the job which was as a buildings inspector, looking after their education premises.

Bristol City Council Education Department
Buildings Inspector
1962 to 1964

It was then early January 1962 and the weather was especially bad, snow and ice etc., However, Jean and I set off by train arriving quite late for the interview so I telephoned and was told that they would wait for me. I remember the first time I saw the Bristol Council House, a quite magnificent building, built with a curved front elevation, in front of which was a moat. The main building was topped with two gold unicorns.

Eventually, we found our way to the interview room and were greeted by senior officials from the education department who congratulated us on making the effort to get there. The interview didn't last long and I was offered the position which, of course, I was delighted to accept.

I gave my months' notice to Jim who understood but was disappointed to see me leave and I have to say that I was quite distressed when actually leaving. It had been a most special time for me with the firm and had been very much more than just a job.

So there in early 1962, Jean and I set off for my first local government position. We had already booked lodging but the weather was still not so good and we arrived a bit late only to be told that we couldn't stay, as we were not married! (It was 1962). So late in the evening, we were rushing around and eventually found a reasonable hotel which wasn't very pleasant as the sheets were very strange, a slippery plastic material which slid off the bed all the time. We only stayed there a couple of nights and then found something more suitable.

I remember going to work the very first day and into the office to meet all my future colleagues. Jean had gone off job hunting.

My very first impression was excellent, they were a very friendly, supportive set of people and I shall never forget them, although by now, most of them have passed away. There was George Reeves (to whom I was attached for initial support), a great colleague and friend, and George Dewfall, generally thought of as the leading inspector (he had been a Major in the army), a really nice person.

George York (he had been a Captain in the army), and Les Wilcox, all extremely nice and very supportive of me, and although I was a lot younger, yet, I felt very much part of the team.

Our function there was to look after the premises of all the buildings under the control of the Education Department. Prepare contracts for small extensions, and above all, supervise the everyday repairs. It was always a pleasure, travelling around Bristol which is a large attractive city, and to the schools where the head teachers usually expected us and were very hospitable and appreciative.

I used to spend quite a lot of time preparing specifications etc., and I shared a room with George Dewfull in a large country house owned by the Council. So life was very pleasant, indeed.

The flat we had first found just after the hotel, was a temporary stopping point when to our great convenience the Department offered us the use of an old house near the university, and within walking distance of the office. I believe the notional rent was just £2 per week, low even then, but it was in need of quite a lot of work to make it habitable. It took me about two weeks to make a kitchen and bathroom, tidy up the lounge and bedroom, and above all, make myself a workroom. There were still a couple of rooms beyond repair. There was even a garage and a large garden. It was heaven.

Our first two children, Julie and Christopher were born in Bristol and I remember well, the enjoyable walks we used to have over Durdham Downs and around the Clifton Suspension Bridge and many others. Yes, Bristol has many special happy memories.

Unfortunately, the only practical way to improve one's career in local government at the time was to move from one job to another and usually, away to a new part of the country.

But my next career move proved easy, for I applied for and had obtained a new position as a Technical Assistant in Bristol's Housing Department, just one floor up in The Council House. Nevertheless, it was a sad day, leaving all my friends in the Education Department, very much so.

Bristol City Housing Department
Technical Assistant
1964 to 1965

Although next door to the Education Department, the Housing Department was quite different. The office I worked in housed five of us, quite a bit younger than those in Education, we were all about the same age, except one, a one-time architect and we were supervised by a senior assistant. I am afraid that now I have forgotten their names but not, of course, the actual people. Just as in Education, they were all very nice, indeed and became good friends. There was a very nice office-atmosphere and we tended to undertake our work in a slightly competitive way. Generally, our work was to improve existing houses and turn them into acceptable housing units. This meant a survey of the present layout and condition, etc. Then the preparation of a plan and specification, ready to go out to tender, supervise the work, then agree on the final account. I remember doing the plans for a new unit and realising that my colleague, alongside me, was attempting to do the same and beat me to the finish. Of course, that was much to the advantage of the Department.

It was a very pleasant working environment, very satisfying in producing newly refurbished houses and flats.
All during this time, we were able to stay in our house and I continued to enjoy my workshop. In particular, I made a chest of drawers (this was whilst in Education). It had a curved front, was inlayed and banded with six drawers and sits behind me as I now write. It had been over to New Zealand and back, see later chapter. The front was made up of 215 little wood-bricks, set and planed to the curve, then veneered and inlaid. A great deal of work and it still looks good.

I should have mentioned before that not so long after we had moved to Bristol, Jean and I got married, which was held up in

Grimsby, where Jean was originally from. Thereafter, we used to make quite frequent visits to her sister and mother and they came down to see us.

We also, of course, went to see my parents who by then had moved to Peacehaven, in Sussex, to a lovely bungalow not far from the cliffs overlooking the sea.

I only stayed in the Bristol housing job for a year when I applied for a job in Southend-on-Sea, in the Architect's Department, as the only surveyor in the department. I remember the interview well. There were about seven of us waiting in an office to be called in for an interview. I recall that I had paid particular attention to polishing my shoes to a high gloss which paid off as I spotted one of the interviewers looking at them. I was eventually called into a room for the interview and it went well, with me being eventually recalled to be told that the job was mine, if I wished. Of course, I said yes please and left the offices in high spirits. Jean and I later enjoyed a celebration lunch downtown. So there we were moving again.

Architects Department
Southend-on-Sea
Sole Surveyor
1965 to 1968

It was, at first, difficult to adjust to the new environment, Bristol had been so nice and there were so many interesting places nearby, whereas Southend-on-Sea was OK, but in a different class. We had found a flat, not so far from the sea but it wasn't very satisfactory, not very soundproofed and we quickly started looking around, eventually finding a newly built semi-detached house on Carlingford Drive, Southend. It had three bedrooms and a built-in garage, which also served as a workshop. The mortgage was a bit tight, financially but we struggled on. We had a very nice neighbour on the right and quite good on our left, so it was OK. Of course, there was the beach which was great for the family and especially, when we had visitors.

The Architect's Department in Southend was in a high-storey block, near to the top and I remember that at the time, and as the children were quite young, I was quite deprived of sleep which affected my memory making it difficult for me to remember where I had left my car, so I stuck a flag on the aerial which made all the difference. It was an open-plan office and I sat there with my drawing board, just like all the other architects. In fact, it wasn't until I was leaving and had made my farewell speech that some of them realised that, in fact, I wasn't an architect.

I am not sure to this day whether that's a good or a bad thing!

Like all local government departments, it had a satisfying and pleasant environment. It must be the selection process that chooses the right people who will blend in and do their stuff.

The chief architect was a Mr Burridge and his assistant was a Mr Astins, who was the one we normally dealt with. Both were very pleasant.

When I first arrived, I sat behind a fellow who previously had been employed by the GLC. He fascinated me in that he did virtually nothing and got away with it. I will not say his name.

He was doing some sort of scheme for work on Southend Pier and I remember it so well, for he would come in, light up his cigarette (one could smoke then), lean back and look at the plan in front of him, tip his head to one side, then after some consideration would rub out a line, then sit back and decide what to do next, which was virtually nothing, perhaps until the next day!

While he was acting this way, I had been out, surveyed a site, drawn up plans, say for garaging, and even gone out to tender. How he ever got away with it, I will never know. But I do recall that when I eventually left the department, I was told that they were amazed at just how much work I had done during my stay there, when at the time I wasn't in my mind, very productive, due to my lack of sleep.

A very interesting project I was given was to design and build a new porte cochère, that is a covered entranceway to their crematorium. I really enjoyed that and it meant frequent visits to the crematorium.

During these visits, I made friends with the two assistants working there, I called them "Burk and Hare". I remember one visit, when one of them offered me a cup of tea whilst he was washing a mug in a bucket with the funeral ash floating on the top! I said no thanks, I have just had one.

It was an unusual experience, as sometimes when I was there, they would be opening up the furnaces to rake up the burning bodies and one time, they opened a door just after the body had been placed in there. The coffin had already burst open in the heat and I could see the flames burning down on the body, which seemed to shrink then attempt to sit up.

No, I decided, when I am gone I shall be buried!

On one occasion, Mr Burridge, the borough architect asked me to join him for a visit to "Porters", one of the few historic places the borough owned.

He had heard of my cabinet working and sought my views on a damaged chest they had there which was apparently of some value. While we were there looking at the chest, two chaps came in who I think had some insurance interest. When one of them remarked to me that he had seen the half-round tables that I had made for an antique shop on the seafront and how good they were. That, of course, was very nice to hear.

I had, in fact, made these tables to earn some money in my Carlingford Drive garage workshop. There were six tables, all made entirely by hand, half-round with the curve made up from little bricks, then veneered and inlaid with drawers at each end and drop leaf flaps. They had four tapered legs with brass ferrules at the base. Then French polished. A great deal of work, six handmade tables. I think I got paid £6 or was it £12 each, which was even then a pitiful sum. But I needed the money. It would be interesting to see now where each one is placed. Over the years, I have made many such tables, some of which sit in Australia, in relatives' homes.

On reflection, our time in Southend was a happy time, especially with the children being young, which meant we made many visits to town on weekends and especially to the beach.

But my career was calling me again and after a good look at what was available, I chose a position, again in an Architect's Department for the London Borough of Harrow. It had the grand title of Chief Technical Assistant.

London Borough of Harrow
Architects Department
Chief Technical Assistant
1968 to 1971

At that time, the Architect's Department was sited just north-west of Stanmore which more or less joins Harrow, the centre of the department was in a very large house, used as the headquarters, surrounded by hutted offices, not unlike those used by the army at their camps, in which we all worked.

For my interview, I went into one of these hutted offices to face the interview panel which was headed by the borough architect, a senior admin officer, and a George Newman, the surveying group leader, he would be my direct boss. The interview went very well and pleasantly, with a great deal of interest shown in me. I liked them all and thought, *yes, I would like it here*. The job was to lead a small group of seven technicians, supervising the maintenance and minor capital works for Housing and Education, very similar, in fact, to what I had already been doing. I think the fact that I was already working in an architects' office helped. It didn't take them long before I was offered the position, which I gladly accepted, producing, almost a sigh of relief from the panel. They said that a Council House would be available for me, if I wished, there in Stanmore, wonderful.

After my usual months' notice, we left Southend and moved into our new home in Sandymount Avenue, Stanmore. It was a typical unimaginative Council House, bland and uninspiring. The worst feature was that the windowsills of all the windows were so high up that when one sat down, one couldn't look out. It also had an antiquated solid fuel boiler.

But it had three bedrooms, a garden and was within easy walking distance of Stanmore, which then was very nice, a bit upmarket from the general Harrow areas. So we were very pleased and grateful.

Unfortunately, the house in Southend hadn't been sold before we left, and the sale dragged on for some time before it finally sold.

Whilst in Stanmore, Jeremy was born, another delightful addition. Though we have always called him Joe, after his favourite TV programme called "Little Boy Joe". He was so delightful and contented and had really lovely looks, so much so, people would stop us while we were out walking and say, 'Oh, what a lovely little girl!' On one occasion, Jean was wheeling him around Bernay's Gardens in the centre of Stanmore, Joe had been looking at an old gardener working there, when he said, 'Look that man has a miserable face!' The poor fellow heard and looked uncomfortable, so Jean apologised and said, 'Oh please take no notice!'

At work I had my own little office, and my colleague of the same rank, Phil Tyler, had his. At the end of the corridor, George Newman had his office where we spent many a time, either getting instructions or giving him feedback. George was a very committed chap, hardworking and extremely conscientious, which, at times, became a bit of a pain. But he was very nice and we even had a very nice social friendship with him. The entire office had a nice feel, better I thought than the feel of the architect's sections.

The work was very nice also, getting around the borough and seeing the work at hand, meeting the contractors and monitoring the work's progress. The three years there seemed to go by very quickly, very quickly, indeed and I have happy memories of my time there, now thinking back and seeing in my mind the old, large house in the centre and the surrounding hutted offices, across the road was some sort of Royal Air Force place, and at the main gate, they had a "spitfire" placed to give effect and character. Now, the entire site of the house and offices has been developed into a modern housing estate.

One of my duties was to look after Grimsdyke, the one-time home of "Gilbert and Sullivan", the famous musical composers, a very pleasant duty. The main house was very large and grand and was surrounded by magnificent gardens, maintained by a very well-known gardener called Mr Baker. It was always so nice on a good day to go there and look around. It even had a small lake. Many, many years later, I happened to be in Harrow and as I had some time to spare, I thought, *I know I will go up to Grimsdyke and have a look around.* When I got there, I went to the bar which was closed.

Then, just as I was wondering what to do next, in came a Chinese-looking fellow with a woman. I immediately realised that it was "Li Kuan Yew", the one-time President of Singapore and perhaps, his wife. He was extremely pleasant and very grateful when I got the bar open and we chatted for some time. I regret now that I didn't ask him if he really was who I thought, but I was just too well-mannered to do so. I assumed that he had been educated at Harrow Public school and had visited there and now Grimsdyke.

Sometimes in Stanmore when I was going along the Avenue, I would look over and see the house where Roger Moor (James Bond) lived and sometimes even see him there in the front garden brushing up leaves or see his beautiful wife and children at the local bank.

Whilst in Stanmore, we often went off on weekends to see either, Jean's parents or my parents who then lived not so far away in Luton.

After a while, we really got fed-up with our house and thought about finding another place. I cannot remember now but somehow we found a suitable house in a new estate, in St Albans. The price was just about manageable. It was a mid-terrace, three-bedroom house, with an integral garage. So we bought it and I then commuted to Stanmore each day, which I enjoyed.

Again, I made my workshop at the end of the garage, which was fine, except the young neighbours were a bit of a bind.

I had been cutting through the wall between the garage and kitchen when the young wife complained of the noise. *A good start* I thought, *just wait until I start my woodworking properly.*

On another occasion, we were quite shocked to see that a contractor had turned up while we were out and had taken up the fence that divided us and reset it just "50 mm more" onto our side. Apparently, the girl's father, an architect and a very stuffy and unfriendly character, had measured the garden on their side and decided that the measurements were wrong. I checked and found that they had come some 10 mm too far onto our side, so I wrote a note on the fence saying so. We never heard anything more. Eventually, I built a 6-feet high brick wall between us, some 3 metres long from the party wall.

On the other side, the neighbour was quite friendly, too friendly, in fact, for one could never just go into the garden without him being there and starting a long conversation. Even hanging out the washing would provoke him.

Across the cul-de-sac road was another neighbour who would come and chat, usually when I was washing my car. He was quite pleasant, a school teacher, seemed like a nice chap.

Then, sometime later, I bought a new car, cars are a big thing with me. From that moment on, he never spoke to me again, unbelievable, one would think that a school teacher would be beyond that sort of petty jealousy.

Eventually, I thought it was time again for a better job, which as usual, meant a move to another town. After some search, I found a really good one, which was for the position of a surveying group leader, within the Architect's Department of The London Borough of Camden, one of the leading London boroughs. So I applied and was called for an interview.

The London Bough of Camden
Surveying Group Leader
1971 to 1975

I was about 11 years old, at school, when a close friend told me that he was moving to New Zealand with his family to start a new life. He told me some of the things he has learnt about life there and it sounded simply wonderful. His excitement was so infectious that it stayed indelibly etched in my mind and whenever I got fed up in my later life, my mind would go there and wonder.

It was in 1971, when I obtained my first major position within the London boroughs, as chief building surveyor in the Architect's Department of the London Borough of Camden, a prominent London borough, within the local authority scene. Actually, the job started out as "surveyor group leader", but was soon changed to chief building surveyor by Sydney Cooke, the borough architect. He was really a true gent, by any understanding of the word and a very charismatic person.

Everybody in Camden was very nice and looking forwards and backwards in my local government career, they were the very best. Even my interviews were different. The first interview was with Sydney Cooke, the borough architect and Len Williams, the office manager, and then afterwards, for Council confirmation, with the Committee. Once appointed, I was warmly congratulated by everybody, then over to the pub opposite the Town Hall for drinks. Even the chief executive was there. Camden appeared to be a very nice borough indeed.

My immediate chief was Trevor Wall, a very nice, capable, hardworking assistant borough architect. So hardworking, in fact, he actually got sick due to overworking a number of times.

There was one person between Trevor and Sydney Cooke and it was the deputy borough architect, Peter Clapham. There was no love lost between Peter and Trevor, though it was more on

Trevor's side than Peter's. I never did find out the real reason. When seeking new surveying staff, I would either be in the interviews with Trevor or Peter.

It was more entertaining with Peter, as he had a lighter attitude to life, in general.

On one occasion with Peter, we had spent some hours without success and Peter said, getting rather impatient, 'What was wrong with those, surely one would have done?'

At that moment, I spotted, through the partially open door, a really beautiful young woman going down the circular staircase, just outside the door, and I said, 'There, Peter, you see that? Now, if she had applied then it would have been an immediate appointment!'

'Really,' said Peter, with a twinkle in his eye. 'Actually, she is my daughter and she is here for a day to help out.'

Whilst working in Camden, I lived in Harpenden in Hertfordshire, with Jean, my wife and our four children, Julie, Christopher, Jeremy and Carole. Each day, I would commute by car to the office in Holborn.

As chief surveyor, my general duties covered an extensive programme, which was the conversion of old housing stock, described in local government jargon as "The Rehabilitation Programme". This was a major political part of Camden's programme. There were also structural surveys and the maintenance of the Council's public buildings, libraries, swimming pools, etc., but excluding the maintenance of housing, which was carried out by the Housing staff.

Some of our projects were very large and demanded considerable management input and design. Some we put to outside firms of specialists, architects, engineers, etc.

I was assisted by a staff of 35, including Trevor James, my deputy, a very nice, able fellow and Alec Harney, the senior surveyor looking after the maintenance group. We never had the full 47 compliment of staff, due to the Council's difficulty in attracting suitable people, hence, the need to place some work with outside consultants.

When I first joined Camden in 1971, the group for which I was responsible, had an overall programme valued at £1.6 million. When I resigned in September of 1975, this had expanded to some 22 million, a great deal of money at the time.

This expansion of work and responsibility greatly increased the pressure and the considerable frustrations of working within the bureaucracy of local government and was a major contributory factor in my final decision to emigrate to New Zealand.

In late 1973 to early 1974, I used to walk down to New Zealand House in the Haymarket, during my lunch periods, sometimes with Trevor, who was the only other person aware of my plans, looking at the spectacular pictures of the country and read up on the possible employment prospects. This way I obtained a good understanding of how it might be to live there.

By then, I had written to numerous people and various public bodies, putting out feelers for a suitable job in the building industry.

Names were passed around and I wrote to many people including about 40 firms. In spite of a mini building boom in New Zealand, at the time, I only had one really interesting response and that was from a fairly large builder in Hamilton, a town in the north island. The firm was called Peter Holman and Co., Peter Holman himself had seen an advertisement I had placed in a local journal and thought to follow it up. We corresponded for some time and eventually, he made an offer including the finding of accommodation, after an initial stay at a motel, all at his expense. I also think he had to pay part of the cost of our assisted passage, by the New Zealand Government.

A critical point in my life had been reached when I had to make a decision that would affect not only me but the future lifestyle of my wife and four children. At this time I had been looking elsewhere in England, just in case I could appreciably better myself and had two invitations for an interview. In addition, I had applied for the post of assistant director in my present department and had I succeeded, I may have rethought the New Zealand venture.

But I was not appointed to that post and looking back feel that the events happening around me in the Council, of which I was generally unaware, seriously affected the judgement of those making the selection.

About this time, the summer of 1974, I was told of difficulties concerning police enquiries in regard to four of my maintenance surveyors.

Each, in turn, began to come into my office and tell me of the interviews they had had with the police, regarding allegations of corruption in their work and all were related to one contractor.

Although this contractor was under the supervision of various area surveyors, I held overall responsibility, albeit with Alec

Harney, the senior maintenance surveyor, who was responsible for their direct supervision.

I was particularly concerned because I had purchased from this very contractor, a range of building materials and a washing machine, all at wholesale prices and to the total value of £250. This came about via a discussion I had with the contractor whilst having lunch with him. I told him of my interests in working on my house and in practical subjects, particularly joinery making. The contractor explained that he owned a wholesale builders merchant, with an electrical side-branch.

He suggested that I might wish to take advantage of the discounted rates if I were to purchase materials from his company. This would also have the added advantage of everything being delivered in bulk, in one go.

One of the main problems in doing any building work personally was the incredible amount of time one would spend in going to various merchants, in getting the materials. It can be a large, frustrating proportion of the entire time anybody involved in the building trade will fully understand, others may not!

I had started the extension to my house in August of 1972, which was the provision of a utility room adjoining the garage and a small extension to the garage itself, all to be finished in May of the following year.

Concerning the making of the New Zealand decision, I decided that to be entirely sure I had better go over there and see for myself, by an exploratory visit. This I did in August of 1974, having arranged overdraft finance from my Bank. I explained to a Mr Britain, my friendly bank manager, the purpose of the request and there were no difficulties. The visit was well-worthwhile and enabled me to identify the possibilities and changes of lifestyle and whether we would be happy there. I met with Peter Holman, establishing that the firm was solid, with an excellent reputation.

It seemed to be a wonderfully fulfilling opportunity, none of the present frustrations and to a really beautiful country. So Jean and I decided, "Yes, we would go!".

I remember feeling so very happy about this decision, so happy that our lives would be so good, with the potential of that wonderful country. One day I was walking through Camden from Holborn Town Hall to a meeting at St Pancras Town Hall when I met the deputy chief works manager. We had a few friendly words and I particularly remember him saying, 'Do you know, I have never seen you looking so good, so well.'

He went on about this, with me thinking, *yes, life is and will be good in New Zealand and already I am benefiting.*

Being aware of the interviews with the police, I was not at all surprised to receive a telephone call from John Green, the assistant director of architecture, informing me that the police would like to have a chat with me concerning the other surveyors and seek an explanation of our procedures, etc. He made a particular point of stressing that the inspector concerned, a Detective Chief Inspector Reader, had said that in no way was "I" under suspicion. I was merely being asked to assist in Council procedure. As a result, I telephoned Chief Inspector Reader and made an appointment for the 1st of May, 1975.

The visit to the police station went as follows. I arrived at Leman Street police station, which is on the east side of London, at about 10:45.

Other than being fined for no lights on my bicycle when I was 16 years old, this was the only time I had ever been in a police station. The desk officer seemed completely unaware that he had Scotland Yard upstairs but managed to eventually locate them and I was then collected by two detective sergeants, a John Hine and a something Reynolds, then taken by lift to the fifth floor.

They sat me down facing them across a desk and began. They explained that Inspector Reader was busy and would see me in due course and that in the meantime, they would go over the general situation. They briefly described the enquiry and that I was no doubt aware of the interviews already carried out with the other four surveyors.

I was then asked if I had received anything at all from the firm Rawlings and Lucas.

'Yes,' I said, 'a whole range of building materials.'

Then they asked, 'Hadn't you received this material as a favour and wasn't it true that you would not be paying for them, and that it was worth about £80?'

I said, 'No, of course, I would be paying for it and that it was worth a lot more than £80.'

I was then quite aggressively pressurised about the time between receipts and the fact that I still hadn't paid, and what about a washing machine? I hadn't mentioned that in with the materials.

I explained again that I had all or most of the invoices and delivery tickets at home but never had a ticket for the machine, which arrived separately and that I was still waiting for an account of it all, having chased the contractor many times to submit one.

This they chose to disbelieve, making the same accusations as before.

I tried to explain that this particular contractor was exceptionally slow in submitting accounts for the Council work and that they had promised that I would get an account in due course and that I was not to worry as I would eventually get one. I was then asked about receiving a gold watch and a car from the same contractor!

At this I became quite angry, explaining that I had bought my present watch during my National Service in Hong Kong, some years ago and which I wouldn't wish to change.

Also, my present car was purchased through a Council loan and it would be very easy to confirm my statements if they took the trouble to check before making such accusations.

I said that I had come down willingly to the police station to assist, but clearly under false pretences and strongly objected to being accused in this way. I believe it was Hine who said that I was not being accused. At this point, one of them left the room and a few moments later, I was taken into another room and introduced to Detective Inspector Reader and a police constable.

The interview with the two Sergeants had taken the time up to 12:50 pm, approximately two hours, of which no notes or records were made. Incredibly, the entire episode was later "denied" by the two sergeants, whilst under oath in the witness box! It was a disturbing and quite shattering experience.

I was completely green to police procedures, had never been accused of anything before and was utterly unprepared for the sudden aggression of the two sergeants. I was, therefore, not in a very happy state of mind when Reader said he would be formally interviewing me and that I would have to read, agree and sign every page prepared by the constable.

I never thought to complain to Reader about the previous interview, as I assumed it was standard police procedure, applied to soften up and speed up confessions from accused persons.

It was only later, years later, in the Old Bailey dock, when I learnt the event had been quite a serious breach of the judge's rules. The interview with Reader was a much more civilised affair. He was always careful, courteous and fairly friendly.

Tea was provided at reasonable intervals and no pressure was applied.

He went over the same ground as taken by the two sergeants and every page was checked by myself and initialled. His constable was also a reasonably pleasant person, almost a friendly face in such a place. I never had any complaints about the way I was interviewed by Reader, at this time or in the interviews held on the 26th of June and the 11th of August, 1975.

Normally, he would telephone me and ask me to come down to the station for another interview.

I learnt later from the other surveyors that he was not as careful or pleasant with them at their interviews, as he was with me. Sometimes theirs were conducted without refreshments. I believe, like most police officials he was taken up with status and titles.

One time, he said to me that he could not find my name listed amongst the senior officers of the Council. He would not, for only people like the borough engineer, planner, architect, chief executive, etc., would be there, as statutory officials of the council. My grand title of Chief Building Surveyor was a good move from that of Group Leader and always seemed to impress people.

Back at the office, I made a point of seeing the director of architecture, Alfred Rigby, Sydney Cooke had retired sometime before and sadly, later died from some blood infection. I told him what had happened and how I had gone down to the police station, under false pretences.

He listened sympathetically and suggested that I should make urgent contact with a solicitor, even suggesting that I use the one he had. In the circumstances, it was a very open gesture of support, and much appreciated. I thanked him and said it would probably be better if I were to find one myself. This I did through a recommendation I had from a friend, on the pretext that I had a colleague who needed a solicitor, one familiar with the building industry.

It was the following day that I met the senior partner of the law firm, a barrister, and related to him the whole sorry story.

It was a very difficult thing to do, to a complete stranger, as I was to learn so many times over the following years. I particularly sought advice on whether or not I should pay the contractor for the materials and washing machine straight away. I explained to him the difficulties I had previously in persuading the contractor to even think about an account, let alone send me one. He thought about it very carefully and said I should evaluate the cost to the best of my ability, based on the delivery tickets, I held and send him a cheque.

The evaluation had already long been made, as I had estimated the cost in some detail, as each of the materials arrived.

So off went the cheque, in the sum of £270.15 and very soon after it was returned to me undrawn by the contractor's solicitor, saying that the police had been informed of events.

On the 11th of August, 1975, I was again invited by a phone call from Reader to attend another interview, down at Leman Street Station. I didn't look forward to this, recalling the aggressive nature of the beginning of the first interview and the accusations made, but this time set off accompanied by my solicitor, who was a bright, young chap called Wignall and I think, though I am not so sure now, that I went alone on the third occasion.

Reader looked a bit like a character from "Z Cars" a TV series. He was of medium height, strongly built, with dark hair, well Brylcreamed back. He wore a suit, which I have always thought must have been his demob issue and had the look of a policeman all over him. Although he always acted in a civilised way towards me, it became crystal clear that he thought I was guilty and after each interview, we would chat quite freely, and from these times I learnt of his views with some alarm!

It must have been after the first interview, or possibly the second that Browne, one of the surveyors, who had already been interviewed by the police, came into my office and said that during a discussion with the police, Reader had said to him, and I quote: 'I am going to get that fucking bastard Edwards if it is the last thing I do!' At that, my faith in the British Legal system waned a little.

Reader once quoted a conversation to me that he had overheard in his local pub, talk between two local government officers, who were discussing illegal gains. Reader remarked that he believed "all" local government officials were, as he put it, "on the take". Thinking of all the people I knew in service, I asked him, 'Surely, you cannot be serious?'

And he said, 'Oh yes, I am'.

The interview ended at approximately 12:50 am and I went back to the office in a troubled state of mind.

The second interview was conducted as before by Detective Chief Inspector Reader, with the constable taking notes. My solicitor also made complete notes, but in any event, I never questioned the contents of those written interviews, always prepared to sign each page as correct.

Each interview seemed less tense as they progressed and Wignall thought that if I didn't hear again within a reasonable time, I should generally assume that they were satisfied and that I need not worry. Knowing by now Reader's noted beliefs and of his remarks to Browne, I was not so sure it would be that simple.

By this time we were totally cleared to go to New Zealand, having had our x-rays, medicals, interviews and so on. My new employer was waiting, with temporary accommodation arranged, and I even had the boat tickets. The house had been sold and all our worldly belongings, crated, ready for shipping.

My car was to be picked up at my aunt's house in Southampton, arranged this way because the ship sailed from that port.

These simple, few words hardly convey the months, the years of planning. The countless letters and discussions, as to whether we should really go or stay and make a life here.

The acceptance that we were really going to say goodbye to my parents, relatives and friends, and that I was leaving local government for good, to be able to fulfil my dream, to work and live in New Zealand. In spite of our enthusiasm, it was still an extremely heart-rending decision.

After a discussion with my solicitor, I rang Reader on the 16th of August with the intention of going down to Leman Street Station and telling him of my emigration plans. He seemed pleased to hear from me and I think it was late afternoon when I arrived at the station.

When I started to speak to Reader I got a distinct impression that he thought I had come down to make a confession! He seemed a little irritated when he realised otherwise and said that he already knew of my plans anyway.

Whether he was telling the truth, or bluffing I never found out, but he certainly didn't seem surprised. The conversation was informal, no notes were taken and it ended by Reader being fairly friendly and saying he hoped he would have enough further questions for his chief to justify sending him to New Zealand, to question me again.

While chatting I casually asked him if he had met Alfred Rigby, the director of architecture.

'Why?' he said. 'What do you know about him?' I was shocked at his comment, implying that he was guilty of something and it only went to reinforce my view that Reader, in particular and possibly all police officers thought everybody guilty.

That they hadn't been found out yet! I have often thought about that comment and still do so, all these years later. Perhaps it's a standard part of police training, to assume that everybody is guilty of something!

We shook hands and off I went, but just before going he sought to know the place and date of the sailing time of the ship.

I had the impression that at last, the police were really satisfied with my evidence.

Why not, I had copied all the building material delivery tickets and sent them on and also provided other information, such as the time Sam Weller, the deputy chief quantity surveyor had witnessed the threatening and almost uncontrolled phone call I had received from Rawlings.

Notice of my resignation was given to the director of architecture in Camden and I had the last week off for leave, to say our last farewells. The acceptance of my notice happened remarkably, by a brief curt note, so abrupt after the four and a half years hard enthusiastic service.

I found out later, much later, that I was the last person to be aware of what was going on, the talks the police had with the Council and those between members and senior officers. An invisible finger of suspicion had certainly been pointing at me!

I have often wondered, these many years later, what those people thought when I was completely cleared, but more on that aspect later.

The days between my leaving Camden and the sailing date were intensely busy. The furniture people moved in and virtually wrapped up everything in the thick padded-paper, from soft toys to garden rakes. The house seemed full of nothing else.

We were taking absolutely everything.

My garage was full of choice pieces of timber from old mahogany table tops to pieces of boxwood that I had cut from the Bristol Hills, years ago, quite apart from half a dozen tea chests full of nails, paints, stains etc., and not forgetting all my numerous tools.

The packing process was quite a strain, both physically and psychologically, after all, we had spent some two and a half years in that house and Carole, our youngest daughter was born there. I also had a soft spot for Harpenden and the Common, which was almost on our doorstep. The process of packing took about two days and my sister Pauline came over from Luton to help out. It was nice to have her around at such a moment.

About two-thirds way through the packing, we went down to Peacehaven to spend a few days with my parents before the final off. Then back to the house to see how they had managed. There was a bit of a mess and few things not packed, just left about. But they had gone, at last and so had most of the house contents.

There was a note left by one of the packers on the telephone. It said that a Mr Reader had phoned and wanted me to ring him urgently. The phone had been disconnected; calls could still come in but could not be made out. So I walked down to the local phone box, wondering what he wanted now.

He said would I go down to the station tomorrow morning. He said come on Friday as he had some urgent questions he must put to me. This was extremely inconvenient as we were travelling up to Jean's home in Grimsby, to a big farewell party with her relatives. But he insisted so I arranged to come down, all the way from Grimsby on Saturday, having dropped the family off there. Then I could return straight away afterwards, hopefully back in time for the party. A bit of a hand full, but I could not see an easier way.

Walking back to the house, I noticed a Mini parked outside in which sat the two sergeants, Hine and Reynolds. I went up to the car and they said that one of them lived out this way and they were calling to make sure I telephoned Reader. 'I just had,' I said and went into the house. Jean remarked they had called earlier and what a strange sinister couple they were!

With the house finally cleared out and swept up, we wandered around the garden and around each room, in turn.

I tried hard to fix them in my mind, the shape and colour and above all our times in them. Then the very last pulling too of the front door, and we were off to Grimsby.

We drove out onto the common, through lovely Harpenden and headed for the A1, wondering when and how much older we would be and when we were next to see the place again.

It is difficult to remember the exact times and dates after all this time, unless they are recorded in correspondence, but I think it was arranged that I would see Reader again at Leman Street Station at about mid-afternoon. It is some 200 miles from Grimsby to London and I drove down, parked the car somewhere near the station and went inside to find him.

Reader was not in his usual room, but a much larger office. I cannot recall, for sure, who else was there except for one of the assistant constables. Perhaps there were more than two of them. I sat down and Reader, somehow looking slightly different from usual, said that it was his duty to charge me and he would read out the precise charges against me, and then ask if I had anything to say at the end.

Three charges I believe, related to the alleged corrupt receipt of building materials and a washing machine.

He asked me if I had anything to say. I said no and he then asked me to empty all my pockets, making a list of the items, commenting on the small amount of cash I had on me. After a while, I got it all back.

During the reading of the charges, I began to appreciate what was happening to me. I felt numb, partially shocked I suppose. It was like watching a play through another person's eyes, except that person was me!

My uppermost thought was our plans for emigration, literally only days away before the sailing date. What would happen now? In fact, Saturday was the planned sailing date.

Reader said could I arrange bail? I would need a surety of so many pounds, so much to justify my release on bail. Preferably two people were required.

The only person amongst the whole of my relatives who might have some money, was my bachelor Uncle Edward, living in Hove and being an ex-policeman himself, was ideal.

Using their phones I rang him up, being lucky to find him in. I explained the situation and he didn't seem overawed by the news and said yes, of course, he would support bail. I thanked him and passed him over to Reader who explained that he would have to go to the local police station in Hove and sign various forms. On completion of these, Hove Station would phone him back at Leman Street to confirm completion. Several calls went to and fro. Reader getting impatient with the slowness of the local police. I rang my youngest brother, Roy living in Alton, Hants, as the other person to bail me and explained the situation to him. I think it was a bail of £2,000 that was required. He obviously sounded shaken and I could hear my sister in law saying to him,

'Yes, of course, you will stand bail'.

Then once more, many more calls made and the to and froing on the telephone between the stations. Either during this time or just afterwards I was required to go to the basement for fingerprinting and photos, a process to be part of the arrest procedure. I sat full frontal whilst the camera was adjusted, in a sliding frame arrangement, and then in profile. I expect whatever they say they will "still" be there, somewhere in the police records. I never saw the results, but they couldn't have shown me at my best!

I wasn't exactly clear headed at the time, even though the attending constable asked me how I managed to remain so calm in these circumstances and was so helpful. It was perhaps that I suffer shock slowly, it possibly being an English trait and not like the reaction one might expect from say a more excitable Greek or Italian person.

Above all, I couldn't believe it was happening. Not even when my fingers were pressed into the black ink for fingerprinting. We then went back upstairs again into the office with Reader and the others. They were pleasant, generally chatting; we had tea on several occasions and possibly something to eat as well.

I had the feeling that they were relieved to be at an end of their stint in that police station and onto something else. Reader said that they were usually the "Murder Squad", I said, perhaps unwisely, 'Perhaps I ought to commit one to keep him employed!' Realising then by the look on his face that he wasn't at all amused.

Quite a long time passed before the bail arrangements were completed. Reader explaining that I was on bail and would have to appear before a magistrate at the Thames Magistrate's Court, the following Monday.

I asked Reader for an envelope and some paper so I could drop a note into the office of my solicitor. For a moment, I thought he was going to refuse. He certainly didn't seem keen to help, but he did and I wrote the note, explaining fully what had happened and said I would be at their offices prior to the court hearing on Monday.

The day of my arrest was Saturday the 14th of September, 1975 and I was due to sail on the 18th. It all seemed quite impossible then, that we would be able to go and miracles were too much to hope for. I left the police station some in the early evening, to find my way back to the car.

All of a sudden, it all became a little too much and I knew that I couldn't immediately drive all the way back up to Grimsby, and if I were to attempt the journey I would be too distracted to be safe on the road. I thought of Jean and all her relatives gathered in a country restaurant for the big farewell party.

A very real precious moment for her and I knew that even if I drove off then I wouldn't be able to make it on time. The best thing to do, so it seemed at the time, would be to drop off the letter at the solicitors and call in on a friend in London, then phone the reception in Grimsby and try to explain the delay.

This I did, my friend being quite shaken by the news, but being particularly understanding. He suggested that I couldn't possibly drive back and it would be best if I stayed at his place until the Monday court hearing. So I would telephone Jean and tell her what happened and that by staying I would be fresh for the hearing, to face whatever was to happen next.

I telephoned the restaurant and with great difficulty managed to persuade them to contact the party by naming my brother in law, Grenville Page. Gren came to the phone and I explained, the best I could about what had happened. He was really very good and said he would do his best to let everybody know.

How he did I will never know. It must have been incredibly distressing for Jean, and all her family and I have often thought about that time, never being able to ask her directly, for fear of reminding her of the pain of that terrible time.

Monday morning came around quickly and I was at my solicitor's office, in the Temple the minute they opened. They were already fully underway trying to locate a barrister. I think the court hearing was at 10:00 am and I wondered if the police had arranged it so I couldn't find a barrister in the short time available. In fact, my solicitor was unable to find one and said that it might be possible to do so at the court.

We drove off in my car with my lady solicitor and we found the court, over on the East End of London. Jean and her sister Margaret and my brother in law were already there, looking very apprehensive, but having come, to some degree, to terms with what had happened. I still had a job in coming to terms with the situation; but will explain that later on, much later on.

Also at the court were the four maintenance surveyors, Browne, Todd, Evans and Beavers. The last was now an ex-employee of Camden, having changed his job. The other three were still employed there. All had been charged with receiving bribes. We exchanged a few brief words, prior to going into court. My Uncle Edward was also there from Hove, to confirm that he was providing part of the bail.

By now, we were looking desperately around for a barrister and, as time was getting on, had no choice but simply ask the first one we came across in the court's central lobby. Then we spotted one, through a large number of people gathered there. This was one of my most lucky moments in the entire wretched affair, for Mr Hartley-Booth, barrister, was a unique find.

He was so enthusiastically efficient and as it later turned out, an expert in one part of the case relevant to my special situation.

Our turn came and I was directed straight to a raised stand with the other four. The court was full of people, with all eyes focused our way.

I was the first and the building charges were read out, one by one, and I pleaded "Not Guilty" to each one of them. My new barrister jumped up and asked for bail terms to be altered so we could, as planned, emigrate to New Zealand.

The magistrate then asked the police to comment. It was Detective Chief Superintendent Page who stood up and formally opposed bail. It was the first time I had seen Reader's chief. I then had to go down to the basement with my Uncle and fill in various documents relating to the bail and sureties. I was also instructed to report to my local police station every 24 hours as if I would now disappear without my family, who were now homeless!

It was at this, my first court appearance, that I felt an association with the "Dickensian" nature of the scene and this remained with me, whilst waiting in the cells and particularly on the dock, and also at the committal proceedings, etc. They all had that atmosphere, one of utter hopelessness, drifting into the inevitable grasp of the vast public legal system. Not being able to do much about the complex developed machinery of the Government's legal system, which seemed set against me personally!

Only my death could ever set me free!

This feeling was very much intensified when I first read, on the correspondence addressed to me. "The Crown v Brian Rowland Edwards" or sometimes "The Queen v Brian Rowland Edwards". What had I ever done to require the Queen to personally challenge me?

This feeling was at its strongest when later I was sent to the Old Bailey, acquiring a strange mental association with all the past unfortunate souls who had suffered there, some later to be sentenced to be hanged, or imprisoned for life and then, later, their wax images displayed at Madame Tussaud's waxworks.

The feeling of public scrutiny and curiosity, and of course, that of assumed guilt. How I ever managed to sleep at nights and not dream of being hanged, or seeing myself in wax, I will never know. It didn't help much either to read the history of the Old Bailey, and the infamous judges, who sat at the trials in the past, famous for their harsh sentences.

After the hearing, we gathered outside the courtroom, my solicitor, the barrister, Jean and her sister and brother-in-law, and my Uncle.

I asked the solicitor, what happens next, and above all, what more could we do to continue to go to New Zealand. I was told that I could appear before a High Court judge in Chambers and seek an adjustment to the bail terms, but this could be expensive and for some reason could not be on legal aid.

It was agreed that this would be the attempted way forward, but time was desperately short. It was Monday the 15th of September and we were supposed to be sailing on Thursday the 18th!

Leaving our legal team to go off and get a hearing at the High Court, the five of us went off to the Kingsley Hotel in Holborn for a Carvery lunch. This was an idea of mine to cheer ourselves up, at my expense, and on my Barclay card. The account for this, after several mishaps, later followed me around the world. After the meal, my Uncle returned to Hove and the rest of us returned to Grimsby, where the children waited.

There was one particular blessing, this was that the children were all too young, right through the entire long saga, to really appreciate what was happening around them, another reason to write this book, so that they may later realise how perilously placed we were all at the time.

The next day Jean and I returned to London, staying at my friends, Rolf's flat, just off the Bayswater Road. By then we had learnt that our solicitor had gained a hearing in front of a Mr Justice Cantley, a judge at the High Court. It was difficult at the time to think of anything else, except how things would turn out in court and would we be allowed to go.

The High Court is a grand group of historic buildings, more like a church than a court, very impressive and very busy. We all met up in the corridor outside the judge's chambers and discussed the case and the points to make. Other people were also milling around, waiting their turn. Eventually, our turn came and in we went.

The room was like a small court with raised benches. The judge and somebody, who I assumed to be a senior clerk, sat on his left, and I sat at the back of the court. Hartley-Booth stood up and outlined the situation, the charges, and my position, our aim to emigrate, how near to sailing it was, and why the court should let us go.

Mr Justice Cantley was very good, pinpointing the relevant questions. He asked the police whether or not they would approve a change in the bail terms. Detective Superintendent Page said they would and then there was a long discussion. If I did go, could the Crown extradite me! What were the arrangements between the countries and the risks, etc.?

This seemed a stumbling block, even though Hartley-Booth explained that by chance he was writing a book on extradition and as a result had intensively researched the whole subject, and was sure that there would be no problem.

It seemed odd to me to labour this point because I would hardly stay in New Zealand with the accusation hanging over me and would wish to return and clear it up, once and for all, even if it meant my returning alone for a couple of months, and then going back to the family.

How naïve "that" thought turned out to be!

I could sense that although Hartley-Booth was giving a great performance, there was settling on the court an air of indecision. After that session, another was booked for Thursday, the actual sailing date, I told my solicitor how I felt about the way it was going and asked what else we could do.

I was told that we could introduce a new face to the scene by way of appointing a "Queen's counsellor", at a personal cost to me. In the meantime, Hartley-Booth was conferring with a solicitor in New Zealand, to clear up the extradition aspect.

Jean and I had to return to Grimsby that day and would come down again on Wednesday with the children, taking them to my parents in Peacehaven, Sussex, then drive up to London and stay overnight, to be ready for the court on Thursday. This plan was the expression of my optimism that we would be allowed to go that day!

So up to Grimsby again, where everybody was a bit bewildered by the events, not really understanding, what it was all about, how serious it was, or what could happen next. I had to report to the local police station as I was on bail and so yet again into an unfamiliar situation.

We had great difficulty in getting all our loose luggage into the car for the six of us to go to Peacehaven and it was a long drive, particularly for the children.

I remember well that it was around Edgware in London, I decided that we couldn't afford the risk of the court hearing going on as before and would appoint the QC. So I stopped the car and phoned my solicitor from a callbox and told him to go ahead, and we would meet them in court, as planned.

I told my parents, it was a 50-50 chance of us being allowed to go, and could they immediately drive down to Southampton with the children and our bits and pieces and we would meet up at my aunt's house in Millbrook, Southampton. We went back again to London and Bayswater Road where Jean and I went to the cinema to take our minds off it all. Next day was the make or break day and we felt a little apprehensive.

We were quite early the following morning at the High Court and were introduced to our new Queen's councillor, who was in the process of being briefed by Hartley-Booth, and the solicitor. He seemed pleasant enough and capable, quickly grasping the situation. Other people were about in the corridor, the police as well, *this time, in for the kill*, I thought. Superintendent Page and a few reporters were looking at us, and at me, rather carefully.

In court, the new QC stood up and after introducing himself outlined the situation, as checked out beforehand with the New Zealand solicitor.

It was more or less said that there were no problems, as far as extradition was concerned. The conversation developed and I could tell quite clearly by the way Justice Cantley was phrasing his questions that the chance of our going was on!

Then the question of bail came up and how much could I put up. At that Jean and I became quite excited, nudging each other in encouragement. My QC and solicitor worked out that with the two sureties already provided, plus the proceeds of the sale of our house, a sum of £16,000 could be raised. Mr Justice Cantley said that was sufficient and then asked Page if he would object. I felt the question was put in such a way that agreement was expected.

I was sure that Page read the situation in the same way and then agreed. The judge then said, together with the bail of £16,000 I was to purchase a return ticket and promise to return immediately when sent for, and then we would be allowed to go! I had then to stand up and confirm that promise. The wording of the revised bail terms was then carefully agreed between all parties and at last, we were out of the court!

The reporters could see that something interesting had happened and started questioning the legal people. I had to get my passport back from the police, for it was about midday and the ship sailed at 8:30 pm that day! We met Page and Reader in the hallway of the Temple and Reader passed the passport over to me. Page then said to Jean, 'Here is your passport, it's nothing personal, you understand!'

Nothing personal, are all police officers lacking in imagination or sensitivity. Their desperate bid to secure a conviction against me had but all destroyed our lives and deeply disturbed many others. We left the court and our first thought was to phone my parents and tell them the news and for them to get underway and take the children down to my aunt's in Southampton. I went into one of the phone booths just outside the courts and made that call.

As I was doing so, reporters were taking photos through the glass. I can still recall my mother's gasp of excitement when I said, 'Yes, we are off, see you at Auntie May's.' We then phoned Jeans people in Grimsby. They would be unable to come down to see us off as it was simply too far at the time available. We were followed by reporters, even when leaving the phone box and walking up the street.

Back in the car, it was obvious that we could never manage all our stuff without another suitcase. The car was totally full of our clothes, the children's clothes, toys, etc., right up to the roof line. So the next thing to do was to go to my bank, in Kingsway and organise the money for my return ticket, get the ticket from the New Zealand travel office, in the Haymarket, then a suitcase from Marks and Spencer.

Finally back to the car and drive like mad down to Southampton. We were in an excited frame of mind doing all this, walking up to Barclay's Bank sited in Kingsway.

Outside the bank was a large news poster on a stand and no doubt sited all around London, it read, "Chief surveyor accused of corruption!"

It hardly registered that it was "me" to which it referred. Inside, we asked for the assistant bank manager, Mr Britten, who knew quite well. He had always been a most helpful and efficient person.

I explained all that had happened and the requirements of the court. He responded well and in no time, he had arranged the money for the ticket. I think I already had the traveller's cheques. With good wishes of the bank in our ears, we hired a taxi and bought a suitcase, my return ticket, then back to the car and off to Southampton. It was approximately 4:30 pm and we were getting seriously short of time.

The day was warm and quite pleasant, right for the journey. On the way through London, I popped into the offices of Rolf, to tell him the news and found another friend there by chance. It's funny, after all these years how I remember the little details.

I remember rushing up the winding staircase to his office and into his room, to find him with another friend, sitting in the corner, the very briefest of words, the catch in the throat, and the goodbyes. The car was parked in the middle of the road so I had to go, then bounding down the stairs again, I heard his lady partner shouting, 'Brian, all the best!' I got into the car, then we were really off.

We stopped off at several places on the way down to tell them in Southampton that we were on the way, but the phones didn't work, vandalised, or so we thought until I realised in my rush I had missed off one digit. By the time we reached Southampton, we were so late that I actually didn't go into my aunt's house. Jean did, she had to, being desperate to visit the bathroom.

My brother and his wife were there and of course, all the children. All the stuff in the car and that from the house had to be put into suitcases, parcels, or anything manageable, and this was done, literally outside the house, on the sidewalk, with the neighbours looking on. It must have been a most bizarre scene for them all, 7 adults and 4 children rushing about packing suitcases. I backed my car into the side driveway of the house, for later collection by the shipping company, said a quick goodbye to my aunt and off we went as a convoy of cars, laden up to the roof, to the docks.

We drove through the docks, under the vast marine cranes and there was the ship, seemingly vast and packed with people, all hanging over the rails to catch a last look at their loved ones. The main gangplanks had been taken up long ago and the ship should have already sailed but had been very kindly delayed by the captain, waiting for us!

We were directed to a deserted part of the dock where a single gangplank went up into the ship at a low level, and a kind-hearted porter took our stuff up the gangplank and stacked them in a huge heap, just inside the ship.

Because of the rush, there wasn't any time to fully appreciate the emotions of the moment, we had no time to discuss anything, just a quick hug, an unmovable lump in the throat and we were up the gangplank into the hold of the ship. My mother came two-thirds of the way up the gangplank to wave and to say take care before it was finally clanged too.

The vision of that moment will be in my mind for the rest of my life. She was a desperate figure, clutching onto the flimsy handrail that was on one side of the gangplank only, afraid that it might be the last time she would ever see us again. She must have been so distraught when the metal door clanged shut. Then I suppose it was about 30 minutes before the ship actually started to slowly move out.

During that time, we had carried out a huge heap of belongings to the reception, found our deck and cabin number and piled our stuff somewhere safe so we could go on deck and wave goodbye.

Alas, I couldn't see my parents or brother anywhere on the dock, however hard we looked.

It was strange how things turned out. Because of the absolute mad panic over the last few days, the sudden arrest and last minute bail appeal, the press hadn't actually caught up, until the day after the ship sailed. So, at least, we were spared that on board. A great deal was apparently said later and my solicitor sent on cuttings of the newspaper reports. The change of bail terms was said to have made legal history. One newspaper declared that we had missed the boat and that we had then flown out to Tenerife and was picked up there.

Another said that the Edwards' family had been provided with the best six-berth cabin on the ship, huh, but more on that later.

Because I missed all the first press comments, I was the last person aware of the general reaction, almost oblivious to it all, in my unawareness. My relatives and friends were not. One friend told me later, much, much later, of going on his normal train and opening up his newspaper, only to find a large picture of me looking up at him, and the shock the news item caused him.

Another work colleague and a good friend of ours told me of the shock it had caused him, making him feel quite ill. Heaven knows the shock it caused our parents, relatives and friends.

Quite a few friends said that when they saw the press comments, and after the initial shock had gone, they just couldn't believe that such a fuss could be made over so small an allegation and therefore, waited, for years, as it turned out, to be told of some huge deed, to justify it all.

It took quite a while for the ship to leave the waters of Southampton harbour, and then we were really on our way. We made our way down to see our cabin. It took us over 15 minutes to find it, being placed in the very bowels of the ship, along numerous corridors, around corners, over high steps and stopping to look at wall maps on the way. In fact, it was days before we could find it without concern and during the first days, we were obliged to refer to the maps all the time.

The cabin was sited just above water level and we didn't have a pothole so it was artificial lighting all the time. Furthermore, it was near to one of the propeller shafts so there was a constant hum and vibration, at all times. Hot water was intermittently supplied, or non-existent and since Carole, our youngest daughter was still in nappies, this made for big problems. Washed out nappies would be left in one of the two basins to soak, to get them clean.

When the ship rolled in rough weather the water would drain from one basin into the next, and vice versa, or over the edge. We had a number of cockroaches and when you lay in the bunk late at night and put out the lights, or put in on, they would tear around the walls and into whatever crack was near. Worse still, drop onto the bunks and disappear into the bedding.

But perhaps I should describe the ship herself. She was under a Greek flag and was called the "Australis". I don't know if she was Greek-built or just Greek-owned and managed. She was claimed to be the largest single-class ship on the ocean, at the time, holding some 1,200 passengers. It seemed grossly overcrowded and it was always a constant battle to get and retain a deck chair. The public rooms and areas were quite reasonable and the cabins at deck level and higher looked positively attractive when compared to ours. Most of the toilets were highly suspect and were cleaned by seedy-looking Greek staff, shuffling along with brooms, pretending to be cleaning up and obviously hoping to come across friendly passengers. They would even follow women into their toilet areas, flicking their brooms about whilst the toilets were in use, smirking hopefully. Jean was always nervous about going to the loo, particularly late at night.

But possibly the worst factor was that the general toilet area drain outlets never seemed to work properly and there was always an evil looking pool of water somewhere around. In rough weather, this pool became a major hazard.

As the ship rolled the water would rush across the toilet floor area, under the cubicles, slosh against the wall and tear back to the opposite wall. Every time it came under one's cubicle you had to time the lifting off your feet and clothing to miss it. Heaven help you if your pants were resting on the floor.

This hazard was made worse in bad weather and when somebody had been sick, all of which added to the mess sloshing about. It was surprising that we never became chronically constipated.

The Greeks had a strange logic about the staggering of mealtimes and especially the priorities. For example, large families, like ourselves had the very early breakfast, about 7 am, so if you had a number of young children to get ready, it was all rush and panic. After a while, we gave up breakfast but occasionally, I would go with Christopher, our eldest boy, we would have ours and take some toast back to the others. But even earlier than that, at 6 am to 6:30 am, the cabin door would open and a tray of tea would come in with biscuits. Had it been later, it would have been very welcome.

A day's programme went something like this. Cabin door opened at 6 to 6:30 am and tea and biscuits were brought in.

Sometimes Christopher and I would go for breakfast and bring back toast. Then the children would be got ready and we would Carole, who was a poor and fussy eater, prior to a general clean up before going up on deck.

For some part of the voyage, we managed to persuade Carole and Jeremy to stay in the nursery unit, though Jeremy got fed up and wanted to be with us. Sometimes we would watch people doing exercises in the main hall or just wander around the ship into the library or the ship's shop, etc. I spent a great deal of the morning in the library, writing letters to friends about recent events. I must have written about a dozen, long letters. Even though I gave the next port of call and time of arrival, I only ever received "one" reply and none ever caught up with us in New Zealand. So about a week of solid writing and perhaps a day of queuing, when the mail came in, was an utter waste of time. Some replies would have been of great value and comfort to me at that time.

Lunch was early, about 12 noon and the thing about food on the ship was that it was, of course, prepared by the Greek staff that had never seemed to hear of "gravy". So you might have boiled potatoes, meat and veg, not too badly prepared but without any gravy, so it was difficult to swallow. The occasional cockroach would dash about the sugar bowls and when the stewards were told they simply hooked them out with their fingers and returned the bowls back to the table. There was a fusty sort of cooking smell about the two main dining halls. This was through lack of ventilation, and this was certainly very off-putting.

For each meal, there was always a queue, even though we had a set position.

The main entrance doors to the ships dining rooms were closed off until the exact mealtime, and then opened for us to go in. Most of the passengers were composed of emigrants, like ourselves, or New Zealanders and Australians returning home.

When we were in rough weather, the dining hall changed character and became like that of a farce. Fewer people were there, only resilient souls like us and in the very rough seas, dining on the ship was something never to be forgotten.

As the ship rolled, the tables near to us, plus the people on their chairs, would suddenly break away and slide, en bloc, to the other side of the dining room and then return on the opposite roll. This was accompanied by the crash of cutlery and dishes onto the floor and the screams of the younger children.

Also, in rough weather, the stewards would pour cold water all over the tablecloths to stop things from sliding about. It worked but meant that you couldn't put your arms or elbows on the table and it was a bit cold and clammy. The food, on the whole, was just about passable, but Carole who was a poor eater became a problem. She would eat a little after hours of coaching and slowly, as the voyage progressed, became less well and even fussier with her food.

We bought well-known tinned baby foods and had them heated up, giving her the things she fancied. At times, she was so off-colour that we had to take her to the ship's doctor who prescribed medicines and tonics.

Although the food was generally indifferent, there was one occasion when it was absolutely marvellous and this was at the captain's Party, which, in turn, everybody attended. All were dressed up in their best clothes. The party was held in one of the large public halls and was well packed with guests. Set out was the superb display of food that I have ever seen, and so much of it. Every dish was well decorated and the basic ingredients were obviously of a very high quality. How the same cooks, who had produced such indifferent fare throughout the voyage, could produce such a display I never fathomed. Drink was plentiful and it was a jolly good party.

The captain walked around with his senior officers in waiting, at his side, saying hello and looking as one would expect a captain would look like at his cocktail party.

Dinner was at 7 pm, a slightly larger menu than lunch, usually better attended. We always attended lunch and dinner, even though there were many times when we didn't enjoy the food at all.

At mid-morning, on the decks, the stewards would serve an Oxo-like beverage and biscuits, which made a break, and of course, the various bars were open, serving drinks, with some serving coffee and cocoa. The ship had a cinema, which we frequently attended and we would usually leave Julie, the eldest girl, looking after the others, especially when the film wasn't suitable for us all. But sometimes we would all manage to go together. When the weather was rough it sometimes made it worse, there in the darkness of the cinema, the sensation of the ship rolling was doubled. People would suddenly get up and rush for the exits and this would set the others off.

Just outside the cinema was a bar that Jean and I would sometimes go to after the film, I mention it because I always remember that the counter would have a cockroach or two dashing from one end to the other. You didn't lean on the bar for fear of one running up your sleeve!

Apart from the captain's cocktail party, the other very good part of the voyage was the evening entertainment. It was popular enough to have a queue of people at each performance, was very professionally staged and in fact, was very good indeed. The chap who ran it was Greek, assisted by a troop of dancing girls.

He was rather effeminate and would sometimes practice during the day, prancing around the dance floor, making weird gestures with his hands and practising his routines.

The whole entertainment was something you would expect say at a good holiday camp, but more tastefully arranged.

After several days out on sea, when at last we could find our cabin without too much difficulty, we returned one day to our cabin to find a note pushed under the door. It invited us to call and see somebody who knew us!

We certainly couldn't think who it might be but called with interest, only to find that there was a family of four who once lived on the same road in Peacehaven as my parents and one of them was a distant relative of my cousin's wife. This was a pleasant surprise, to know somebody and then later, through them to make friends with their friends. They were emigrating to Melbourne, Australia. Gladys was Australian and Rodney English. They lived in Melbourne before, where Rodney met Gladys.

A few days later during a lunch break, the "Tannoy" system, which often made the occasional announcement, said, 'Would Brian Edwards please go to the wireless cable room?'

This worried us both as we could only think that one of our relatives was ill or something of that sort.

In fact, it was one of the newspapers, asking me how I felt after the High Court hearing, how things were going, etc. It seemed a strange conversation, crackling there on the high seas over cable wireless, like some old black and white TV film. I never did see the report in a newspaper and as usual, I seemed always to be the last one to know about anything.

The highlights of the voyage were the calls at the various ports on the way. Our first stop off was at Tenerife, in the Canary Islands, where we joined a day tour around the island.

The next call was at Cape Town, on the tip of South Africa. It was a fairly rough day as we sailed in, but brightened upon landing. Another trip around Cape Town itself, which was marvellous, around the shops and into the country to see a Dutch farm. The flowers everywhere were exceptional, but most unusually it snowed in Africa, just lightly and wasn't too warm, although bright.

From then on it was a very long run, right over to Australia itself, on the west coast to the Port of Freemantle. But before this, we had a variety of weather conditions, from very hot, when all the crew donned their whites, to very rough. So rough that I believe 6 people died during accidents on this part of the voyage.

One, put off step by the rolling of the ship, just outside the lift door, at the third floor, staggered against the lift doors, which like the rest of the ship was suspect, they opened and she fell to her death.

Another fell down steep steel-steps on the deck and I think the others died possibly from heart attacks, brought on by the extreme weather conditions.

Ropes were fixed around the public areas of the ship so one could hang onto something and in our cabin things became quite hectic!

Apart from the wash-hand basins draining into each other in turn, and then draining onto the floor. The suitcases, which were under the bunks at each side of the cabin, would suddenly break away and tear across the floor, crashing into the opposite wall, then do the same in reverse.

The stepladders, serving the bunks would fly out at an almost horizontal angle and we would have to strap ourselves in the bunks to avoid being thrown out.

Altogether quite exciting and we all enjoyed it, especially the children.

As a family, we managed to stay fairly free from sea-sickness, except for Jean on a couple of occasions, one of which was in the cinema when suddenly, the ship started to go up and down.

On landing at Freemantle, we took a taxi into Perth, which is fairly close by and had a look around.

It was our first taste of Australia and seemed very attractive. The taxi driver said he could easily nip into the bush and get a "red-backed spider" to show us if we wanted, but we were not that keen! As usual, it was a fairly confined day trip which soon passed as we had to be back on the ship quite early. The process of getting on and off was pretty tedious, having to queue for quite a long while, both in and out, but it all made a refreshing break from the routine on ship.

Melbourne was next and our friends were getting off to restart their lifestyle, getting very excited. Melbourne was quite different to Perth and we were particularly lucky in having a friend meet us at the port and drive us around Melbourne, showing us the sights. What a bliss it was, to drive into town and to a good restaurant and have a really good meal, with gravy! Christopher was carsick before we got there so he couldn't eat much, but that aside, it was a very nice break.

Our host was kind and very understanding. By chance, he happened to be in London when my problems became press worthy. In fact, he saw all the newspaper coverage that I'd missed. In spite of that, to his credit, it appeared to make no difference to his attitude towards us and his kindness itself.

We went into some of the larger stores there and they were absolutely first-class. Back to the ship, we were tired but well-fed and happy, then on with the next long haul to Sydney.

My eldest brother David lived in Sydney and at that time had already been there for some five and a half years. It was especially nice to be met at the harbour by him and his wife Anne, with their two children Robin and Stewart, and then to be taken out by them for a superb meal in a revolving restaurant at the top of one of

Sydney's new spectacular buildings. A short tour of Sydney central and then off in his car to his house in the suburbs. Two of the children swam in his pool and we had a very good get-together, until dark when we had to go back to the ship, to be ready for departure. We said our goodbyes, having already thought up exchange holidays between Australia and New Zealand for the coming Christmas and other exciting prospects ahead.

David and Anne drove off back home and we went back on board only to learn that the ship's crew were on strike and the ship wouldn't be sailing for at least another day. I went down the gangplank again and phoned David to explain what had happened.

He said get a taxi and come on straight back out again. This, we did with great pleasure and very much enjoyed the extra day with them.

I had already told my brother of the events preceding our departure from England, whilst walking up the steps of Sydney Opera house. Strange how clear one's memory of that moment is. It is difficult to assess the total impact, trying to explain what had happened. A mixture of shock and disbelief, though of course, he accepted my account.

Eventually, the ship left for New Zealand and we looked forward, at last, to be able to start our new lives, having waited so long. The last part of our journey went quickly but going into Auckland's harbour was a bit of an anti-climax after Sydney's spectacular harbour. Nevertheless, we were very excited and couldn't wait to get ashore. On berthing, I was again called on the Tannoy system to meet with somebody at reception. Again, Jean and I speculated as to who it might be. It could be the firm I was going for, so I went to the point stated. The two men waiting there for me were reporters, from the New Zealand Herald.

We had come some 13,000 miles and the press were still pursuing us! The leader of the two said he knew what had happened in England and how did I feel about it all? I said we were very pleased to be able to come to the wonderful country of New Zealand and looked forward to the day when it was all totally sorted out. He asked me what plans I had and I told him that I had a job with a firm of building contractors in Hamilton (which is on the North Island and is the largest inland city) but I said I didn't want his paper to take pictures, or publish the name of the firm, as obviously, it wouldn't be the most helpful thing to do.

They seemed pleasant people, for reporters and agreed, asking me to let them know of any new developments. Jean was surprised to hear of this and we wondered what would happen next.

Before leaving the ship, passengers had to go through an official checkout procedure where New Zealand official asked questions, then stamped the passports etc.

We queued up; the six of us in line, shuffling up to the first checkpoint sited in one of the ship's lounges. I handed over my passport, which included the children's as well. Seeing my name, he gestured to another official sitting on the other side of the room and sent us over to him. He was particularly pleasant and helpful, explaining that they had learnt of events leading up to our departure from England and would have to stamp our passports as limited to 6 months stay only, pending events in regard to the accusations set against me.

This rather took the wind out of our sails a bit, for we had given up everything to come here, only to be told that it was not confirmed as permanent! He said the local office in Hamilton would be in touch later. Getting our huge heap of belongings together again we struggled to get them into a pile on the docks.

People were thronging about and there were many excited reunions. The chap from the firm I had met during my previous exploratory visit came forward to greet us and we piled our stuff into a pickup van driven by his colleague, getting ourselves into his car to drive to Hamilton. New Zealand, we have arrived!

New Zealand

Arriving in the town of Hamilton, which is about 60 miles from Auckland, we booked into a Motel receiving a very warm welcome. It was called the "Ambassador Motor Inn" and was owned by the company. By now it was late afternoon and we were all a little tired, especially after getting up so early, and such a hectic day. The motel only provided breakfast and Laurie Cave, the manager, suggested that we could purchase something from the "Kentucky Fried Chicken Shop", across the road. This we did and it was so nice to hear those friendly New Zealand accents and see the lush green vegetation again.

Our unit was at first-floor level. Along the outside balcony and near our entrance, was a grapefruit bush in full blossom, as well as other plants around the walls. Monday was to be our move-in day. Outside the motel, some workmen were building a swimming pool and it was interesting to watch them shape up the sides of the pool with pumped concrete.

On Monday morning, I went to see the firm and to meet my new employers. Of course, I had met them before, about a year ago. Their offices were in a single-storey building, all very pleasant and well-arranged. Alongside the offices was a huge level yard where various heavy plants were placed. Next to the yard were a number of fairly large workshops and stores. I met one of the directors and then into a room to meet the principal director, Peter Holman, after whom the firm was named. He greeted me with obvious pleasure and after we had chatted generally for some time, I thought I had better explain the situation as I had left it in England, just before sailing for New Zealand.

Again that difficulty of explaining it all to a comparative stranger, how it all came about, what the allegations were and what had happened. It is difficult to do so, especially in so short a time, and I was never really sure how the other person took it, whatever their reaction. I also explained that I anticipated being called back the following January when I was reasonably confident that either the case would be thrown out or very quickly dealt with. "Oh what naïve predictions"!

He seemed to accept my explanation and then told me how he first became aware, whilst driving to work. Out of the blue, it all came out of his car radio.

He was quite shocked and couldn't contact me, as I was on the high seas. So he wrote to Camden Council. His letter, unfortunately, did not go to the director of architecture but ended up in the main Town Hall, where some kind individual, and I think I know who it was, simply wrote back, enclosing copies of newspaper cuttings. No word that Camden Council had every faith in me and hoped for a happy conclusion. The newspaper cuttings, of course, showed everything in the worst light, just as a prosecuting counsel would have presented, something so newsworthy. Heaven knows what Peter Holman thought at that moment. But to his great credit, he was completely open-minded, extremely kind and considerate, very helpful in settling us in, being very generous in all he did. However, looking back over the years at our time in New Zealand, it did make a difference.

It must have affected the way the firm thought about us and the immediate opportunities for the future. Just another good reason for writing this account.

The rest of the firm did not seem to know anything about it, except, of course, the executives of the company, who never mentioned it.

We went up to the house they had found for us on Sunday, taking our trunks and suitcases in the firm's van. Before moving into the house on Saturday, Jean and I fixed up the schools for the children. The one for Jeremy and Carole was only around the corner from the house and was beautifully constructed from local woods. It was so polished, so clean, with a number of colourful Maori children. On Monday, I started my new job and it was so strange sitting in new offices and getting into the picture.

We all settled in quite easily, but with the case always on our minds. Every opportunity was taken in getting about and to do so we hired a series of small cars, with just enough room to squeeze us all in. Weekends were especially good. We had shopped on the Friday, sorted out the dinner to come on when programmed in the oven and set off for one of the beauty spots, and there were plenty. One big advantage of living in Hamilton, in the centre of the North Island, was that one did not have to go too far for a complete change. Up to Auckland and onto one of the beaches, or down to Lake Taupo and the hot volcanic lakes. Perhaps over to the east coast beaches, or simply into the country to see some spectacular sights, like hot springs, or superb unspoilt scenery. It was also so very easy to get about on the empty roads.

It wasn't long before we saw a marked change in the children. Carole, in particular, picked up amazingly well, rapidly filling out and getting quite tubby. Jeremy used to bring home from school, attractive young Maori friends and they would all run around the garden New Zealand style, that is, barefooted. Christopher and Julie settled in quickly and happily and all seemed just fine, except for that huge black cloud on the horizon.

After some weeks in the office, I was asked to look after and finish off the pool and surrounding works at the Ambassador Motor Inn, the one we first stayed in. Back to the tools, really as general foreman, setting out and supervising, organising materials and working as one of the men. What a change after sitting behind a desk at Camden, organising a large surveying group and all that went with it.

Now I was actually pouring concrete into formwork that I had helped erect, with the sun blazing down and giving me a red back, the sweat dripping off me in the blazing sun. I remember walking home and getting there utterly exhausted, so much so that I had to lie on the bed for about half an hour, to recover.

It can get really hot in New Zealand, and fairly often with the most amazing blue skies that I had ever seen, then or later, the lush New Zealand ferns, not forgetting the wonderful green grass and that incredible clarity of light.

The average New Zealander worker, although mostly of English origin, works much harder than his present-day counterpart in England. This meant that I had to lead and keep up! It was so tiring in the first days until I became used to it. A few friends wrote from England telling me how things were. It all seemed light years away, in comparison. Christmas holidays in New Zealand are, of course, their summer holidays and we had two weeks with a hired car doing a complete tour of the coastline of the North Island. Christmas Eve and Christmas day were spent in a Motel at Lake Taupo. In all life was idyllic, even though I earned a lot less there, than in Camden but was still renting a car and house at fair cost. But in spite of that, we were living better, doing more things as a family and feeling free and healthier.

New Zealand holds a special place in our hearts, and our short stay, from the October of 1975 until the April of the following year seemed so pitifully short.

My solicitor wrote and told us about the magistrate's hearing in October, at which the magistrates were apparently put out that I didn't show up! To hear that when everything was going so well, and still, there was still no sign of a case forming up with the Crown.

After the Motel scheme was finished, I moved onto various small jobs. The firm had in mind for me to get involved in a very large multi-million dollar scheme, for the Huntley Coal Board and that looked like quite a challenge and an opportunity.

In the New Year, we received a registered letter from a Magistrate's Court, seeking my attendance at a committal hearing. The Crown had set a date for the 27th of January, 1976, which was later changed to the 27th of May.

I had promised Mr Justice Cantley that I would return when sent for and this was it! Jean and I discussed what we should do, having in mind that the best thing to do in the long run. How secure would she be if I went on my own?

But that was impossible, what would they all live on! All our capital was tied up as bail, only to be released on my return and application. Anyway how long would it take to get cleared up, it could be months. How could she possibly manage? There was no way out but for us all to return. In any event, we would never feel settled, or secure until the ghastly mess had been properly cleared up.

I had phoned twice and written once to the New Zealand immigration authority when I learned that the January '76 committal date was not on. They eventually replied, saying that the limited stay must still apply, so that was that!

I wrote to my Uncle Edward, in Hove, Sussex and he cabled enough money for us to return to my parent's home in Peacehaven, Sussex. I already had my ticket, the remainder cost something in the region of £1,600, to fly us back including a two-day stopover in Hong Kong.

I told Peter Holman, my employer, about the situation, and first of all, he seemed to understand my dilemma and was very good about it. Then after a few hours, he appeared to turn a bit cold, just as though he had been got at by somebody with a harsher point of view.

In any event, we really had no choice, other than turning when sent for. For not to return when sent for, having made my promises to the High Court would surely destroy my credibility, right from the very start, so we were set.

During the last days, the firm took back the utility van that I had used to run about in and we were reduced to foot, as we couldn't afford to hire any more cars. This was especially difficult when shopping as we had to hire a taxi or walk miles and miles, clutching the hands of the children and our shopping. New Zealand doesn't really have a proper point to point bus service so there was no easy way out. A friend in the firm who had been over from England for about two years kindly took us to the town centre and we picked up our last hire car to take us to the airport.

I said my goodbyes to the people in the firm; the management were still talking, but only just. Goodbye to our friends, and we were off once again. On the way, we stayed one night in a Motel in Auckland, then in our large overloaded shooting brake, headed for the airport.

I shall never forget that ride, never, it was a perfect day, one of those spectacular days with a vivid blue sky, even better than the usual wonderful days that one got so used to. There was a sort of calm in the air that blended in somehow with the clarity of the New Zealand light. The tide was just coming in, creeping up all the little creeks and inlets alongside the road to the airport and it was just too beautiful to believe.

We stopped the car outside the airport and unloaded it and waited for the plane to carry us back to what we thought would be a reasonably quick solution to our problems.

When we realised just after Christmas that we would have to return, we had to consider what to do with all the furniture, so we wrote urgent letters to the removal people, telling them "not" to send anything on but to store it all until advised further. But we had no response, even after several letters, eventually, some odd notes arrived from them stating that our furniture was on the way and should now be in "Philadelphia".

No proper replies were ever received after any of our desperate letters. My car which I had left at my aunt's in Southampton had been picked up by the firm and driven to Birmingham, to a car compound. The car itself was costing £550 to ship and the furniture some £1,800. So I wrote to my younger brother, Roy who went up to Birmingham and after a bit of fuss, drove the car back to my parent's home in Peacehaven.

We learnt later back in England that the wretched shipping company had gone bust! So there we were, back with our entire household belongings stuck on Auckland docks. This more or less included everything, our clothes, papers, bed sheets, everything, except our travelling suitcases and trunks.

We had planned a break in the long flight by stopping off in Hong Kong, a place that had a special meaning for me and where I have served my National Service.

It looked the same as I remembered it, except it was better, more interesting. We had booked our Hotel in advance and even though it was the Hong Kong Hilton, it was surprisingly competitive in price.

We had two main bedrooms and our own bathroom but didn't eat in as it would have really cost too much, so we had all our food out. The taxi from the airport, in fact, we had two taxis, to cope with the entire luggage, stopped outside the palatial front of the Hotel and unloaded the luggage. A huge heap quickly formed, most embarrassingly, a line of plastic carrier bags with their handles tied together with coarse string. Not a pretty sight for such a smart hotel. The staff quickly moved it all to our rooms.

Together with New Zealand, Hong Kong has always been one of my hopes, as a place to live and work in. In view of this, I had already arranged to see a friend there and the very next day I phoned him to arrange a night out. I also made contact with various firms who eventually put me in touch with one of the largest property companies in the colony. Luckily, one of the executives of that company agreed to see me and we fixed up a lunch that day. Who knows perhaps there would be some interesting possibilities for work in the future? When I met him he was pleasant and hopeful, saying that he was particularly interested in what I had to offer and would keep me on the top of his pending list. He was confident of something happening fairly quickly.

I didn't, of course, attempt to explain my present predicament, as I believed then that after a few months it would all be cleared up. I learnt later that the company had indeed contacted Camden Council, to check up on my past service and my job particulars. Most regrettably they were given the same return, in the form of newspaper cuttings etc., as had been given to my New Zealand employer.

Almost certainly it was the same person, who for some twisted reason spoilt any chance that I might have had. I wrote several times to the Hong Kong firm, but never received a reply of any sort.

Eventually, I wrote to the chief executive of Camden Council, protesting at such unfair and savage a treatment, but of course, I never learnt of the effect and I expect that the Council officer concerned, retired unscathed having caused me untold damage.

It is sometimes better that we go through life unaware of others feelings and views of our selves. For whatever we do in being kind, decent and honourable in our dealings with others, there is always someone who is sadly screwed up with petty jealously or just simple spite.

For example, when I did my National Service training and was told that I was one of about a hundred of the lucky ones to be posted to Hong Kong, I was delighted beyond measure. It was the best posting in the British Army. Prior to going, we were marched up to a clothing billet to get our tropical kit. It was my turn to go in and when I did, there behind the counter was a colleague from my previous building firm, Richarson & Bottoms. He was one of the Devlin brothers, related to Len Bottoms.

It was a pleasant surprise and we joked together, that we should, by chance, meet in such a place. He wished me well and I fell back in with the others. A friend who had followed me in came out afterwards and said to me.

'Do you know that fellow in there, behind the counter?'

'Yes,' I said, 'I used to work with him'

'Well,' he said, 'the minute you left he went on about you, wishing you hell and disaster, and much more. Hoping the world fell in on you!'

So there we are, back in the firm I didn't see that much of him, but when I did we exchanged pleasantries and the time of day, etc.

I thought of him as another nice chap working for the firm, and there he was wishing me hell. I never forgot that event. It was such a disappointment in human nature. It still troubles me all these years after.

Our two days in Hong Kong were very pleasant indeed, even though the weather wasn't too good. The shopping arcades were so spectacular, the food there is cheap and very good and we all thoroughly enjoyed the stopover. It was a long time since I did my National Service, back there in 1955 to 1957, and now it was even better and appeared more exciting and beautiful.

Many years before when I was working as a surveyor in the Architect's Department of South-end-on-sea Borough Council, a job was advertised in the journals for "deputy chief surveyor to Hong Kong University". It was right up my street, excellent salary and prospects.

We would even have servants. So I applied and filled in the application with the greatest care. It was three months later when I was called for an interview at "Clarence House", in the mall and where the Queen Mother lived!

Jean and I went up that day filled with excitement at the prospect. The interview was held in buildings at the back of Clarence House, facing onto Pall Mall. There were about five members on the interview panel, with a very grand character leading as the chairman. Everything went well and when the chairman asked me where on earth had I learnt to make such a good application and I thought I had got the job!

It was another three months before they wrote and said that the position had been given to somebody else. A big disappointment, but much later, when I was working for another local authority, exactly the same job came up again and so I applied again

The usual three-months wait, then the same interview in the same place, even with the same chairman, who again congratulated me on my application. Three months later, they wrote and told me the position had been awarded to a "Chinese" applicant! So it seems I was not destined to live and work in Hong Kong.

Now, it was time to pack all that stuff back into two cars and head for Kai Tak airport and then we were really off this time, landing back in England fairly early on the bright morning of the 3rd of March, 1976.

On that very day, the New Zealand emigration people had put a letter through the post box of our home there, saying that our restricted stay of six months had been extended and we could, therefore, stay there until further notice!

Bitterly ironic when viewed against the way later events materialised.

Another car was hired, this time a Volkswagen van and off we drove, heading for Peacehaven.

My parents were so very pleased to see us, especially, of course, the children, then after the excitement of the moment had passed we unpacked all our stuff, as best we could, into their bungalow. This meant that there were "eight" of us staying there, in a two-bedroom bungalow, with my parents who were quite elderly. It was a crush and I often think back to that time, as now, both my parents are sadly gone and realise just how remarkably kind and generous they were with their hospitality when like everybody, they must have been very worried about the final outcome.

After a few days, I telephoned my solicitor and made an appointment in London with them, with a view to get updated on events and particularly, where we stood. Jean and I drove up and met one of the principal partners of the firm. He explained that "nothing" had happened, but that a committal date was being urgently sought!

Quite staggering, all this flap to return, following those recorded letters and nothing had been set, which meant another two-months wait. In the meantime, we would have the various briefing sessions with my solicitor and the barrister. I then realised that we had nothing left to live off. We couldn't possibly sponge off my parents, who were pensioners, struggling anyway. So off I went to the local labour exchange, which happened to be at Newhaven, near to Peacehaven.

In all an experience, as less than eight months ago, I was chief building surveyor to a large London local authority, now I was reduced to handouts, on the dole! On the first occasion I applied, the children came along for the ride, as I drove just past the entranceway, where all the applicants were queuing, Christopher looked at them and said, 'Look at that lot, you would think that they would be able to find a job somewhere!'

They didn't know that it was precisely where I was going. I said nothing, parking well around the corner, so they couldn't see where I went. When inside, and after waiting for about half an hour, I eventually went into a room to be interviewed and assessed by one of the staff.

Immediately, I felt intensely uncomfortable in my attempts to explain why I was there. It had been such a long complicated saga. The young woman interviewing me could see my discomfort, almost distress, and said I didn't really need to go into all that detail, just say that I was unemployed, let them know my qualifications and experience, and that I was looking for employment. She was very kind to me, the stranger.

The weeks went by and I queued up regularly, collecting my dole money, shuffling up to the counter with the others, never, ever getting over the embarrassment of being there.

The family never knew what an ordeal that it was for me. Later on, as the months went by I could feel the resentment of the various post office staff paying out, to what appeared to be a perfectly able person. How could I tell them that to no fault of my own I had been rendered unemployable by the Crown, in fact, the Queen herself?

We got the children fixed up at local schools again, that wasn't too difficult. Though it was difficult and always has been, to explain why we returned so quickly from New Zealand without going into long complicated stories, which I was never sure would be understood.

I am sure now that if we hadn't left so quickly, after the High Court hearing, to go to New Zealand, then even the contractor might have called things off until I had been cleared.

On one occasion, a good friend of mine fixed up an interview with a particularly well-known contractor in London. It was a good managerial job, so up I went, full of my usual optimism. The interview went fairly well, but again I had to explain the predicament I was in. How do you explain that you are waiting events after corruption allegations had been made against you? How could I ever expect them to take me in those circumstances, whatever they thought of my suitability?

After about five months in Peacehaven, it seemed very unlikely that I would stand a chance of finding work, so far from London and in any event, the overcrowding was telling on all and was particularly unfair to my elderly parents, and to Jean. It was amazing that we all had managed so well so far. Jean and I decided it would help if we attempted to find temporary accommodation nearer to London, with reasonable car commuting distance. So off we set one day to explore the area around Camberley and Frimley, in Surrey.

After some wasted visits to a number of estate agents, we found one agent who offered a specialist service in letting accommodation belonging to army personnel, those posted abroad for the usual two or three-year tour. We selected a three-bedroom semi in Frimley and went to look.

It was just right, nicely furnished, with a garage and near to the schools and shops. The owner, an army captain and his family had been posted to Germany and were so pleased we would take it.

I had to explain that initially, we would take it for six months, as our future was a little uncertain. I didn't go into any other detail, how could I! They were nice people and accepted us as suitably responsible. I wonder what they would have thought if they had known of my situation. I wondered afterwards, as my situation became newsworthy if they had become aware.

A new date had been set for the committal hearing, for the 28th of June. That came near and was cancelled because the prosecution were not ready! Finally, a date was set for the 22nd of July and after the usual pre-briefing, Jean and I went up to the Magistrate's Court in Marylebone. My barrister had advised us that he wouldn't reveal our hand at that stage. I wasn't entirely happy with that approach, as I had always felt that the whole thing should be squashed with the utter contempt it deserved. So to strengthen their position, they thought to tie me in with the others, on money charges. Some mud is bound to stick, and I may be more likely to appear guilty by association!

I can easily imagine such a meeting at the offices of the director of public prosecutions, when without compassion and following the biased viewpoint of the police, they decided to follow that line. After all, it was a game to be won, or so it seemed, and I was being accused of corruption.

It was impossible to give us a date for the Old Bailey. It would obviously, be months away. So we went to Frimley, to try and see what to do in the near future. We stayed in that house, quite liking the area and the children settled again quite happily in the local schools, in fact, progressing remarkably well, with one headmaster telling us to be sure to get Christopher into a good school, when we moved from Frimley, as he had exceptional possibilities.

I think I obtained two interviews with London firms whilst living there. Both very kindly arranged for me by ex-colleagues. I remember them well, describing my career to date, then the awful business of explaining to a complete stranger how I came to be in my present predicament, queuing up, as it were to appear at the Old Bailey. One never forgets that look on their faces, of surprise, then sympathy, possibly thinking, 'There but for the grace of God go I!' An air of curiosity and the final handshakes, saying, 'We will be in touch.'

Of course, they never were. I am not sure if I ever heard anything at all from them. But they were kind and made an impossible situation a little more civilised.

I was still on the dole during our six months at Frimley and still hadn't become used to queuing up each week at the Newhaven offices. But they were very kind and phoned me in Frimley, saying that arrangements had been made to pay me at the Frimley offices.

So I made contact, seeking an appointment with the lady supervisor. It was almost a repeat of my first visit to the Newhaven offices, after our return from New Zealand. The children were in the car so I made a point again of parking out of sight, with Christopher again remarking about people lining up to get handouts on the dole. What could I say, except I just had to pop in somewhere and wouldn't be long! Then the discomfort of yet again explaining one's situation to a stranger.

For six months, I joined that queue, hoping that one of my new neighbours wouldn't see me, though it was always about mid-morning and therefore, less likely.

I was kept fairly busy, writing to my solicitor, preparing long reports and screeds on the questions raised. It was sometimes necessary to attend long conferences at their offices. Then I had my first meeting with my new QC, who "I" had sought to defend me. He had been recommended to me by my friend Rolf Rothermel, who as an architect had carried out a commission for him. I remember so well Rolf saying that he had been doing some design work for a QC and what a character he was, mind like a razor, a terrific presence and "boy" would he hate to get on the wrong side of him!

But if one ever needed a QC, he would be a very good choice. Little did we both know then that I would eventually be in such a position.

The meeting was very genial and at that time I was only concerned with charges relating to the receipts of materials. I remember leaving his chambers and with him saying, as he shook my hand, 'Don't you worry, Mr Edwards, we have a strong case and there should be no problem in sorting it out!' or words to that effect.

The second visit was quite different. I went to my solicitor's, and then we walked around to Campbell's chambers, situated there in the Temple. It was a very impressive setting, sited in a grand historic manner, alongside the Thames, giving the impression that we were indeed going to see somebody very important. This impression was confirmed when entering his office and seeing the style and quality of the room.

Mr Alan Campbell, QC is a most impressive person, of medium height, stoutly built, very dark hair and thick, bushy eyebrows and with a swarthy complexion. He positive oozed charisma and personality. He had a strong theatrical air of authority and with eyes that stood no nonsense, seeing right through one. No messing about and straight down to business.

A very crisp effective meeting, but his attitude towards me had changed, from being on my side, to being testy! Almost as if he was annoyed over being made aware of the added money charges, almost as though he had been duped by me earlier on, when only the material charges were in question. He tested me with almost the exact amount of aggression the two detective sergeants had applied at the police station, all that time ago. After a while, I felt myself becoming a little more than irritated, after all, he was supposed to be there to help me! Not to put me down. Anyway, I'd explained it all so many times before and had written so much about it all, surely between them they had every known fact. Then I realised, that of course, it was a ploy to test me and my story. If I couldn't stand up to him, in his own chambers, I wouldn't be expected to survive in court, under great pressure. Nevertheless, it was an unpleasant experience and I could see what my friend had meant. A very fierce gentleman indeed! He didn't shake my hand this time, as I left, but promised to readily sort out a satisfactory end result, not sounding so convincing as before, as though there was still a question over my honesty.

However, with the strength of his personality, that he was a "recorder'" in his own right, and with my friend's recommendation, I felt happy he would be defending me. Also, of course, there were the special talents of Mr Hartley-Booth, and that of my solicitor.

As the months ticked by there were several other meetings in Mr Campbell's chambers, all quite detailed briefing-meetings, relating to exchanges between the Crown and himself. There were quite terse pressing letters from him to the Crown, some important ones which I believe we never received satisfactory replies to.

So the months went by and in March of 1977, we understood that the contractor and his manager, that is Leonard Rawlings and Laurie Pearce, were to stand trial. The Crown agreed that I could see the proceedings from the public gallery. Jean and I went into court that day, to court No. 8 at the Old Bailey and waited to go in. Much to my surprise, there in the entrance lobby was Len Rawlings, with his father and brother Ken, he said. 'Hello, Brian, how are you?' How does one respond to such an event? After all, it was his initial comments that had set the police and Crown on an irreversible course of action, had cost me a small fortune and huge distress to everybody around me. I think I said something like 'Hell' and left it at that.

We went into the gallery, looking down into the courtroom. Rawlings and Pearce stood in the dock. The Crown made a long statement, describing the circumstances and the assistance the defendants had given to the police.

Neither was asked to speak, they just stood there giving the impression of having been briefed and to look attentive and seem sorry for themselves. A decision was not made that day, but later my solicitor advised me that Rawlings had been fined £10,000, and with an 18-months suspended sentence. I have forgotten what Pearce received, but I think it was a much lower fine if any and a similar suspended sentence. So that was that!

It was then the turn of my counsel to try and expedite matters concerning me. He explained the circumstances relating to the charges, the unfounded case, the long delay and associated stress and how I was rendered totally unemployable, even though my co-defendants still enjoyed full employment. He also dealt with the New Zealand aspect and loss of opportunity.

The judge, Alan King-Hamilton, then asked the Crown to comment, who after a great deal of waffling, more or less said that they were not ready and needed more time!

My counsel pointed out that my arrest for the money charges were made on absolutely no more evidence than that settled at the time of my first arrest, for the material charges.

After a great deal more talking about various aspects, the judge conferred with the clerk of the court and a date for the 14th of November was at last fixed.

Having arrived at my parent's home in March of 1976, then in June going onto the rented house in Frimley, Surrey, there came a time when it was abundantly clear that I had been made completely unemployable. Heaven knows how much longer we could simply mess about trying to occupy ourselves. After all, at the end of our six-month stay in Frimley, it would be nine months of the weekly dole queues and its associated humiliation. Whatever the future held we had to try and get an established home, somewhere. Our furniture was still in New Zealand, attracting storage costs. So about autumn time, we decided the best thing to do was to get an old house and do it up, thereby occupying ourselves until the trial, after all my particular skill was rehabilitation and I had practical skills and knowledge as well. After much searching, we eventually settled on a small humble terrace house in Hove, Sussex. The reason being, it was cheap, near to the shops, had potential and was not too far from my parents in Peacehaven. I suppose I had the thought in my mind that if things really went wrong, and after all, hadn't things gone amazingly wrong so far, the family would be secure, and not too far from my parents. Also, it was a practical proposition, which furthermore, would have some definite aim.

After some difficulty, my solicitor had managed to obtain a release for the balance of money locked up in Bail fees.

I think the balance was about £4,300. That was all after the years of struggle and hard work, the balance lost in legal costs. A great deal had been spent on furniture transport costs, over and back from New Zealand, solicitor's fees, travel expenses etc.

When we found the house, which was about September of 1976, I paid a visit to my bank manager in Kingsway, in Holborn.

They had always been remarkably kind and understanding. I explained what I hoped to do and that even if it went wrong, at the trial, the bank's money would be secure. It didn't take them long to agree to loan me enough to complete the purchase and have sufficient money to improve the house. It was wonderful, amazing and to the bank's, or should I say the personal judgement of the manager, great credit in supporting me in the most insecure situation imaginable. Now all these years later, it would be unthinkable, for the Banks seem to have lost that human touch, the relationship between managers and their long-term clients. Instead, we have super-efficient young whiz kids with many "A" levels, telling mature people how to manage.

Although the bank had been marvellous, it was necessary for them to have some security on the loan, apart from the value of the house. This took place in the form of another security, attached to my parent's house in Peacehaven. Something they agreed to without a moment's thought, amongst their endless acts of kindness.

We planned to complete our six months stay at Frimley and move into the house in Hove straight after Christmas, so I set to surveying the house, drawing up plans and getting the necessary approvals. Then we would all go to my parents again, every weekend, leaving the two youngest with them and get cracking on the house. I also went by myself a good part of each week, stopping over at my parents, starting up early and returning about this time. All the children were still, of course, attending schools in Frimley.

There was a lot to do as the house had been let to deteriorate to a point when it was not a viable financial proposition for local builders to purchase and restore. The house featured prominently in all the problems associated with my troubles, in sheer terms of endurance and commitment, over those difficult years. For it required enormous physical effort and enthusiasm, for all of us, over a very long period. A period when during the later stages of completion I was never sure what the court outcome would really be, although I was always blindly optimistic in my faith of the British Legal System.

Later, when I had more experience, the term "Ignorance is Bliss", comes to mind.

The house, though sound as a structure was in a very bad way, that is in terms of general repair. A new roof was needed, also new ceilings throughout. A central heating system was required, all the services had to be replaced and numerous repairs throughout. I also planned to build a new extension at the rear of the house, on 'top' of the present extension. Wildly ambitious to say the least, as there were no ceilings on the top floor at all! It also had poor basic provisions. The one toilet in the basement was reached externally, through the darkest cobweb clad, Dickensian-style basement imaginable. That was some problem at night. In the basement annexe, was a low stoneware sink, on rough brick piers, fed by a solitary cold tap, and even the electric lighting didn't work.

Apparently, the house had been lived in by the daughter of the builder who built it, and those surrounding it in the area, in about 1873. She had lived there right up to her 90s. But in spite of the gloom and general disorder, the house had quite a pleasant atmosphere. I always feel that is very important, either one feels at ease there, or not.

We aimed to get certain basic things done to enable us to move in after Christmas. There were certain essential priorities, like putting new ceilings up to the entire top floor, fix up temporary electric lighting, by fitting leads all around, subdividing the front main bedroom into two bedrooms and install a wash hand basin so we could wash, and generally do a host of other vital jobs, enabling us to exist there and continue to work to our plans.

So we worked particularly hard during those months. Countless skips were filled up by the family, working like a Chinese chain gang, carrying bucket after bucket, down through the house, along and up from the basement to the skip. By the end of each week, we would all be thoroughly worn out, filthy, dirty each day, aching all over and then stagger back to Frimley to recover.

Our six months was up at Christmas time and we decided to move all our belongings ourselves, by car. We managed to cram all we had at the time into the car and to do this I even had to borrow some steps to put the final things on the roof rack. Then off to my parents again for a couple of weeks, prior to our move into the house. Buying some second-hand bunk beds, solved the bedding problem for the children, as a result, we were able to fit into a three bedroomed, fairly small house.

Our actual moving day, was the day after the furniture turned up from New Zealand. It had been sent back totally uninsured because to reinsure it would have meant unpacking it all on the docks in New Zealand, making an inventory, repacking and then shipping. This was totally out of the question, in financial terms.

So it all came back uninsured, although a great deal was damaged, with most of the crockery smashed, the washing machine badly dented and lamps were broken, nothing at all went missing. It was really amazing since it had stood in the docks of New Zealand for six months. Our bed had severe water marks and a few things were scuffed up. But I suppose in view of the fact that the original shipping company had gone bust, we were lucky to even get it back. It was exciting, yet sad, to unpack all we could into the Hove house, quite apart from being extremely difficult.

After all, it had all come from a four bedroomed house, with study and double garage, into what basically was a two bedroomed terrace house. Above all, work on the house was in the very early days, so from there on, I had to work around it all, which of course, made it hard work and every single task more difficult. A lot of stuff had been bought specifically for New Zealand, the lounge suite was particularly large, being right for an NZ style spread out plan.

A great deal of our clothing was bought for a warmer climate, so even though it was back, a lot was unsuitable, one way or another. Being stacked in one large heap made it almost impossible to find certain things and often they were so well wrapped up in that cushioned paper that only unwrapping could identify the contents. It was exciting because the children's cherished books and toys were found, and terribly sad because absolutely everything had NZ marked all over it, as a big reminder. Now years later, this marking remains on some items, as an ever-present reminder of what might have been, even to this day. On the days when we felt a little low, the coming across of this marking made us feel even lower.

We had, of course, fixed up schools for the children. The two youngest going to the new primary school at the bottom of the garden, most convenient, they didn't even have to cross the road. The older two had to go to schools not so far away. So we settled in best we could, in a practical way.

I remember my mother standing in the middle of the house, looking at the bunk beds, the general state of the place and disorder and proclaiming that she never thought a child of hers would ever be forced to live in such conditions!

But we were reasonably happy, in our ignorance, we had our stuff back and above all, I could occupy myself. Nevertheless, the first months were very hard and uncomfortable. The youngest children wouldn't use the cold outside-toilet in the middle of the night, and I couldn't blame them. Instead, we used buckets. The lights were on the end of long leads draped all over the place, over which we were forever tripping over. All six of us washed in a single basin. I had fixed up one in one of the bedrooms with hot water via a kettle. Jean cooked on a second-hand cooker temporarily fixed up on the ground floor. All the washing up had to be in the stoneware sink in the gloom of the basement.

Surrounded by our furniture, building materials and the work in progress, it was extremely difficult for the six of us to get by practically, and luckily the children were unaware to our overall situation, a big blessing, but for Jean and myself the total uncertainty of the future was always in our minds. Would we ever finish this mammoth task! I knew that an experienced builder would take at least six months to do the work, and that is with a team of tradesmen. All `I had was myself and the family of labourers, available most of the time. Being a professional I could image the finished job, but everybody else, who perhaps found decorating, even in their own lounge a daunting task, would find my intentions impossible to imagine.

Part way through my bank manager came all the way down from London, especially to see how I was getting on. I shall never forget his expression of almost disbelief, as he first looked into the house. Then he kindly took me out to lunch, to a very nice restaurant in Hove. His visit was such a supportive gesture, and he never once mentioned the pending trial at the Old Bailey.

I was so glad, at the end to prove his judgement to be correct.

So I worked on, every day, all weekends, never-ending, somewhat like one person attempting to paint the Forth Bridge, but practical hard work is a wonderful occupier of the mind.

The whole venture was, in a way, a rather hard convenience, to take my mind of distressing thoughts, in the circumstances.

Occasional visits were made, as usual to the solicitor's. Letters going to and fro, although a date for the trial had been fixed for the 14 November 1997 there was still a great deal to do. For example, the three newly formed bedrooms were not fitted with doors until very late on in the completion of the works. As a result, we could all lie in bed and talk to each other last thing at night and first thing in the morning. Whenever I see the TV series, "The Waltons" and John Boy talking to all his family, I think of the house in Hove, and saying, 'For heaven's sake, Carole, go to sleep or you will be no good for school tomorrow.'

Bit by bit, as each room was totally finished the furniture would be set up, thereby reducing the large pile of luggage in the Lounge. But the house was far too small to take it all, especially the larger items, so all the surplus had to be packed into the roof void. In the end, there seemed as much stuff up there as in the rest of the house. Luckily the house had a good large shed at the bottom of the garden and this I used as my workshop. I had bought an electric woodworking machine and spent countless hours preparing selected second-hand timber, making doors and windows, preparing skirting boards, and so on.

The mental pressure during this time was extreme on both Jean and myself. Not one second of the day would pass without some thought racing through our heads and I knew that I couldn't possibly work so hard, seven days a week and then lie there in bed at night worrying myself silly. So I did something I have never managed to do after this period and that is, I would lie there in bed each night and I would consciously empty my mind of 'any thought'. I mean any thought, leaving myself with a completely blank mind. It worked; I would awake the next day reasonably refreshed, for another day's work.

There is one thing I do regret particularly and that is not visiting the seafront more often on weekends, instead of working. I don't think that we did that more than just a few times in the entire period.

Now I have reached the most important part of this book, a very difficult part, sadly unaware, even then of how long things could still drag on I didn't keep a diary of events, but I did keep a few notes, particularly on the time devoted to my case, which in proportion to the entire trial period roughly occupied one-half of the total three-month trial, in comparison with the time spent on the other four co-defendants. There is, of course, the official court transcript of the trial, there I presume for possible recall or re-trial, but for how long that remains intact I do not know, but I believe for only a few years.

Throughout the trial I did manage to remain composed, however hard the questioning and accusations became, except when asked to speak about my New Zealand times, after which I calmly dealt with the rest.

Then, at last, the actual trial started on the 14th of November, 1978 at 10 am, in court number 8 in the 'Old Bailey.'

The Trial at the Old Bailey 14th of November, 1977, to the 8th of March, 1978

I have now reached a very important part of this book, a very difficult part, sadly unaware, even then of how long things could still drag on I didn't keep a diary of events but did keep a few notes, particularly on the time devoted to my case, in proportion to the entire trial period. Roughly, my case occupied one-half of the three-month total trial period, in comparison with the other four co-defendants. There is, of course, the official court transcript of the trial, there I presume for possible recall or re-trial, but for how long that remains intact I do not know, but I believe for only a few years. After the trial, I wrote a draft account, now some 40 years later, I am re-writing this account, with the benefit of hindsight. With the aid of my draft notes and memories, which will never fade, and will in fact always remain vivid in my mind, I am able to accurately describe the precise events, setting the atmosphere, how it progressed and the descriptions of the major events. However, it was odd, for in a way I felt my mind detached from my body, with my eyes looking around, and my brain taking it all in.

For the first three days, we drove up from Hove but soon changed to travelling by train. In the early days, I was accompanied by Jean and my Uncle Edward, who also lived in Hove. We parked the car and went into the Old Bailey, for the first time, through the revolving doors, the ones you see on TV News reels, to be questioned by one of the attending officers, just inside. Explaining that I was a defendant, he checked and then we lodged our coats in the reception coatroom and made our way to the first floor to meet my legal team. It was clearly quite an event, for many of us. In that particular foyer, outside court number eight, and the adjoining courts milled dozens of people. They were potential Jurors, Witnesses, legal people for the defendants, ushers etc., it was a great hive of activity. The building is quite impressive, just as one would expect it to be, solid like the banks or building societies. About ten minutes to ten, we defendants met with the others and their legal teams. Then we were asked to go into the dock! Jean and my Uncle went up to the gallery.

It was an odd sensation, never to be forgotten, in walking into that court, up a couple of steps and going into the raised dock, with the attending Warders in the dock with us, sometimes one, sometimes two. The court filled up, my legal team, Alan Campbell QC, my barrister, Mr Hartley-Booth, my solicitor and all the other defendant's teams. About 18 barristers in all! Just before ten o'clock we defendants were taken out of the dock into the joint waiting room behind, serving two courts and leading down to the cell and court services. The gallery was full and the press were there in strength. There were also many relatives of the defendants and the Crown's two prosecuting council, called treasury counsel, reported to be the fourth highest graded in the country. They were assembling their papers and, making last minute preparations, together with their junior counsel. Alan Campbell, as the most senior defending QC, was placed with the best vantage point that is next to the jury benches.

At precisely ten am the Usher called for all to be upstanding to receive his Honour, Mr Justice King-Hamilton QC, a thin-faced not an unkindly-looking man and looking terribly important in his judges robes and wig. When he was seated, and we could see all this through a small gap in the door, where the Warder was watching the proceedings for his queue. Then when the time was right, the Warder opened the door. I followed directly behind him and the other five followed on behind me as we entered the dock. All eyes were turned on us as we entered and took our seats and then remained on us for some time, this was the first and one of the most dramatic days of the trial.

The first thing to be dealt with was the selection of the jury. A group of potential jurors had been brought into the court and as a court official called out their names, they walked towards where they would sit. During this time we, through our solicitors, had the right to reject three, as far as I can recall, as unsuitable, and the Crown were also able to reject and did for reasons not always obvious.

The selected persons looked much like each other, but one did look particularly scruffy, as though he hoped to make a living, sitting in the warmth. Some of those selected went up to the judge and in hushed tones gave him reasons why they would be unsuitable to serve.

If it satisfied him, they were immediately dismissed. Eventually, the 12 good and just men (including some women) were selected and sat in their allocated places.

An official of the court then stood up and read out the charges against the defendants. The Crown had made me the first and most important defendant: so charges relating to me were read out first. Six were related to the materials and three to the alleged money items. Both sets incensed me because instead of just applying one charge, covering all the materials, which I had estimated, including the washing machine, to be £270.15. The crown had made up charges for odd amounts of material and for one possible reason, to expend the case and impress the jury. No other reason to do so could exist. As for the money charges, it has to be remembered that the two detective sergeants originally had accused me of corruptly receiving a gold watch and a car! It wasn't until I had appeared at the Committal proceeding at Marylebone Magistrate's Court that I was charged with the alleged corrupt receipt of money. Charges based on no more evidence than that which had been compiled through the interviews, ending in August 1975. The money charges were made in February of 1977, some 18 months later! In my opinion to cover up the Crown's acute embarrassment in finding me back in the country with my family. Also in their desperate desire to prosecute m, they had arranged that I would be charged alongside the others, whose charges were quite unrelated to mine. A point strongly objected to by my Council. The very construction of the case against me was a corruption of the basic principles of justice and was ironically applied to one accused of corruption!

On hearing the charges, the judge, almost, it seemed apologetically reduced the nine charges to six, confirming in a sentence that the Crown were overdoing it a little!

One by one, the charges were read out relating to the other defendants, whose names as they sat on my left were. Bill Browne, Cliff Evans, Trevor Todd and Paul Beavers. They were all maintenance surveyors for Camden, employed right up to the trial, with the exception of Paul Beavers who had left for another borough, in the May after my first arrival in Camden in March 1971.

It then fell on the Crown to make their opening speech, a task carried out with enthusiasm by one of their senior treasury council, a Henry Pownell QC.

He was a hawkish-looking man, better suited to acting in Dickensian or Shakespearian plays, judging by the dramatics he used. He dealt with us one by one, and craftily, collectively, in a simple dramatic fashion, pausing to gain effect, making wild gestures and acting up to the jury and court alike. As far as I was concerned, I just couldn't believe the comments levelled at me. One would have to have the case transcript re-typed to recall the exact words, and they were wildly overstated for the best impact.

By opening the case with the prosecution's speech, they have 'considerable psychological' advantage, mainly because it is the first thing anybody hears, whilst fresh and interested, and before becoming bored by the tedium of months of court proceedings. Above all they are able, and do, make up the very worst case for the prosecution, based only upon their allegations. One has only to compare their opening speech against their closing speech to appreciate the difference. So there settles in the mind of the court, above all the jury, what villains we are, then picked up by the news people, to broadcast to all and sundry.

My uncle was in the gallery with Jean, being an ex-policeman, with the trained conviction that we are all guilty, yet to be found out, he privately thought me guilty, but as I was his nephew he supported me throughout. This, I know to be fact and is illustrated by an incident much later. I was staying at my parent's home in Peacehaven, also visiting was my Uncle and an old friend of the family of my parents, a Horace Odell. All three of us were walking around the garden enjoying the sunshine. I hadn't seen Mr Odell for a very long time so we were catching up, when out of the blue he suddenly said.

'My word you were lucky, weren't you!' implying that I had got off when guilty. I was shocked and incensed. Some long-time friend he was, but he had been talking to my Uncle. I forgot to mention that after the opening remarks of the prosecution my Uncle seldom attended the court, except for the verdict.

I strongly believe that the procedure for allowing the prosecution to start off with an opening speech is fundamentally unsound and should be discontinued.

The next day's newspapers made a big splash, with pictures of each of us. Throughout Pownell's opening speech, all eyes had been turned towards us, some openly hostile, others curious, very few it seemed to me to be dispassionate.

That one is innocent until proven guilty didn't appear to be the feeling of that day! It also didn't do our moral one little bit of good.

Throughout the four long months of the trial, it ended on the 8th of March, 1978, on my father's birthday, I never had the slightest problem in sleeping well, or beforehand, thanks to the technique I had developed to empty my mind before sleeping. This was perhaps because of my total naivety and wild optimistic faith in British justice, a faith now much bruised.

Throughout the trial, many, many days were taken up with complex legal submissions, at times almost a kind of legal chess game, all sides enjoying themselves, and on occasions taking so long that the jury were able to stay away all day. Part way through the trial King-Hamilton said that during these submissions we defendants could also go home if we wished. The others did but I chose to always attend, out of pure interest, and in case I missed something.

At a request from council, the judge also allowed us defendants, to leave the court for lunch, a considerable blessing, because on the first day we had to go down to the cells, amongst dozens of people waiting, or in the process of trial, from the various courts. The area of the cells was awful, filthy dirty, unkempt, with food thrown about and sticking to the ceiling! Scruffy characters laid out on the benches, as though in parks and dubious types plotting in corners, quite an unsavoury atmosphere altogether. The food was cold and almost inedible. Not a place to spend an hour every day, whilst thinking about all that was going on upstairs in court. The judge also decided very early on in the trial, that a coffee break was essential and they would regularly break off for half an hour, that is, everybody except the defendants who apparently had stronger constitutions.

When the extent of the case against me is fully appreciated, it becomes apparent that this was a remarkable effort by the Crown to secure a conviction, by 'any means' open to them. The cost of the trial and that is in 1978, was reported to be about half a million pounds!

That means the Crown spent some £250,000 of the taxpayer's money in an attempt to 'convict me'. Impossible to comprehend, but I'll expand on that at the end of this account.

It was suggested that Rawlings, the contractor, had kept a red notebook, listing all cash payments to the four defendants. 'No records were alleged to have been kept referring to me!'

This simple fact was ignored for its true meaning throughout the trial. Why would Rawlings keep this methodical record of these payments to the others and people outside the case, and not myself? Surely, it supported my evidence, that I did not receive any payments.

There were days when the clerical staff of Rawlings was questioned in the witness box, by both sides. Some were just bookkeepers, and their comments seemed hardly relevant to the case, against anybody. Some responses even helped our case. Then Jean Hussein came into the witness box. I had already learnt from the other defendants that she had been Rawlings mistress, whilst working for him. She said that she was well-aware of the large amount of material delivered to my address, but said in a way that implied all sorts of things. She denied vehemently that she'd been Rawlings mistress, and when questioned by Campbell, the examination became much more effective. Campbell clearly established that she had been the 'grass' to the police and, after quite a fuss by all the defendant's counsels, the prosecution confirmed she had phoned the police at Scotland Yard when after some persuasion, disclosed her name. She told them of likely payments made to a wide range of people and presumably, of the materials that were delivered to me.

She became quite upset when Campbell accused her of being Rawlings' mistress and phoning the police in a fit of "sour grapes", after being dropped by Rawlings.

The only difficulty Campbell encountered was the initials BE, written in 'capitals', in pencil, in a cash book, against a sum of £100, which of course, the prosecution alleged was a money payment to me. The argument then raged as to whether or not it was anything to do with me, but simply 'Building Expenses', possibly paid to one of the directors for pocket money. I had after all, been referred to as BRE, or Mr Edwards, or just Brian, never BE.

The initials BRE, in the professional building world, are particularly significant because they stand for 'The Building Research Establishment' and would be immediately recognised as such by anybody connected with the industry or the professions. As a result, the initials BRE became associated with my own initials, Brian Rowland Edwards. There were even jokes made about it in the office when trade newspaper cuttings used the initials, and some rag would adjust them to imply that it was me.

It was, therefore, illogical for such a strong connection to be misquoted. The thought crossed my mind, but not apparently to anyone else, that perhaps the police conveniently pencilled in BE, but slipped up in not being connected with the building industry, did not know how my initials would be interpreted.

How easy it would have been for them, and why not, it would justify their time and present little risk to themselves. And of course, all local government officers were on the "take", according to Reeder. Looking back now I know very well that they did, making the entry, for they had absolutely nothing else to go on.

It was established that somehow Rawlings had received a tip-off about a pending police raid and had managed to burn a great deal of stuff in his back garden. How such a thing could have happened is impossible to imagine? At times in the court, it became terribly tedious, even for us, protecting our futures and with everything at stake, but for everybody else, it must have been, at times, a great bore and of course, at other times, intensely exciting.

Laurie Pearce, Rawlings' manager, with whom I had dealt with on occasions, came into the box. He looked grey and submissive. A number of questions were put to him by the Crown, one of which was, 'Did he ever deliver a brown paper envelope to me in my office?' He said he did, and it was given to him by Rawlings to deliver to me. He was asked, what was in it? I think he said he wasn't sure but assumed it was an invoice.

He claimed that he could only get work in local authorities and private companies by bribing those he made contact with, otherwise, the work dried up and that his accounts, more or less showed this up. During one of the breaks in which Rawlings wasn't in the box, the judge turned to the court and said, 'Doesn't Rawlings show up as a credible witness?'

My God, I thought, *how can he say that of a man so self-confessed to that extent of corruption*? This reference by the judge was an omen of some consequence and indicated very clearly where his support was placed. He would never have said that about any other witness in court.

At the end of the day, after we had all left the box, I sometimes saw Rawlings some yards away, phoning his office and asking to be connected. I kept well clear, of course.

This part of his examination was reasonably placid but interesting for the court. Then came the most important part for me so far, the questioning of Rawlings by my Council and those for the other defendants. Rawlings looked very apprehensive over the prospect of a cross-examination, and well, he might.

Campbell made a dramatic entrance into the court, stalking to his usual place, looking neither left nor right, not even at me and gathered his papers together, taking his time. His dark eyes flashed and he looked towards Rawlings, as an eagle would look at some insignificant prey, choosing his time and moment to tear him apart. I knew what was coming because I had been pre-warned, yet the court did not. Campbell's entire demeanour was so intense, and it was clear that he obviously built himself up into a fierce state of aggression that an atmosphere descended on the court which I had never seen the like, in either film or TV play. The air was positively electric in anticipation. The jury leant forward and complete silence fell as Campbell started.

He, immediately, tore into Rawlings, accusing him, that in a fit of hysterical pique, of fabricating lies against me. He named schemes I hadn't even been involved in, saying that I had received money from them. Rawlings had in fact, named two schemes with which I had no dealings, whatsoever, a fact quite clearly proven in the court proceedings. That in fact, the money allegations were a tissue of lies and that he never intended an account for the washing machine and building materials, hoping by doing so to have some hold over me. He went on to aggressively questioning Rawlings in detail, pressing unclear answers for more detail and ridiculing others.

It wasn't long before it became clear that Rawlings was becoming seriously rattled. In fact, on the verge of completely losing his cool.

At this point, an amazing scene developed. Mr Combes QC, acting for the Crown jumped up and interrupted the questioning on some insignificant point, as he did, the judge started questioning Campbell's approach and line of questioning. This infuriated Campbell who flew into a rage when he knew he was on the verge of breaking Rawlings and he turned to the judge and said, 'You know what you are doing, you are deliberately interrupting my cross-examination, at a point when it is becoming effective. You purposely put me off my stride!'

King-Hamilton said, 'Mr Campbell,' in an attempt to put Campbell off.

'Don't deny it,' said Campbell, waving his papers around.

'Don't wave those papers at me,' said King-Hamilton, getting riled and he then called for a short recess to let tempers cool. But, of course, the Crown had succeeded in allowing Rawlings time to regain his composer, and from then on he remained unruffled and although Campbell gave him a rough time, he got no further than before. Rawlings was questioned in turn by each of the counsel for the other defendants, but few inroads were made in further discrediting him and he finally left the witness box looking greatly relieved.

It was at this point that King-Hamilton commented again on the credibility of Rawlings, as a witness. Clearly, a strong rapport seemed to exist between them, later identified to be there also with the police, as though a special understanding or affiliation existed between them.

At some point earlier on in the trial, my junior counsel, Mr Hartley-Booth had a serious car accident and was out of the trial. This was a sad blow for my defence since he knew so much of what had gone on beforehand and was so obviously quite outstanding in his service. Campbell and Hartley-Booth had become an excellent team and he was clearly a great help to Campbell.

However, his replacement, a Rex Brian was an absolutely first class replacement and he quickly got into the case, at one point praised by the Crown, who had come across him before and commented on his ability. It didn't take long before Campbell was able to considerably depend on him. Another witness was called for the Crown, he was a solicitor who worked for Camden Council. I had never come across him when I was working there.

He arrived dramatically on a stretcher, having broken a leg. His entrance added a little excitement and flair to the court proceedings. For some technical reason, he wasn't allowed to say much, thanks to Campbell and left the court looking very much deprived of his day.

At one point in the trial, possibly after the time when Rawlings had left the dock and first thing one morning, Campbell stood up and faced the judge, looking a bit mused, he asked the judge to excuse the jury, as something had to be said. The jury went out and Campbell said, that as senior for the defence he had been asked to express a view on behalf of all the defence counsel.

The point they wished to collectively make was that they were unhappy the way the trial was proceeding. In particular the close relationship between the judge and Rawlings and the way he appeared to bend over backwards to give Rawlings credibility. This view of the man's appalling record was quite unacceptable and positively unhelpful to their clients.

King-Hamilton looked furious, he went white and quiet and looked daggers at the court, saying that he would consider what they had said and would come back to it later. In fact, the following morning the jury were kept out whilst he responded, having a go back, in return. But I thought the point had been made and recorded, should there be a retrial, or appeal.

During the course of the trial, many very cross words were exchanged between Campbell and King-Hamilton, who also had the same problem with the other defending council. But he seemed to remain unaffected and unrestrained.

The point was now reached in the trial when the first of the defendants, that was me, of course, was due to go to the witness stand. Obviously, a point of great interest in the trial and on which the newspapers duly reported.

It was during this period when the defendants appeared in the witness box that the press decided to take our photographs. They would lie in wait at the end of the day and catch us as we left the court, coming through the revolving doors, or catch us first thing in the morning, on arrival. They caught me one morning, arriving for the day and photo appeared in the press with me looking a little grey and strained, as such photos tend to look.

I didn't feel particularly uneasy going into the witness box. In fact, I had waited years to do just that, and answer the charges.

To have my say, from the beginning, from my first arrest in September of 1975, and if my counsel hadn't pressed to get an earlier hearing it would have been much longer. The Crown was obviously completely indifferent to the distress caused to the accused and their families, making a myth of the supposed keystone to British justice, in that one is supposed to be "innocent until proven guilty".

So into the court I went that morning, to my place in the dock. After the usual ceremonial start off, I was called to the witness stand. I left the shelter of the dock and walked around to the stand, which was at the same level as the judge, and not too far away.

All eyes were upon me and I looked around the sea of faces, at the jury, who appeared to be a good cross-section of sensible people, the 18 barristers and their attendant solicitors, the ushers and the press and the galley, looking down into the court, rapt in their attention.

Defendants are examined the other way round, that is the defendant's counsel initially cross-examine, to be followed by the Crown, topped off by the judge, who may butt in at will. Campbell and my solicitors are not allowed to make contact with me when in the stand, from the start to the finish of the examination. Not even after the court closed each day, so one is really on one's own. But Campbell, in his usual flamboyant style, did one better. He stalked past me, as though I never existed, not even the slightest suggestion of recognition. Not the merest hint of sympathy, or favour, in fact, quite the reverse. One of the dock officer later told me that Campbell was harder on me than the Crown! Possibly he did it with great skill and cunning and this approach evoked sympathy towards me from the court, for after all wasn't he there to defend me, not to pull me apart. He really was an amazing character and would make a truly awesome full-time judge.

He started off asking me about my qualifications, which were read out at length, my period in Camden, and my responsibilities, the size of my surveying group, the financial programme and council control procedures. He asked me about various contracts and how they were placed and what was the normal procedure. Then he asked me about specific contracts, the improvements and repair work of Holborn Town Hall. Why was such a large contract organised on a "Day-work" basis and who gave authority to a Day-work method of control?

I explained that such works were extremely difficult contracts to control, being carried out around staff engaged in pressing programmes, as a consequence, at no time could we vacate large areas for easy working. To seek competitive tenders in the normal way would mean that each contractor pricing would have to thoroughly cover him since he would never know how long each area would take. Therefore, his contingency time would be a large safety factor in his price for which Camden would pay very dearly and would probably end up in contractual claims, for lack of access. So the contract was placed with a proven contractor, on a "Day-work" basis, and this was a correct way to proceed, providing a continual check was kept on the running expenditure.

It was a form of contract, that could, if it went wrong, be easily stopped and another contractor appointed, thereby safeguarding the Council. I also said that in my view it was, and still is the only way such work could proceed.

I was then asked what liquidated damages are and was requested to explain to the jury exactly what it implied and meant. This I did, turning to the jury, explaining that in applying the damages, the Council, as the owner, were recovering the true cost of the lost opportunity of letting the property, due to the contractor's inability to complete the work, within the set contract period. This seemed to please Campbell, who adopted one of his special little smiles, making sure the jury noticed. Rawlings had carried out some re-roofing works to 'Keat's House, the home of the famous poet in Keat's Grove, Hampstead. This job had not gone very well and we had great difficulty in getting anywhere near a satisfactory job. Rawlings had been asked to do the works in the first place because up to then he was the only contractor engaged in maintenance work of the house. In fact, he had a first-class decorator who did the more difficult rooms when due and had achieved a very satisfactory standard. Such a good standard in fact, that nobody else was allowed to touch the work, except Rawlings. Not long after the re-roofing works, it was decided to restore the entire house including the fabric, particularly as the local press had been publishing letters on its apparent deterioration. I had personally sought advice from the GEC's restoration division, on the most appropriate consultant to consider organising this work, choosing a well-known local architect's practice who had worked nearby.

This practice suggested that because of the unknown nature of the work, the requirements of which could only be defined when parts of the property were taken apart, it would be sensible to organise the contract on a "Day-work Basis", suggesting a negotiation with a well know Islington firm of builders with a good reputation in the area. This proposal received sanction from the committee and the restoration works were eventually very satisfactorily completed, to the credit of both the architect and the builder. Furthermore, the final account was well within the estimate approved by the committee, upholding this basis of contract, when properly controlled.

This was, of course, a useful point for the court, more or less proving the basis of Day-work, when applied to Holborn Town Hall and to Berkshire House, and I am sure of interest to the jury. Sometime later, after the works to Keat's House was completed I attended a re-opening celebration, held in a marquee on the lawns of the house. Very much later, after I had returned from New Zealand and was working so hard on my house in Hove, I stopped for a tea break. All of a sudden the children were shouting, 'Look, there's Daddy on TV!' I rushed into the room and sure enough there I was, drinking white wine whilst talking to somebody in the marquee at that celebration. Strange life's little twists and turns.

At some point, after this run of questioning and answers, and well after settling down after lunch, Campbell turned to me and said he was now going to ask me questions about my emigration to New Zealand. I think the judge said, 'Is this necessary?' Campbell replied, 'Yes, it is.'

I cannot quite recall now what were the few initial questions, generally asked on the subject, but then he asked, 'Why did you return?'

'We had to return because we were…'

At this point, a very strange thing happened to me. Up to then, I had been confident, only pleased to be asked questions and be given a chance to answer fully, but when asked why I had returned from New Zealand my mind seized up! A strange numbness seemed to creep up the back of my head and I became almost, at once, both too hot and too cold. I just couldn't speak.

I could feel my temperature racing up and down, out of control. I looked at King-Hamilton, there, close to me, I was unable to speak, just try to say something with my hands, trying to say sorry. I can't get it out! In a way attempting to apologise for my inability to respond to the questions, but King-Hamilton simply turned away. He couldn't spare just one minute for me, but had all the time in the world for Rawlings! Through the mist that had dropped over my eyes, I could see the shocked faces of the jury. I believe one woman was quietly crying and was holding a handkerchief to her face.

I could see the shocked face of my solicitor, not far herself from tears and I could hear Campbell apologising to the judge and to the court, for the totally unexpected reaction from me, saying he had no idea I would be so affected. I felt acutely embarrassed, to be intensely witnessed at this point of extreme anguish. King-Hamilton said he thought it was time to finish for the day, as it was near to finishing anyway.

I left the box to pass John Green, the assistant director of architecture, who had obviously been sitting there alongside the police and prosecution. I looked at him and he looked white and shaken. In the following day's newspapers, it stated in large print.

'Edwards breaks down in the witness box!'

This further embarrassed me, I imagined all my ex-colleagues reading each day's events.

In fact, I hadn't actually broken down. I had a virtual mental seizure and as I try to understand my own reaction, I believe the absolute frustration of the protracted events leading up to the trial, above all the deep psychological deprivation I felt in having lost the opportunity of settling in New Zealand, with my family, and all that it meant to me, was a loss of such magnitude, that I simply was unable, or prepared to talk about it to anybody, least of all the court!

For the court represented all the frustrations and hang-ups of the State bureaucracy and as such could never understand that they themselves had deprived six English people of living a wholesome, complete life in possibly the safest and most sensible and beautiful country in the world.

How could I ever attempt to explain all I had felt ever since the age of 11? What it had taken to make up our minds to emigrate, and all the soul-wrenching emotional upheaval this brings about. To be brought back and accused over more fanciful charges. I simply believe my reaction was a mixture of anger and anguish, which just overwhelmed me and made it impossible to speak about it.

I got back to Hove that evening, obviously looking very shaken. Jean looked at me and was sensible enough to say nothing, leaving me to recover the best I could. It is an odd thing to say but we never discussed what would happen if they found me guilty!
I just couldn't see how that could happen and I still held on to my naïve faith in British Justice. I know now, even though we never talked about it that she had plans in her mind for this eventuality, but I have never asked.

I arrived back the next day in the witness box, looking and feeling rather numb, thinking to myself that I must pull myself together and not make a fool of myself with a performance like that of yesterday. I had slept reasonably well and had wondered, as the train travelled along, what the other passengers would have thought if they knew I was to be, in a few hours, appearing in the witness box at the Old Bailey!

The court settled down and Campbell poised himself to continue the questioning. He said he was going to continue with the same line of questions, on New Zealand.

'I knew again I was in trouble.' I knew I would, whatever I tried to do, have the same emotional control problems and already felt that odd feeling coming over me. It was a potential disastrous situation for me. Fortunately, King-Hamilton leant forward and said to Campbell.

'Mr Campbell, I don't think we will pursue this line of questioning further!'

I was terribly relieved, yet I had so wanted to tell the court what a fiasco the Crown had made of our lives. Strange now after so many years on if I was faced again with that court scene and that same line of questioning, I would probably react the same way. Even writing about it after all this time and re-living the loss we suffered, makes me feel deeply distressed.

Campbell asked me about the materials and washing machine I had purchased from Rawlings, about how I came to get them that way.

I said it was really very simple. I was lunching with Rawlings and his brother Ken and their manager Laurie Pearce when, as often happens, they asked me what I did during my spare time. What interests did I have? So I told them I had quite a few. Car maintenance was a serious interest, and I also made reproduction cabinet furniture, made homemade wine and did a lot of do-it-yourself jobs around the home. In fact, I was just about to build a small extension to my garage and form an external utility room. I said I would do everything myself, bricklaying, carpentry, plastering, everything etc. enjoying it very much.

Rawlings then said he could possibly help because they had recently bought a Builder's Merchants and could supply all the materials to my home at very favourable wholesale rates. All he would need initially was a list of my requirements. I said that that would be very helpful because one of the most frustrating things about doing work myself, was the hours and hours spent at the counters of various builders merchants, waiting for some small fitting, only to find that they were short. I had, therefore, been obliged to go to another merchant, join the queue and wait all over again. Yes, several lots delivered to my door would be a great help, not forgetting the trade discount. So it was left that when I was ready I would supply the list and they would deliver the materials.

I almost forgot about it for some time, as it takes quite a while to get statutory approvals, for permissions, like the building regulations, and planning etc. Also Jean had our youngest child, Carole, in November of 1972 and for the first time, the extension became of secondary importance. At this time our washing machine, which I had repaired countless times, was giving trouble and we thought about getting another one. Then I thought, perhaps Rawlings, with his trade connections could get me one at a wholesale discount price. The discount on electrical goods was the highest of all trade discounts. When I asked Rawlings he said, no problem, just give him the model and spec number and he would organise it. The machine arrived just after Carole was born and when Jean's Mother was at the house, helping out. I soon fixed it up and with four young children in the household, it was a great help. It was the only item delivered by Rawlings that arrived without a delivery ticket, even though Jean asked the delivery chap at the time and I also asked Rawlings many times. He would reply, 'Oh, don't worry you will get an invoice eventually.'

The other building materials didn't arrive in nice clear lots but came in oddly complied batched, often seriously holding me up, when I had taken leave off from work to do something specific. In fact, I had to chase Rawlings several times when it was becoming quite a problem.

At the end, I wished I had organised the materials myself, as I seemed no better off.

We carefully kept all the delivery tickets and I listed them, estimating their approximate value collectively, to compare against the final account. Campbell asked me where the original delivery tickets are now and I replied that I have them all, at home.

At this, the jury caught the judge's eye and asked that they would like to see them, also all the correspondence on the New Zealand job offers, travel arrangements etc. I said yes, I would be pleased to provide them and would bring them along tomorrow.

I could see that King-Hamilton wasn't too pleased and knew I had gained an advantage, because, for one thing, the court seemed surprised that I held all the delivery tickets myself, with lists of their approximate value, even though I'd stressed this point to the police, commenting that I would hardly keep all the tickets if I didn't want a bill! The police never once asked to see them! I also stressed that I did absolutely everything myself, not one day's labour was done by anybody else. Strange also my comments never appeared in my statements.

I knew the New Zealand letters would help my case and so did King-Hamilton. That night I carefully collected them all together, numbered them and prepared a covering list, writing at the head. "Please return these when finished with". I didn't want them conveniently lost.

The next morning, from the witness box I formally handed them over to the jury. On looking at them, King-Hamilton looked amused and said, 'Somebody has written on top of the list, "Please return when finished with".'

I said, 'Yes, it was me, they are important to my case.'

The summary list also contained brief comments, like the one referring to the letter from the New Zealand Government, saying we could stay on, and I made the comment that this letter arrived through the front door of our New Zealand home the very day we actually landed in England! I did get the letters back, eventually, after my Council had pressurised the Crown, several times over.

I was asked about my relationship with Rawlings and said I met him earlier on in my Camden days, not long after I had arrived in the borough, when Brown, one of the maintenance surveyors arranged a meeting. The meeting was friendly, with Brown there and we discussed their long-standing work period with the Council, particularly their work at Keat's house.

Rawlings said he was also interested in rehabilitation work and would like to have a go. I said we were looking very hard for additional contractors, for that type of work and that I would think about the idea. We then decided to have a look at Keat's House for which Rawlings was the sole contractor. In looking over the house I met the Librarian and Archivist, Christina Gee who was stationed in the adjoining library building; she came out to give us her view of the most pressing problems. A pleasant surprise for me because a surveyor I worked with previously in Harrow, Jim Lee, had one time lived in the basement of Keat's House, with his parents, his father had been the caretaker.

At the time of the works to Keat's House, other jobs were also in progress with Rawlings, particularly Holborn Town Hall and a rehabilitation job in Oak Village. They were important jobs and I made sure that I was up to date on their various stages of work. In doing so and during the overall period, I had lunch with Rawlings on a number of occasions, sometimes with him alone and sometimes with his brother Ken, or his manager Laurie Pearce. The nearest place to my office in Holborn Town Hall was the "Sportsman's Club" at the bottom of Tottenham Court Road, of which he was a member. Convenient to me since I could walk there within five minutes. It also had a very good restaurant and during lunch times the prices were quite reasonable.

I never dined or socialised with Rawlings, or anybody associated with his firm at any time, other than lunchtimes. The

Crown was to make a great play at this so-called wining and dining. Quite amazing really, using it as the main plank of their case, which in my view placed their case in context!

In my position then in Camden, I lunched out reasonably frequently, possibly no more than any other businessman in London and almost certainly a lot less than the average bank manager or city official.

Often it was a ghastly bore, with the host bending my ear in selling his companies services. At times, of course, it was enjoyable. Always and for at least 70 percent of the time, the main subject would be the area of work in which they were placed, with me explaining what services the Council expected and how the system worked.

Almost without exception, everyone was told quite simply, yes, the Council has a very large programme and providing they were efficient and competitive, the Council would be only too happy to let them compete.

These lunches also served a purpose. They were always by the invitation of the contractor or serving consultant, who when new to the council would meet me, as chief building surveyor and were sometimes, not unnaturally a little nervous. Sometimes I tried very hard to put them at their ease and they would sit there in front of me, in a suit they were not used to wearing, perhaps being a working partner in a building firm, being more at ease in an open neck shirt and overalls. But after lunch, a few jokes and a couple of drinks they would relax and one could get a better impression of the real person. Learning a great deal about the man and what made him tick, his aims, his degree of responsibility, possibly just how reliable he might be when hard put. It was in effect like conducting a relaxed interview. Following the declared interviewing techniques, to put them at their ease and gently progress into a full interview without them hardly being aware. Sometimes, I became very wary of the character of the man being revealed to me and can think of one occasion in particular when my worst fears were upheld. Due to the pressure of the situation and lack of available builders to carry out some emergency work, we had to ask one of the new builders. It was a job that required a great deal of pre-planning and at the very last moment, he completely let us down. It was the taking over of squatted property. He had, over lunch come across as a bit of a braggart, but at that time we, as a Council, were almost obliged to give him a try, for lack of available builders.

On the other hand, Rawlings had made a good initial impression on me, from the first meetings, on Keats House, where, in particular, he came highly recommended and for some time afterwards. He was obviously very bright, very personable, easy to talk to and came over as sincerely wishing to further his firm and give a good service. After all, he had worked for Camden for a long time before I arrived and also for a number of other London Councils, always a safe sign in local government, and plus a wide range of private companies. At the beginning, he seemed a sound choice to try, apparently well proven. But as is often the case, his company did not match their fine aims or service and gradually his involvement with the Council reached the point of becoming strained.

All his work, including Holborn Town Hall and Keats House, were looked after by other surveyors, plus the assistance of clerks of works. This meant that his accounts had to satisfy most of these people, then my deputy or another colleague would see them for the final certification. An interesting point, which was never entirely grasped by the Crown, perhaps as far as they were concerned, rather conveniently was the Oak Village rehabilitation job, which was extraordinary late in being completed, as an example.

But one of his major problems seemed to be that his own surveyors would issue invoices and accounts with insufficient information in them, and as a result, my surveyors could not certify them, thereby delaying payments.

Rawlings would telephone me directly and ask me why his invoices were not being passed. I would usually say. 'There is no problem, other than their shortage of information. Complete what my surveyors are asking and I will be pleased to pass them, but cannot otherwise.' This sort of exchange went on for some of the time.

On one occasion he telephoned me at home. It was Saturday morning of the 16 June 1974 when we were going up to Jean's mothers, in Grimsby. We were quite ready, the stuff in the car and the children organised when the phone rang. Jean unlocked the house and discovered it was Rawlings. I got out of the car and went into the study and said.

'Hello, Len. He was obviously in a bit of a state, sounding very odd and immediately went into a tirade about the problems of late payments and other problems, saying his accounts were perfectly fine.'

'Len, I said I have told you before there is no advantage to the Council to delay payment if justified, all you have to do is to make sure the questions of my surveyors are answered, then they can be paid.' At this he seemed to go into hysterics, quite impossible to make any sense of, or be able to talk to, ranting and raving away, about the effect on his firm and I believe he said he couldn't build his office extension because of lack of funds. He put the phone down in the end and I got back into the car, telling Jean what had happened. It had been a wild phone call, quite the wildest I had ever received and it stayed with me all the way up to Grimsby.

So much in fact that when I got there I wrote a letter to the office, telling them what had happened and saying that they may receive a similar call, be prepared.

Unfortunately, my letter was never found and only my word and Jeans' confirmed the event.

Sometime later, in October 1974, when by absolute good fortune, Sam Weller, the deputy chief quantity surveyor was sat opposite me in my office at Berkshire House, when the phone rang. By chance, Sam and I had been discussing outstanding Rawlings & Lucas accounts.

Again it was Rawlings, clearly extremely agitated, to put it mildly. He was obviously either totally drunk or utterly hysterical and immediately started on the same vein he had used when phoning me at home. He complained of lack of payment. My response, when I could get a word in, was the same as before, satisfy my surveyors and you will be paid. Again this sparked off complete hysteria, and the phone went down. I turned to Sam and said. 'Phew, I never want to receive a phone call like that again.' I then told him briefly what it was all about. The phone call had rattled me, in the calm of the day, suddenly bursting through the phone like that. I did say to my surveyors, see what you can do to clear them up as soon as possible, even if you have chase Rawlings for more information. Which they did, but it didn't seem to improve matters very much.

We later learnt in court that Rawlings was owed something like £17,000 by Camden and I understood that this was never paid, because of the case. This was surprising if he was really owed the money.

I was asked either by Campbell or the Crown, what efforts I had made to pay Rawlings for the materials and washing machine. I said many, I had repeatedly asked him how my account was getting on, and when I could expect an invoice.

Also every time we made contact in the office, I asked him again. He was always coming into the office, in regard to day to day maintenance work, that he was doing for the various surveyors. His answer was, 'Don't worry about it, you will get one in due course, anyway it's saving you interest.' Or he would say, 'I will do it when I get around to it, but at the moment our books are in a mess and we are being sorted out.' This I believed because he'd mentioned it several times that he had taken on, a swish upmarket firm of West End accountants to reorganise his booking systems.

I even went down to his office one day and got the same old story. On that occasion, we had a drink in a pub around the corner. I think it was at that time, or it could have been the time we looked at some sites where he had applied some new roofing covering, a process developed by his firm. It was lunch time and there was some sort of activity going on at the pub's far end, rough stripping to music. The pub was filled with smoke, which always gets into my eyes and the noise was totally deafening. We couldn't talk and be heard at all and I didn't stay there long as I had to return to the office for a meeting.

I added to my reply, that by then it was becoming obvious that I was getting nowhere, in trying to persuade Rawlings to let me have an invoice. Then I learnt of the police questioning certain of my surveyors. My immediate reaction was, apart from the shock at what was going on, and now perhaps, at last, I will get an invoice. But I didn't and did not know what to do.

If I pushed Rawlings harder for an invoice, it might be misunderstood, so perhaps wrongly I waited until eventually I myself was questioned, on a false request to attend at Leman Street police station. This I told the police in my first statement, and the two detective sergeants, who later denied this under oath.

After that, the first one, I phoned my solicitor and met one of the Principals who, after a lot of thought, advised me to estimate the total cost and send a cheque to Rawlings. This I did, in any case, I had already made a running estimate for my own guidance. Eventually, it was returned from Rawlings' solicitor, to my own, saying that the police had been advised.

Later on, it became very clear that Rawlings never intended to bill me, hoping to have some kind of hold over me.

The questions from Campbell eventually came to an end and he said so to the judge but sought the right to re-question me, when necessary.

It is odd, in the circumstances, but now, all these years on I cannot recall whether it was Parnell or Combes who started to question me. I think it was Combes, Pownell, the most senior of the Treasury Council had excused himself from the trial sometime during Campbell's questioning of me, to go to a case in which he would be more certain of victory.

I remember having the distinct impression that, it wasn't going quite to his liking, so he left the case, to make sure his reputation wasn't tarnished. Combes, the second most senior Council was then left with Parnell, his junior counsel, Parnell was a baby-faced character who seemed to find our fate continually amusing, funny enough to go into long girlish bouts of giggles. When one is placed, as I was, in extreme public scrutiny, fetched back from New Zealand, as it were, purposely to demoralise me by keeping me hanging about for years, his reaction was at the very least most irritating.

I liked Combes, he seemed fair, honourable and never stooped to tricks or turns, appearing almost detached, yet applying his questions with skill and care. But inwardly I objected when he complained to the judge that he had difficulty in 'Thinking on his feet!', and especially when the judge sympathised.

I felt like saying out aloud, 'What about me, what about us then?'

My entire response had to be thinking on my feet (even though I sat), yet they were able to prepare their material in advance.

Combes picked up a bundle of papers and passed them up to me in the box, he said.

'Mr Edwards would I, I liked him for his courtesy in using Mr and I think I would actually have objected if he hadn't. Would I take my time and examine these accounts, which were by Rawlings and Lucas, to Camden Council and for works for which he had contracted. 'He said in no way was I to feel hurried, just have a good look'. So I did, with the entire court watching intently, finding it a little more exciting than so far. Combes then said.

'Mr Edwards, have you studied them long enough to appreciate what they are?'

I said yes, he then said.

Would I agree, and he emphasised his words, that they were perfectly satisfactory accounts, in my experience, and adding, said would I have a closed look, if it will help.

This I did and answered by saying.

'No, they are not in my opinion satisfactory accounts, because I was told that they had been through my department and in particular the quantity surveyor's department.

No quantity surveyor, worth his salt, would thoroughly check these account without methodically ticking off each item, even in coloured pencils, or by commenting here and there. These accounts are totally unmarked, unheard of in the circumstances. Then I spotted something really interesting. Heading the accounts was a summary sheet and in comparing the summarised totals on the top sheet against a related under sheet, I found a simple arithmetical error! This I pointed out to Combes, with some pleasure, saying again.

'No, I certainly wouldn't say that they are satisfactory accounts. I have examined them for only a few minutes, and even then have found a simple mistake. If I had hours, or even weeks, as they possibly had in the preparation, then, no doubt I could pull them apart!'

Combes looked very unsettled and Campbell positively smirked, I noticed that even the jury seemed to enjoy the turn of events.

I was questioned again about the so-called dining out. Having in mind that I never dined out with Rawlings, other than at lunchtimes, and accepting that the places were certainly grand, the actual lunches were designed as business lunches and were not over-expensive. He went through the routine of re-calling the lunches and with whom. It all seemed to me to be a desperate measure to make something of them. Surely, they didn't believe I would sell my soul for a few lunches! They managed to fit an allegation that I had been paid money during one of the lunches, at the Sportsman's Club, on Tottenham Road.

I was asked at some length about my statements made to the police, when they were taken, were they properly conducted, did I go with anybody etc.

After the first interview and accusation, I had taken a solicitor, who was later to say that he thought I should hear no more.

It was either Campbell or Combes who asked me about the first visit to the police station and again I related the story and the aggression applied by the two detective sergeants, Hine and Reynolds. I can't recall now, but some doubt was raised that they would have pressurised me this way. I became very irritated, then angry and I turned to the judge and said, 'Hine and Reynolds are lying, the jury know that they are lying, the whole court knows that they are lying!'

King-Hamilton looked very uncomfortable. I don't suppose many witnesses react this way. Sometime later, when travelling from Hove to London, I spotted in a newspaper a short article referring to two police officers accused of perjury. One was Detective Sergeant Hine. I was quite excited at finding this and passed on a copy to my solicitor, suggesting that they follow it up, because if he was a proven perjurer it would be of benefit to my case. Nothing came out of my request and I never found out whether or not he was found guilty.

Rex Bryan, my barrister said to me that if he had been able to have a go at them, in the witness box, he would have been able to establish that they were lying. It was a comforting comment and I wished he could have been given the chance.

It is very strange now, looking back and with the benefit of hindsight that I never pushed Campbell to include two persons highly relevant to my case.

One would have been Detective Chief Inspector Reader. After all, he controlled both Hine and Reynolds and above all, it was him who had interviewed me so many times and made whatever recommendations he had to his superior, a Detective Superintendent Page.

The other one was Alex Harney, the senior surveyor directly responsible for all the maintenance surveyors and reporting to me.

Sometime later I realised why, both were certainly "Free Masons", and perhaps even the judge!

I am now certain that had I take up one of many offers during my many different local government positions, to join the "Free Masons", I to would never have appeared at this trial! I really believe this.

Eventually, my days in the witness box came to an end, by then I got the impression that Combes had eased up, accepting that he would gain nothing for the Crown by continuing. However, King-Hamilton thought he'd have a last go.

Turning to me, and he was quite physically close to me there, at the same level, only a few feet away, he said.

'Mr Edwards, when you had all this material and the washing machine and couldn't get an account from Rawlings, why didn't you estimate the cost yourself and send Rawlings a cheque?'

I said because I was sure at the time that I would eventually get an account and was not put off by the delay, especially as

Rawlings was so hopeless at quickly sorting out his accounts for the Council. Also as Rawlings had said, which I knew to be the case that his whole office accounts were being sorted out by that swish West End firm of Accountants and that his accounts were in a mess.

There were no more questions and I then left the box with some relief on the 20 January 1978, at the end of this four-day session and returned to the dock with the other defendants.

The trial continued with a number of defence witnesses being called, all ex-colleagues from Camden and I watched them one by one, each with visible nervousness go into the witness box and give evidence.

I am not completely sure whether they were called for the defence or the Crown, certainly in every case their evidence was supportive to my case, even when quite clearly the prosecution seemed to be relying on their support. In these cases, Campbell easily extracted useful support to my case.

Sam Weller, the deputy chief quantity surveyor at Camden and the one who witnessed one of the phone calls I had received from Rawlings, was called and confirmed all I had said. It never really seemed to sink into the court, that here was a witness who confirmed this agonised phone call to me.

He was a witness who hadn't even been interviewed by the police, even though I had thoroughly described the events in my statements to them.

It was as though the police only heard or acted upon evidence that upheld their personal view of the situation.

Campbell never questioned the police about this aspect of the case, why I can never really understand, I had also fully reported the matter to my solicitor. I considered the off the cuff comments made by the police to me, and to Browne, one of the defendants, to be very important.

Browne had come into my office early one morning, early on in the events, in the first instance, when the other defendants were being questioned by the police. He said that he had been down to Leman Street police station and had been interviewed, then roughly described what had happened. He said that after his interview had finished, Detective Chief Inspector Reader asked him about me, ending up by saying.

'I'll get that fucking bastard Edwards, if it's the last thing I do!'

A very disturbing comment to be passed on in the circumstances, remembering that I had at that time purchased materials from Rawlings and hadn't been able to get a bill. I think it was after I had been down to Leman Street Station at this time, at my own wish, to tell them in advance that I was planning to emigrate to New Zealand, that Reader opened up a little, saying that in fact he already knew. I couldn't imagine how, I told nobody other than my colleague Trevor James and I knew that he would be discreet. In fact, I had kept it to myself for the very simple reason that it is a very long process, emigrating with a large family, and if at the end of the day one didn't get a job there, or simply changed one's mind, having declared to all at work, then my continuing work situation could have been jeopardised as they wouldn't know whether I was coming or going. It was at the same meeting that Reader casually remarked, 'That all local government officers were on the take!' as he put it, and this was proven to him when he overheard a particular conversation in his local pub, when he said that, I couldn't believe my ears, and I said.

'You are seriously saying that in your opinion all local government officers are taking bribes,' thinking of my colleagues and all those I had worked with over the years.

'Yes,' he said, he was sure they were.

A chance remark perhaps, made when off guard, but in my view the most significant comment made in the entire saga, of that long year. I say this because Reader, in holding this biased view, advised and convinced his superiors and the director of prosecutions, that I was guilty and what they had found was the tip of the iceberg!

Being armed with this view and never quite appreciating that although I was titled as Chief Building Surveyor, I was nowhere near the status of a listed "statutory chief officer", like the director of architecture, the Council's planning officer, etc. My actual status was merely that of just another group leader, in a large department. But all the press had on the case as "the biggest corruption probe since the 'Poulson Affair'", possibly themselves being advised initially by the police, and of course, quoting the opening remarks of the Crown's prosecution, made at the beginning of the trial.

Once the Majesty of the Law had ground into action and settled itself on a course, there was nothing a person like me could do but attempt one's best defence and be swept along by the system. Only death would keep me from the process.

Eventually, Jean was told by my solicitor that she would be required to give evidence and to be ready at court the following Monday, even though they didn't know precisely when. The court wasn't, in fact, ready for her until the end of the week and although she was reasonably ready on Monday, she obviously became more unsettled as each day passed, feeling off colour on the day she had to appear.

For a witness like her, appearing in the witness box, suddenly in from the corridor outside, to appear in front of the pomp and glare of the court to be stared at by the jury and public, not to mention numerous counsel, must, in itself, have been a frightful ordeal. For myself and the other defendants, we were used to the public scenes, committee meetings and other meetings, and were somewhat better prepared. Not, of course, the ordinary housewife, or average man or woman in the street. She wasn't in the witness box for more than half a day, yet for me, it was the worst part of the trial. Watching her being questioned by both Campbell and Combes.

King-Hamilton, who had bent over backwards to be helpful and kind to Rawlings, didn't put himself out for Jean at all, evens appearing a little testy! He asked her why she didn't think it appropriate to estimate the cost of the materials and send a cheque to Rawlings. She said because she thought we would get a bill.

He then asked her if she had ever heard of the "Poulson Affair". I can't remember now if she said yes or no, and eventually, she left the witness box with obvious relief.

The trial then continued, dealing with each of the other defendants, in turn. Setting aside the reason I was there, it really was a unique experience. Browne had elected not to appear in the witness box, but to make a statement from the dock. His part in the trial was, in itself, unusual because it was clearly established by expert medical witnesses that there he had been a long time alcoholic and all the time he worked in Camden. I knew, like the others in the office, that he liked a drink, but never ever suspected that he was out of control and neither did my colleagues.

In the dock, he had been heavily dosing himself with a variety of pills and looked thin and drawn as he walked with the aid of a stick. King-Hamilton, thinking he was attempting to gain sympathy instructed the dock officer to administer the pills, as prescribed, and this was done. His statement from the dock was really good, very well presented, in circumstances and a very good effort.

Evans and Todd both went into the box, in turn, putting up a good defence. Where their evidence was different to mine was, in regard to their treatment by the police. Setting aside the first interview I had with the two detective sergeants, they claimed to have been far more pressurised than I was and were threatened with a term in the "Peter", a term for jail, and one I'd never heard before. They also claimed to have been deprived of food and drink, and generally, the police were not so civilised with them, as they were with me, in my formal interviews. They all, one way or another held similar views of their treatment. My contrasting interviews couldn't have helped their case. I believed their evidence and in regard to the difference in treatment, I put that down to the over emphasis the police had placed on my job title.

Beavers didn't appear in the witness box either, electing to say nothing, but his previous dealings with the police had irritated them as he was said to have been uncooperative and cheeky. Being in reasonably close contact with the other four defendants during the trial period gave me a chance to know them better. After all, when I was in Camden I was fairly remote and they had addressed me as Mr Edwards, except Bill Browne, who never followed the pattern and sometimes called me Brian. In getting to know them better I got to like them during the trial period, and their wives, fathers and friends, meeting them in the court canteen or outside the courtroom.

Odd as it may seem, the dock officers were remarkably nice people, impartial and very friendly, in a civilised way, perhaps chosen for their patience and understanding. They were of considerable moral support and comfort to us throughout the trial.

The days of the trial progressed into weeks and then into months, the comforting feeling of being wanted returned again, it became very much like going to work, in a regular job, catching the train to and from a set point, the same computer faces, being recognised by the court attendance, just as one would by colleagues in a normal days work.

During one journey from Hove to Victoria, I recognised a person on the platform who was a senior official in the Department of the Environment, and one in fact with whom I'd had many a meeting on Camden's work. He obviously saw me then, and as many times afterwards, went quickly up to the other end of the platform. On another occasion, when I was having a coffee in a café near to Berkshire House, near my old office, I saw next to my table a senior planner from Camden. She made no attempt to say hello, even though she knew me well, then she quickly finished her coffee and left.

These were some of the very few occasions when I was actually shunned. It felt odd, hurtful and more than anything, annoying. Later, years later in fact, when I was at that time employed by the London Borough of Islington, and on a similar visit to the Department of the Environment, I saw again the same chap, he was sitting there, in the department's canteen. This time he conversed as though nothing had happened, oh but it had, hadn't it!

The time was then reached in the trial for the summing up by both the prosecution and the defence. With Pownell gone to gain recognition elsewhere, the prosecution speeches wouldn't be anywhere near as dramatic as the opening ones. Combes was obviously a fairer, more honourable person and would stick to the facts. His remarks in regard to me were almost complimentary and I got a distinct feeling that in my case he had almost given up his role as prosecutor, at this point saying that in regard to the police aspects of my case I would have made a very good prosecution witness! I wasn't entirely sure what he meant by that and one may speculate endlessly. Did he mean that because I said, setting aside again the interview with the two sergeants, that my interviews with the police were civilised and controlled, of help as they conflicted with the evidence of the other defendants?

As a good deal of the time of the trial was devoted to this aspect of the evidence of the others, it possibly was of help to the Crown, especially as I hadn't been able to talk about the comments made by Reader.

King-Hamilton didn't look too happy with Combes who had been almost nice to me and it was easy to see when he disapproved, looking tetchy and nervous.

Combes was much harder on the others, especially as with two he had virtually extracted minor confessions of guilt. I thought quite unfairly in one aspect. Todd had obviously been utterly honest with the Crown, explaining how he had kept a bottle of whisky, with a £10 note attached to it. It was on Todd's behalf that we heard in the court the best character reference I had ever heard. It was given by an ex employer of Todd and it was really quite outstanding, moving even. However, King-Hamilton looked completely unmoved, far less than he did over his support of Rawlings: in spite of Rawlings own confession to have bribed over 20 councils, large companies and even the Metropolitan police itself! Sadly, a fact not one of the defending councils used in their closing speeches. Combes finished his speech, he looked more than tired and more than relieved to have finally finished.

It is certainly a hard and highly skilled task to be a senior counsel as such a large trial when every word could be eventually picked up at a possible appeal.

The following day it was the turn of the counsel for the defendants. As usual, Campbell was first to start. He stood up slowly, his back ramrod straight and his head looking up with a benign smirk on his face. He looked around the court. I thought, *if he keeps this up he won't even need to speak*! He likened the Crown's entire case to somebody selling a property in which the foundations were cracked and at fault, and in knowing this purposely set out to deceive the would-be purchaser, by papering over the cracks. He then proceeded to pull down, step by step, any credibility left in Combes statement and continued by recapping on all the evidence given by various Crown Witnesses, Jean Hussein, Rawlings ex-mistress, as he put it, the secret police informer who had contacted the police in a pique of sour grapes, having been set aside by Rawlings and in particular how the Crown, quite illegally had tried to cover up this very important part of the evidence.

He then commented on aspects of principle, how the contract for Keats' House was a success when organised on a Day-work basis. Also, that had the concerned keep a closer watch on Holborn Town Hall, that would also have turned out satisfactorily.

How right at the very point of applying damages to contracts on which Rawlings was a fault, I was supposed to be receiving money, on jobs that must have lost money! He referred to the two hysterical phone calls I had received from Rawlings. I didn't recall him mentioning the lack of interest shown by the police in not interviewing Sam Weller, the witness to one of the phone calls. Neither did he mention that at the time police interviewed me, just prior to my planned going to New Zealand, when at this time I was some £3,750 in the red, they had enquired of me, how my bank manager had accepted such a large overdraft, at the very time I was being accused of receiving sums of money!

Campbell's speech took so long towards the end it became a little dry. One of the women solicitors told him, during a break, "to ginger" it up a bit, which he did, courting the jury with his usual skill and reacting to their responses, just like some Shakespearian stage actor. He eventually finished with a flourish and sat down.

The other defendant's counsels were quite different, and were much shorter, but had a different type of case to answer and based a lot on their logic on the premise that the police were lying, particularly in regard to the various statements. All went that way around, setting aside the consequences to be resolved at the end of the trial. It was fascinating to watch each counsel handle their speeches. They were all very good, some quite outstanding. Some had confronted King-Hamilton, and others had rebelled, quite the opposite.

Brown's counsel, like Campbell, had several goes at the judge and had received, in return, several wiggins, none of which had any effect at all! Campbell had told me that this particular counsel was a bit of a "maverick" and of course, it helped Campbell in his approach, apart from entertaining the court and the jury, who were always pleased for some excitement.

Having been through the whole trial and watching the many interviews with junior and senior counsel, I must say that I was very impressed with their competence, their superb grasp of the English language, their reports and statements, involving the most complex situations, and they were absolutely masterful. They certainly needed a sharp brain, had to give close attention to detail and above all, if these attributes are to be effective, a sound sense of the theatrical. Campbell would have made ten out of ten on each count.

The following stage in the proceedings was the judge's summing up speech, divided over each of the defendants and of course, starting with me.

Campbell has earlier on referred to him openly in court, as a compassionate judge, but I think it wasn't necessarily Campbell's true opinion, just a bit of tactful flattery. When the trial started, I also thought the same way. King Hamilton to be fair and with a good sense of humour, nevertheless clearly biased towards the Crown, hence, his conspicuous support of Rawlings. I had possibly, like most people who had never entered a court before, thought all judges in the British system of justice to be tough, but always scrupulously fair and impartial. Was I in for a shock!

He said he had done his best, but he had a tough time getting it all down, all that I had said because I spoke at the speed of an express train, but he had managed to get down some 50 pages! I have always spoken too fast, it is a bad habit of mine, maybe because I think fast when writing and find it a job to get the words down before I have thought ahead. Also perhaps because I was at times a little nervous. Then he made a remark, that to my ears astounded me.

He said he thought my evidence or statements inconsistent. Inconsistent! How could he say that, when simply relating the facts. The whole matter was vastly too complicated for me to be able to make it up over such a long period and keep getting it right, especially when being interviewed by my own solicitor and the examination by the counsel. Furthermore, the prosecution had never suggested such a thing, or even hinted at it. I felt incensed. He knew in his heart his comment was simply not true, yet made it with the full awareness of what he was saying and the effect it could have on the jury. Judge's speeches are extremely important because they are supposed to be an impartial summary of all that has occurred in the trial, from both the defence and the prosecution. Above all, it is the last thing the jury hears before retiring to consider their verdict. I still feel incensed when I recall that comment because it was simply not true! When he finished his summing up on me he made no other consequential comments.

I tackled Campbell during the break, saying what I have just said and asking him how the judge could say that in the circumstances. Campbell himself then made the comment that I shall never forget. He said King-Hamilton and many other judges consider "any" defendant brought before them, "guilty". This was the view of a part-time judge who would know the system.

Out of the window went my utter naïve faith in British Justice. To think that every now and then there is a strong plea to do away with the jury system, even by some of the highest placed legal brains in the Land. Looking back on the trial, having in mind that it cost the British taxpayer over £500,000, in 1978, for the entire trial, it is worth considering that perhaps the Crown needed guilty verdicts, almost whatever, to justify the legal administration farce.

King-Hamilton would have said a great deal more had not Campbell been there glaring up at him, taking notes of anything said, anything slightly contentious, just in case it might be needed in an appeal. A fact he made abundantly clear several times during the trial. I learnt later that Campbell had a case on appeal against King-Hamilton and both were more than aware of this fact.

King-Hamilton completed his summing up on the other four defendants, going into how they chose or did not choose, to go into the witness box and how that fact shouldn't be to their disadvantage. A statement made, when everybody in court is suspicious of somebody who purposely avoids being cross-examined. The jury was then asked to retire and consider their verdict. So they went out at 10:50 on the morning of the 7th of March, 1978 and were out for two days before reaching verdicts on all of the defendants.

The long nerve-racking wait then started, not that I personally was uneasy, in spite of King-Hamilton's comments. I still retained some faith in British justice, especially the jury service. Every defendant had a close relative up at court. Jean was there, of course, and so was my Uncle Edward from Hove.

Evans had his father there, an extremely nice person, with a strong Welsh brogue. Browne had his wife and daughter, and Todd and Beavers, their girlfriends.

We sat together quite a lot of the time, during the long wait, talking to each other and occasionally to counsel, as they came in. Somebody heard from another court, that the jury were getting really down to it and were, by the sound of it, all screwed up, as shouting had been heard from their room. That made everybody think hard! Then we were told to go back into the court.

So everybody assembled and a great air of expectation hung over the court. After the jury had returned, King-Hamilton turned to them and said, 'Have you reached any verdicts yet?'

The answer was 'No'.

So he said, 'Well, it's a difficult case and I will accept a majority verdict. That is up to 10 in agreement of the 12, holding the same view'.

The jury would, therefore, have to stay overnight in a Hotel and were not to discuss the case with anybody else, other than themselves. Out they trouped and we all returned home for the night.

I don't suppose many of us slept well that night, but I did and always did, throughout the long four months, thanks to my self-training, in being able to turn off, simply emptying my mind of any unsettling thoughts.

The following morning in court an air of intense apprehension hung over everybody concerned with the case. Nobody anticipated any verdict, nobody had proclaimed innocence, or even discussed that aspect. Some of the defendants' wives looked extremely strained and one, whose husband was still working for Camden, was obviously very distressed over the whole affair. One could imagine our friends and colleagues thinking about it, at home and at work. It was now the 8th of March, 1978. I had left Camden in

September of 1975 and had been unemployed from March of '76, until the trial.

The other defendants, by the grace of Camden and one other Borough, had remained in employment, doing their respective jobs. Newspapers had, of course, reported almost daily, in both the national and the local papers, particularly those associated with Camden. I had on one occasion heard my own case being referred to in a discussion programme when I was driving in London.

The remark was made during a statement expressing the sad state of public morality and that I, as an ex-chief building surveyor was awaiting trial for corruption, giving a strong implication of presumed guilt, thereby indicating the damage already done, whatever the outcome!

We heard a further rumour, that the jury were still angrily arguing and we had visions of another night of waiting. Incidentally, we had been advised to pack a bag of essential personal things, as we might need them if we didn't return home with our wives, or others, that night! That simple statement really brought home the wild possibility open to us all and I wonder what was thought as each bag was packed. It was almost like going to the front line, during wartime, not knowing if one would return.

I had discussed with Campbell what possibilities lay open to me to claim compensation after the case was over. The subject had been raised before and I was told of the possibility of making a case to the European Court of Human Rights, at Strasbourg. But Campbell said I shouldn't discuss that aspect with anybody yet! Finally, we had a call, late in the afternoon, to assemble back in court.

So we went to the court, back to the familiar dock, our wives, relatives and friends around the side of the court. The public gallery was full and the press were there in force. While we were waiting there for the jury to return I heard and saw Campbell busy telling the press that we were off to Strasbourg, for compensation, which surprised me, as he had said to keep off the subject.

The jury returned, filing along to their allotted places and sat down. Seeing them was a bit of a shock because they looked extremely agitated, white-faced and very, very tense, looking at nobody in particular, especially us in the dock.

The atmosphere in the court was like that of an execution chamber, all of us suspended in our minds, in mid-air, when possibly the next few moments would let us continue with our lives, or destroy us, with all we had worked for until then. Even

King-Hamilton looked grey-faced and told the clerk of the court to proceed.

The clerk of the court had said nothing before, except at the beginning, when he read out the first charges and it was strange to hear a fresh voice in the trial. He said to the jury.

'Have you reached a verdict?' The answer was yes, in regard to the first defendant, to Edwards. I was then asked to stand up. I did so, with all eyes glued to me and stood there as tall as I could, back straight and head held high. High enough for the press to observe and comment on afterwards. Thinking to myself, I am not going to let the system pull me down, whatever happens. But inwardly thinking, without even forming the words to myself, that I would not be found guilty, but knowing deeper inside that if circumstances beyond my control had got me so far, there really is no limit to what could happen. The clerk then said, 'I will read out each of the six charges against the defendant Edwards, in turn, and will ask the jury to state his verdict.'

In quite a loud voice he did so, and in fairly clear, but not so loud a voice came back with the answer. 'Not Guilty', until all six charges were covered.

I immediately looked at Jean and smiled a little. Everybody in the court looked pleased. I can't remember whether there were any loud comments, claps or anything, as I was a little numb!

I said everybody looked pleased, Campbell positively beamed all over and I felt so pleased that his hard work had been justified. He had told me that he wouldn't have stayed on all through the trial but felt he had to see me through it all. For a person of his standing, and with the obvious demand upon his services, it must have been quite a commitment.

King-Hamilton clearly did not approve, even though it was clear everybody on the jury next to him did. I am sure he would like to have said something but was unable to do so. So he said what he was obliged to say, 'The defendant may stand down!'

I did not, in fact, stand down immediately. I do not really know why, except perhaps, having received a favourable verdict it seemed discourteous to abandon the others in the dock.

King-Hamilton said to the jury that they would again have to retire for the night, so they filed out, having received the same warning, not to talk to anybody. I then left the dock to be surrounded by the press.

One newspaper reported that the first thing I did was to kiss Jean. I did not then and there! Everybody drifted off, the wives and relatives of all the others, all looking very depressed over having to wait again. I hung about a little while to catch Campbell and my solicitor. I couldn't go without thanking them for their marvellous support. Campbell had tactfully kept clear of the back-slapping but was still oozing satisfaction. All the other counsellors had congratulated me, wishing me well. At last, having thanked them all. Jean, my Uncle and I made our way out of that court, for the last time, heading for Peacehaven, a most aptly named place that evening, where my parents were waiting. I had already telephoned them, rather than leave them in suspense, hearing their gasp of delight when they heard the news.

So I left the Old Bailey about 5 pm on the 8th of March, 1978. That day was my father's birthday and I don't think he needed another present, other than that one telephone call!

On the way to the underground, my Uncle said to me, 'Now you are completely cleared, why don't you see if Camden will take you back!' I was so surprised by this comment that I stopped and said,

'What do you mean, take me back. I left originally on my own accord to go to New Zealand, why should I want them to take me back?'

This conversation was most significant because it highlighted a complete misunderstanding of what the case was all about, from somebody close to me and who had also attended some of the trial.

I was to learn later that at the time of my arrest, several people, of whom I would have thought better, had made comments to the effect that it seemed odd that I should suddenly rush off to New Zealand. Rush off! It takes an inordinate time to emigrate to New Zealand and I had spent well over a year working hard at it. Expensive exploratory visits, over 40 letters to prospective employers and during a so-called boom period, to finally getting a job offer.

Then all the family to receive private medicals and get x-rays, interviews at New Zealand House, film showings, then all that one has to do in arranging the removal and shipping of all one owned, plus selling off the family home and tying up of affairs at the Bank etc. It is not surprising that the comments suggesting a hasty retreat irritated me.

In fact, at one time Combes had implied the same question, and having produced the letters I held onto regarding job applications, the eventual replies from my future employer, plus my general comments, even he had to make it especially clear to the court, that in no way were the Crown suggesting I had run away to New Zealand.

Of course, I didn't go back to the court the next day to watch events. That would have been in very bad taste. I did hear eventually of accounts of the court scenes, which struck me as almost horrific.

The wives of the other defendants, almost certainly having gone without sleep for the two preceding nights would have been nervous to the extreme.

Then to sit there at the side of the court and watch their husbands being lambasted by King-Hamilton, and the verdicts being tortuously announced, one by one, they must have suffered hell. It would be s scene that will no doubt fester in their minds forever.

Yes, they were all found guilty, sadly. Sadly for themselves and above all, sadly for their families and their loved ones. I won't increase the distress by yet again spelling out the sentences. Some had suspended sentences and one a two-year term of imprisonment, I believe, suspended.

But what is most sad is that the entire series of accusations against the accused could have been dealt with by an internal inquiry by Camden Council. To compare, for example, Todd's crime of receiving a bottle of whisky, with a £10 note wrapped around it, to that of the 'Poulson Affair', is totally ludicrous and for him to be there for nearly four months, an 'incredible injustice'!

Whilst Rawlings, who had bribed, by his own admission at least 20 local authorities and numerous companies, even the Metropolitan police itself, had been fined £10,000, which he or his firm could easily afford, and an 18-months suspended sentence. After all, wasn't he an impressionable and satisfactory and convincing witness, as King-Hamilton had gone out of his way to try and establish.

The trial had lasted 75 days, starting on the 14th of November, 1977, in court 8 at the Old Bailey, and finishing for me, on the 8th of March, 1978. For the others, it ended on the 9th. The cost was said to be about half a million pounds, with the case engaging 16 barristers, plus their supporting solicitors, all of whom, I assume, and I was right, were paid for by legal aid. Another hefty sum for the taxpayer to cover and a ludicrous mismanagement of the legal system.

At the close, presumably on the 9th of March, King-Hamilton had paid a special tribute to the police team, saying their interrogation of the suspects had been masterly and completely fair. Really, what about the long interview I had with the two detective sergeants when all the judge's rules were so flagrantly broken. What about the utterly biased viewpoint of the senior police officials, which had been the very hinge point of the continuation of the case against me. What about the people they hadn't bothered to interview, in my case, which would have substantiated my statements of innocence.

The papers, of course, had a field day and in my case with headlines like, "A victim of spite! Bribe's jury clears Edwards, not guilty after three years of agony". Other more general comments had described the trial as the biggest corruption probe, since the "Poulson Affair". This was an utterly ludicrous comparison.

King-Hamilton, QC had appeared in the press virtually throughout the trial and was described as a 73-year-old judge, a permanent Old Bailey judge, since 1964, and had been connected with many notable and sensational trials. A particular one being the "Jesus poem prosecution", involving "gay news". Furthermore, he had at one time been a resident of Camden, which I thought interesting!

I found it all rather disturbing, for here was one of the senior Old Bailey judges, who openly and without the slightest qualm made personal comments about the police and the case, which he and a good majority of the court knew to be untrue.

A person very near to the peak of British justice and all it stood for. He knew my case was an administrative fiasco, but stuck with it, obviously decided, that across the board, and as far as justice had to be 'seen' to be done it would be convenient if I was found guilty. It would justify the quarter of a million pounds spent on the trial, a good portion of which was on my case. No thought at all for the losses sustained by myself and family, or the morality of his approach.

Many years later, I turned on my TV to see Alan Campbell speaking in the House of Lords.

He had become "Lord Campbell of Alloway, QC", a conservative peer for Ayrshire. He looked roughly the same, a little greyer and stouter, but still, the imposing figure one always remembers.

I had throughout the long months of the trial been continuing with the work at weekends and evenings that is when I wasn't preparing some notes for the court. I had at times wondered if I'd ever be allowed to completely finish it, and had they locked me away, would my family still be there when I got out!

Heavens knows what sentence King-Hamilton would have imposed on me, but clearly the Crown, in their desire to obtain a conviction, had tried to make me a lead figure, just holding short of a conspiracy charge, had that stuck then he would have made a public example of me. Campbell, at one time, did hint to me that had "he" been the judge, and found me guilty, then a seven-year sentence would have been applicable! Could educated and knowledgeable men, leading in the Law process, be party to such an event? In this world virtually anything seems to become possible, providing the situation is allowed to slowly develop and to build up, then becoming acceptable. The reality of what is happening then becomes confused in the aim to seek the end, simple logic and justice become nicely blurred.

My family, parents and friends were all delighted with the results of the trial and we settled down to a daily routine, almost identical to that lived before the trial. That is, to queue yet again in the dole queue every week, having told them that I had been cleared and wouldn't need my money sent by post every week. Still, every single attendance in the dole queue was a humiliation for me, especially if the queue happened to extend outside the building and into the public view. The people behind the counter were exceedingly efficient and kind, and obviously understood that things were not as they often appeared to be.

However, two other things were now new to our life style. For one, I could now apply for jobs, both back in New Zealand and in England. I wrote off to my ex-employer in New Zealand, telling them that I had been cleared and thanking them for their initial faith in me, leaving it open for them to respond, hopefully, with a new offer, but I never heard any more from them again. New Zealand by then was well out of its minor boom period.

Rowley, the then Prime Minister, who had inflated the economy when I was out there, was now out and Maldoon was in office, on a purge to cut back. I was to write many times to many places in New Zealand for a suitable post, either directly, or through a contact, but never achieved anything.

By then I had passed the immigration age limit of 45, at which point, my lifetime's ambition died a death and I knew I would only ever go back as a visitor, a very sad realisation which never totally sinks in, except now rarely, when I have such a longing to recapture some of the moments that were so delightful during our brief months there. Or when something reminds me of New Zealand, and the special beauty, above all, the absolute sense the lifestyle made there, when one had time to enjoy life and not rush to one's grave.

The second thing which was to occupy us for a number of years in keeping up our spirits was our quest for compensation. This was centred on Strasburg where we understood our only real hope lay of receiving a proper overall understanding and therefore, where our compensation hope rested.

We commenced on a long series of meetings and correspondence with our solicitor. However, before seeking that our case be considered at Strasburg, we were obliged to explore and exhaust all domestic possibilities of redress by likely other means. That is via the Crown! With this clear aim in our minds, we again sought the services of the barrister, Rex Brian, who after many meetings prepared and submitted, what I thought was, a quite brilliant application to the Home Office. He condensed the application into a potted history and covering the financial losses, which when considered at that stage in 1978 were some £38,200, for expenses only, not future salary considerations etc.

The Home Office on receiving this formal application on the 20 September 1978 and after the usual long delays and chasing by us, replied, saying that it was under consideration, but that as it was also construed to be a formal complaint against the police. I would have to accept that aspect and agree to be part of a reinvestigation of all aspects of the case. On discussing this with my solicitor, I was advised that my claim for compensation could not proceed until that was out of the way, so I agreed.

Eventually, an appointment was made at my solicitor's office for me to be interviewed by a detective chief inspector and a detective chief superintendent, on the 14th of December, 1978.

It gave me a funny feeling to go into that office and face that scene all over again, sitting there in the office with my lady solicitor in attendance. After my previous experience, I would never advise anybody to be interviewed by the police without being legally represented, especially when formally complaining about their previous behaviour. They appeared quite pleasant, impartial, not as intensely inquisitive as I would have wished or expected. The chief superintendent made some notes on the substance of my complaint, which was essentially that the police never interviewed, or seemed interested in seeing key witnesses to substantiate any claims of my innocence and that because of this and their compounded prejudice, confirmed by police comments made to me and others, the case proceeded, as now, against me.

I would have been much happier if it had been an examining barrister, appointed to attend to the complaint, and one appointed, say by the Law Society.

One can easily imagine one police officer talking to another on such a matter, there is bound to be, somewhere at the back of their minds, a feeling of understanding and sympathy. After all, 'there by the grace of God go I!' or in this case, one of them. I can never imagine the general public being happy with this state of affairs. I would never be convinced that there hasn't been some sort of cover-up. In any event, I never got the very clear impression that they were taking this investigation seriously, not at all, merely doing what they were obliged to do. As expected 'nothing came out of their investigation'.

It now seemed the right moment to take the next step forward and approach the European Court of Human Rights, so I wrote to my solicitor suggesting we acted accordingly. Not long after sending this letter, I was asked to come in and discuss the present situation. *At last,* I thought, *now we can really get down to it and plan the future way forward.* My hopes were short-lived. A partner in the practice led the discussion, assisted by a solicitor, new to my case, either the sixth or seventh person to get involved in my affairs from the same practice.

It was explained to me that I wasn't eligible for legal aid, as I was now earning a moderate salary and in any event, the legal aid would unlikely be forthcoming to petition the Court of Human Rights. In these circumstances, it was suggested that in consideration of my present local government career, and peace of mind of my family, I best call it a day and let it rest here! It was a bit of a shock to sit there and have this advice. All I had been through, for nothing, but the experience. I could see, very clearly that without sufficient money, outside of legal aid I would get nowhere. So I had to accept that we stop off there, at that point. Certainly, I had no money of my own and was, in fact, desperately hard up. However, I shall have to go back in the story to just after the trial to complete that part of events. I did later, in July of 1981 write to my local MP, asking him if he could, on my behalf, approach the Parliamentary Ombudsman, as this case was of public mal-administration, or so I thought. Yet again, the reply came back in negative terms.

People remember that you had once been accused and after all, there is no smoke without fire, is there? Indeed, I have known that my very own Uncle, an ex-policeman, thought me guilty, and also a close family friend. How many others did, I wonder and how many opportunities were closed to me because of it? I know very well that I would never be called for jury service, or could ever become a magistrate, for although the police, at my request, told my solicitor that all my police files were destroyed, I do not, for one moment, believe it.

However, it was now time to get on with my life and start again.

Off to Rovno in Ukraine with Members of the Project. (1990/91)

At a Trade Fair in Moscow (1990)

National Service, Aged 23

Romania, Ceauşescu's Palace

Museum

National Service Hong Kong (1955–57)

Macau (1956)

National Service Hong Kong (1956)

Around Moscow

Around Moscow

In Kremlin

In Kremlin

In Kremlin

The London Borough of Islington
1978 to 1984

After the trial, I began to look very hard for another local government position, for that's where my most recent experience lay. Each week, Jean and I would go down to the Brighton library, to the reference section, collect all possible magazines showing jobs in the building section, sit down at a desk and look for suitable ones to apply for. It gave us a positive purpose and a way to hopefully immediately organise our future. We did this regularly for over six months, applying for so many jobs that I eventually gave up recording my applications. A good number of those jobs were those that, had I applied for them some two years previous, from say my job in Camden, I would almost certainly have been called for an interview, except some were for lower grades than the Camden position. I recall two interviews in particular during those long months, one in local government and the other with a contractor. But I was unsuccessful with either. Then in September of 1978, I applied for a job in the Architect's Department of Islington Council and was called for an interview.

It was with some excitement that I attended that interview, meeting again John Booth, the chief building surveyor. I had met him once before whilst at Camden. John was a good surveyor, a very sound fellow, but a rather grey, unexciting character. The others on the panel were the lead person, Alfred Head, the then borough architect, a marvellous person, somebody like Sydney Cooke, Camden's borough architect and similarly much respected by all his staff, Alf Head's deputy, Don Fletcher and a senior admin person. The interview went marvellously well with good spirits and interest on both sides. In the course of our discussion, I mentioned that had my father the necessary £200 when I was about 16 years old, then I would have become an architect. This seemed to please him, as he said, laughing, that I was the first surveyor he had ever met who actually liked architects! Lunchtime came and I was asked to come back at 2 pm. I had just left the room when Alf Head came out and said to me that he was very impressed with me and would be recommending my appointment!

I couldn't find a phone booth quickly enough to telephone Jean and tell her the good news, and in the afternoon I was offered the job as a "principal surveyor" and would be leading the housing rehabilitation programme, along with another principal surveyor. This other surveyor was, in fact, a Peter Warhurst, my principal surveyor when I was with Camden, he has seen my application and had strongly recommended me Alf Head. It was really great to get this job, as I particularly wanted to get into employment before the year finished.

Of course, it was Peter's strong recommendation that really helped me and I am always grateful. In fact to this very day, so many years later, we are both good friends and meet up every now and then.

So here I was again in November of 1978, some three years later, back on exactly the same grade, in the same kind of work, yet again for another local government authority, a situation from which I'd finally decided to opt out for a wholesome life in New Zealand of 1975.

It wasn't long after I had started there when I heard that another chief officer, within the Council, had asked about my integrity.

It was reasonable to understand that people will be curious and will indeed wonder, that is human nature, but to raise, even casually such a question, after all that time and after a three-month trial, that was something that galled me. Being found innocent, wasn't that enough? In the first week that I had started my job, I was making myself a cup of tea in the small tearoom next to the office when one of the architects came in to do the same. 'Oh,' he said, 'so you are the infamous Brian Edwards!' he said in apparent good humour.

He was a direct descendant of the famous African missionary, Albert Schweitzer, one of many interesting characters in the office.

Like Camden, the people in the Islington offices were really very nice. It must be something in the local authorities vetting process that ensures their employees are sound responsible people, as well as qualified for their respective tasks. Before going to Islington, I had always thought of it as a less consequential Borough than its neighbour, the famous Camden Borough. But I was wrong, it was just different.

Word gets around, at the end of my first week an admin person in the office, Lydia Kuzura pressed into my hand, with a receipt, my first week's salary, later, and like the others, I would receive a monthly paycheck. The first cash payment was an expression of kindness, being aware of my circumstances and thinking me hard pressed.

So there I was one of two principal surveyors, under John Booth the chief surveyor in a group of surveyors within the Architect's Department. Our main task was to supervise a programme of rehabilitation, primarily to single houses acquired by the Borough, to the refurbishment of large housing estates. This was very much a prominent political programme of the Borough.

When I was working in Camden I had limited dealings with Frank Dobson, who I found to be a most likeable and able Councillor. He was then chair of housing in Islington, there was a number of Councillors who, including Frank Dobson were later to become ministers within Tony Blair's new labour government. These were Chris Smith and more prominently, Margaret Hodge, at one time Leader of Islington Council. She, in particular, was very bright, personable, confident and very capable, but like all ambitious Councillors could be quite ruthless.

Later, I was to regularly attend Committee Meetings and it struck me that there they sat, trying to give off the image of working-class labour members when in reality some were very well-off personally and many were holding double University degrees!

I shared an office with Peter Warhurst, as I said my principal surveyor when I was at Camden, he was now my equal and without him, I possibly would not be there. Peter is quite a character, an ex-district surveyors man, he told me correctly, that he would be invaluable, when I interviewed him in Camden, absolutely correct, as it turned out. He was very positive, knowledgeable and had a great sense of right and wrong. He was also blessed with a great sense of humour. On one occasion Alex Schweitzer came into our office, for some reason or other, Peter said.

'Stay there, don't move'. Peter then went to a cupboard, came back with an aerosol can of deodorant and sprayed Alex from head to toe. Alex hardly said anything, perhaps thinking we were mad and left. But it brightened the day. Being a good loyal friend Peter had spotted my application and went out of his way to strongly recommend me to Alf Head, a friend to have indeed. However, he could be overzealous. In our role, we also supervised a number of consultants, who assisted with the programme. I remember one occasion when Peter was called to Alf Head's office, for I believe Peter was having problems with one particular consultant. Alf Head had smoothed troubled water, but not to Peter's liking for he returned to our office quite white with rage, ranting on about that useless consultant. I thought it prudent to make a few site visits, leaving him time to cool down.

During the first weeks of my new job, I remember feeling quite depressed at being back in local government, where I had been in spite of being so glad to be back in employment. Slowly as I got involved in my work and became absorbed in the many problems of such a programme my spirits lifted and I started to enjoy myself. I especially enjoyed the company and friendship of both my colleagues around me and the consultants who helped. I was even going down again to the Department of the Environment, in Marsham Street, meeting with the same officials, Gerry Webber, the regional architect who was a most likeable chap.

I even met again the highly placed Admin official, the one who had for a time shunned me, until I had been cleared. The meetings were to agree on scheme proposals for large house rehabilitation.

The surveying office consisted of John Booth, Peter and I and I think it was 3 surveying groups, each headed by a Group Leader. Likeable fellows, like Jeremy Keep, whose leg I always pulled by referring to him as 'Jeremy Thorpe', the disgraced politician, and others like him, like Ted Pearce, John Ellis etc. Like Camden, there was a good spirit of togetherness in the office. I believe that this happy committed atmosphere which could be felt in the offices of both Camden and Islington could be solely attributed to the borough architect's themselves, Sydney Cooke and Alf Head.

Whilst in the department I had gone through a range of cars, a large Peugeot I really couldn't afford to run, to a small Renault 4 I had restored completely. Peter accused me of taking the bumpers off each week to clean behind them. Then I had an Alfa Sud, a small two-door coupe which I used to regularly take to pieces, thinking I was making improvements

Once weekend I had the cylinder head off and refitted them with thinner head gaskets, to increase the compression ratio and hopefully improve the performance. When I got to the office car park on Monday the engine felt a little strange, too tight. I was so concerned I telephoned Jean and told her to come to the office in her car so she could tow me home, some 35 miles. Dutifully, she came but without a tow rope so I said go and get one from the nearby car parts shop. She did but it was a rather strange wire one. 'Ok, I said, I have booked the afternoon off so we had better start for home.' We tied on the tow rope, bumper to bumper and off she drove, taking my bumper with her, there being no give in a wire tow rope. I persuaded her to go again to the shop and get a more flexible rope one which she did and we fixed, as a bore, but with better results. Part way home, in the High Street of Hadley Wood, Jean was obliged to stop at a pedestrian crossing controlled by lights, so of course, did I. Whilst there a friend of mine, one of the local architects saw me and came up to the car to say hello.

I had my window down and were having a very nice general chat when Jean's lights changed colour and off she went, leaving me with no choice and so did I, leaving my friend open-mouthed in the centre of the road, for he hadn't realised I was being towed!

I particularly enjoyed one of my roles, to liaise and instruct the assisting consultants, engineer, architects and surveyors etc. One architect, Max Hutchinson, later to become a big wheel at the RIBA, and also to appear, as a presenter on TV.

I made some very good friends among the consultants, and this is an aspect of my life that I miss greatly, even all these years later on. Being on the same wavelength, in a combined effort to achieve a set purpose, the friendship and mutual respect. There were many notable characters, as well as Max.

Roger Pollard of Pollard Thomas and Edwards, architects. Roger is the very epitome of the English Public Schoolboy. He is tall, imposing and has a very strong English accent, very self-confident and capable, he got on well with everybody. He was even applauded at committee, for the quality of his presentations.

Rolf Rothermel, had been in the same practice but left to form his own. He was deceptively capable, giving off a relaxed impression. Before becoming an architect he had been a senior planner at the Greater London Council. Rolf won, in open competition a prize for the best submission of a design for a new hotel for the Saudi Royal Family. He held one of the biggest prizes ever won by a British architect.

Dick Bateman, a quantity surveyor and one I had known back in Camden. Dick had the unusual ability of freely expressing his mind, on any subject openly and honestly, his views could be quite startling, but always honest, and those we all invariably held but withheld for fear of possibly offending. Donald Hicks was another quantity surveyor who had worked together with Dick in the past.

On one occasion, I had to take to task Max Hutchinson and his colleague, Donald for their rather overbearing control of a specialist contractor considering that all were equal in their own right and specialised field. But I liked Max, I liked his warm friendly approach, his enthusiasm. Come to think of it I liked each and every one of the consultants and got on very well them.

Peter Bell was another very positive architect, engaged before my arrival to improve one of the biggest estates in the borough. A little difficult initially to manage but soon we were working quite happily together to get the job done. I had to defend him a number of times from minor conflicts with a couple of councillors.

There were many others and the programme would never have been achieved without them. We all gained from their input and I gained personally good friends who put me right on many an issue. However, I learnt that my friendship with them had been questioned, as being "too" close. Particularly as they were all well placed, well off and a little upmarket! *A little ironic*, I thought, *to form a Labour Council who had members such as Bankers and some with considerable personal wealth.*

Jean and I decided we had better move to find a home in Hertfordshire, which we knew well. Of course, we had already lived in Harpenden before. So we put up our home in Belfast Street, in Hove, for sale, having already sold the self-contained basement flat. Our maisonette sold very quickly to a young local builder.

The minute it was sold I made point of telling our friendly bank manager in Holborn and eventually took a case of red wine around to his home as a gesture of appreciation. He had been so wonderful in his personal support, it was the very least we could do.

It was a very sad day when we left our Hove house. All that work and heart ache, at such a difficult time in our lives. Looking back, I cannot imagine how I ever managed to complete it all. It will always remain a milestone in our hearts and when I go back to Brighton for a day out, I find myself outside the house thinking back with an aching heart and mixed emotions. The very day we left, my Mother and Father came to see us off, so very sad that again we were moving away from them. The furniture had been packed and we were to follow on in my car.

Just before we drove off my Mother came to the car window, obviously feeling very emotional and said never to forget that if we ever wanted anything she would always be there. It was so very much like the time at Southampton when she saw us off at the docks.

We had chosen a house in St Albans, a new house in a new estate. It was a four-bedroom, timber-framed house with double garage. I had struggled to raise the necessary mortgage and later, I extended the back and built myself a good workshop, so I could carry out my main hobby of cabinet making, something I do to this day. I made many things in that workshop from which considerably contributed to the family income, albeit working hard and long hours. One of my architect friends, Rolf always looked out for me to find me work, it helped him, where his customers were stuck, and me financially. One job he found was a very large pyramid shaped window, size about 8 feet high and 20 feet wide! It was to be made in mahogany. When finished it was so big that a furniture van had to come and take it to the site. Then I had to go there and fit the many casement windows. It was one of the many jobs I did whilst at that house. I had always supplemented my income this way, ever since I started work.

Many years ago, when living in Southend-on-Sea, we had bought a new house and as usual were extremely hard up. We only had Julie and Christopher then, living on a comparatively small income, and as the only surveyor in the Council's Architect's Department.

I had discovered a very good antique's shop on the seafront and asked the owner if I could make him anything to sell, suggesting that before he decided he come to my house and viewed a bow-fronted chest of drawers I had made. This chest I had made when living in Bristol, it had taken months to make, and the very bow-shaped front consisted of 215 wood-bricks, bonded together like a brick-wall, to form the curve, then veneered and inlaid etc. It, at this very moment, rests behind me in my present home. Anyway, he came, was impressed and offered me £15! Even then that was an insult, so I said no to that but would make him "six" drop-leaf veneered and inlaid curved table with a drawer at each end. The tapered legs rested in solid brass feet. The agreed price for each table would be £12!

A small sum, but I was desperate. It was hard work, all by hand, 24 tapered legs, 12 drawers with hand-cut dovetails, each French polished etc. But it helped our position at the time.
About a year later, I was still in the same job, the borough architect knew about my cabinet-making and asked me if I knew anybody

who could view and price the restoration of a fine table in "Porter House", one of the borough's few historic houses. The antique firm I knew were interested and did this sort of work. The expert they employed had already seen my six drop leaf tables and remarked upon their fine workmanship, it was praise indeed.

During my time in Islington, I worked hard in my spare time, always making something. One Friday afternoon when I was one of few surveyors left in the office, all the others had gone out on site, I had a call to go upstairs and see the borough architect. I was concerned initially form my security phobia, but soon that changed when I entered the room and found out why I had been called. The room was full, Alf Head, Don Fletcher, John Booth, the office manager and Chris Price, the chair of housing. They were very warm towards me, offering me tea and good wishes. *Hello*, I thought, *what's up!*

Apparently, Chris Pryce had been getting very excited about finding a suitable replacement for the fellow who ran the so-called "Post 48 Estate Programme", part of a very hot political programme.

Unknown to me, I had been chosen!

The programme was in its early design stages with all the consultants already appointed, partly briefed. Now it was in disarray and without direction. All hell was going on. This programme was run from the Council's works division, in different offices next to the work yards. A Janet Payne was the chief building surveyor for that section, though, in fact, she was an architect who previously worked in Alf Head's department. I would work under her.

"What did I think of the idea?"

What could I say, I had no choice, so I decided it was prudent to accept gracefully and then make the most of it. The relief around the room was most obvious and I was almost slapped on the back. Oh, by the way, I was to start next Monday!

I couldn't say at that moment I was very happy, I enjoyed my position in the Architect's Department, the prestige. I had become rooted and comfortable, but as mentioned not fully secure. So on Monday morning, there I sat in my new hutted office, overlooking the bleak environment of the works yard, with everything in front of me new and challenging.

Janet came into my office and called me to her room, to meet her and for her to set the scene. I had seen her around before in the Architect's Department before she was appointed, though I had

had no contact. Janet was an attractive fresh-faced young woman, articulate, positive, extremely intelligent and with a slight stutter, usually apparent when she was slightly nervous. She was well able to look after herself and would be a presence at any meeting. As time went by we became good friends, within our working environment. She explained that the Post 48 Estate Programme was designed to improve and raise standards to estates built after 1948 and was a significant part of the Council's programme and also that that of the Governments. Certain estates had to be selected and the basic programme and work content agreed, via Committee. Certain consultants, architects, engineers, etc., had already been selected and commissioned.

This was a factor I was glad about as I couldn't be blamed for making wrong selections. Some of the estates were very large, like Priory Green and the Mayville Estate. Every estate had strong tenant participation, at all staged. Everything had to be agreed up front, all around, with tenants, committees etc. and the DOE. Each consultant's scheme had to be appraised, approved, tenders sought, numerous tenant liaison meetings held, then put to committee.

After committee approval the schemes commenced with very close consultant, contractor and tenant liaison. In fact, the programme was a potential minefield. No wonder the previous post holder had left!

So I started in earnest, going through each scheme, calling in the consultants, visiting each estate, talking to the tenants, approving tender lists, having pre and post tender meetings with consultants and contractors. As I became more deeply involved and aware, so job satisfaction increased, and I really began to enjoy my new position.

Janet was great and she taught me a great deal! Although I communicate freely and happily with my colleagues and immediate superiors, I have never been really comfortable when exposed in committee. A deputy chief executive once referred to me as a modest person, perhaps that is it.

Then in one way that changed. Early on after my arrival, Janet took me to one of the larger tenants meeting held in a large hall. I was there on the platform with her and she stood up and started to address the meeting. Being a young attractive woman with a slight stutter they gave her respect and it went well. Then I had to go forward and explain the technical issues of the proposed new refurbishment scheme. This was the first time I had ever done so in front of a large public gathering. But it went extremely well and without the slightest problem and to my great surprise I really enjoyed it. In fact, I actually looked forward to all the future public meetings and enjoyed them all. Janet had greatly boosted my public confidence.

Some estates were more pleasant than others, depending upon the make up of the team of consultants, contractors and tenants, and the work involved.

The Mayville Estate was a nice one to be involved in and the consultant, Webb & Tapley, who had a very good man on site, who was Eric Self. He was a charming friendly fellow who got on well with everybody. The tenant's representative for the estate was a Ross Ruck, an attractive young woman, very socialistically minded. It took me a long time before she really understood that I had the tenants real interest at heart and wasn't just another Council official. I attended many tenant liaison meetings with her and it was always very entertaining. At public meetings, it could be more than amusing. At a meeting with me on the platform speaking, she would raise difficult questions and I would answer, with her knowing very well what I would say. It became some sort of game. Not even the members realised the rapport between us. One of my problems has been the rather official appearance I gave off. This can best be illustrated when at one time I was visiting a local car showroom, to see the latest model of a particular make, the salesperson came up to me and said, 'I bet you are a local government official!' which identified me to a tee.

I had similar events of this nature later when I worked in Southwark Council, and when a tenant wouldn't talk to me as I was too official! In fact, I was far from it, as my closest friends will testify.

Life continued agreeably this way and the programme for the various estates progressed as satisfactorily as one could hope. Of course, there were ups and downs. The Priory Green Estate, for example, was overspending with Peter Bell getting criticised for not controlling it properly until it was pointed out that the overall programme had been reduced in specification content so that more estates could be tackled and this was a good political tactic. Peter Bell had, in fact, included the work originally, until cut by Committee. Then there was the Spa Green Estate, near to Priory Green and almost as important.

On one occasion, a member of Parliament asked to meet me at the estate, with the project architect, to discuss issues on the estate, raised by his tenants. We met one afternoon in the site office with an architect from Peter Bell's office, a pleasant capable chap. The MP, I have forgotten his name, ranged all over the place with his questions and we gave him, what I thought were good answers and reasons. I thought the meeting went well and was concluded pleasantly enough.

About a week later, Alf Head passed me a letter given to him by Margaret Hodge. The MP had written to her complaining about a number of things, not specifically referred to our meeting. I was asked to prepare a response. I read it and I was incensed. He had used our meeting to latch on to a number of matters that he and his party (opposite party to that of Margaret Hodge) had, wishing to score off politically. I read it through carefully and prepared a response, pointing out that on a number of issues he appeared to have deliberately misrepresented the facts and ignored those which didn't help his objectives. My letter went back to Margaret Hodge and I understand that she sent it off to him unchanged, not being able to reply herself in the manner I did, me being a mere principal surveyor. Word eventually came back that he was livid and asked, 'Who is that surveyor who dared to write to me in such a fashion?'

Quite a long time later, I saw him again when he was a guest at Janet' and Chris's wedding. He looked at me across the room and glared angrily.

Serves the sod right, I thought to myself.

I settled into the job routine after some time and into our house and life progressed agreeably. Every now and then, a consultant would arrange a social event, like a golf match, Henley or something similar.

Then one day I was invited to go to the Derby races. Taking the day off, I went with an architect friend and a few others from the office by coach. On the way, my friend Rolf said, 'Hey look at this, just the job for you Brian!'

He passed the newspaper to me to see, pointing to the particular advert. It was for 'The Head of Technical Services', in the London Borough of Southwark, in the Housing Department. *Hmm*, I thought, *not bad, I might as well have a go at this*. Not long afterwards, I sent off my application and virtually forgot about it.

At that time, I was in the process of buying a new car, getting it cheaper by going to Ireland and picking it up.

Jean and I went one weekend, flying to Dublin and staying overnight before returning with the car the next day. We hadn't arrived back home more than one hour before the telephone rang.

'Hello,' I said, 'can I help you?'

'Hello,' he said, 'I am John O'Brian, I'm telephoning you about your application here at Southwark for the Head of Technical Services post, and to see if you can come down for a preliminary interview.'

'Would be delighted to,' I replied, 'With the director of housing I assume, what's his name?'

'That's me,' he said, 'I am the director!'

'Oh,' I said, 'I beg your pardon.' He laughed and so we set a date. I told Jean and said how nice he sounded. So I went off to Southwark, for the first time to the director's office in Rye Lane, Peckham, where I met his colleague who held the position I was applying for.

John O'Brian is a reasonably tall, large rounded person with little hair, giving off a benign friendly, yet positive impression, smiling and sometimes laughing. I quickly learnt later that he was indeed very positive, could be a little bullying, even aggressive, but nevertheless was an extremely capable chief officer

Sitting comfortably and having tea we talked about the job and my previous jobs and experience, a few friendly questions from both sides and similarly from his colleague who I hadn't realised wasn't the office manager but was John Wade, the present holder of the post. He was different, quieter, very professional, very articulate, immediately giving off a very good impression.

I left the meeting feeling it had gone well and was told I would be notified in writing, should I be selected for a member panel interview, and so it was some days later.

Going to the member's panel was a bit of an ordeal. It was held in a committee room in Southwark Town Hall, at first-floor level, backing onto Peckham Road. I had arrived early, as usual, parking the car on the side road, I sat there for two minutes collecting my thoughts together, and then walked to the Town Hall.

I think about six people had been invited for an interview, though I didn't see any of them before my interview. I was called into the interview room quite quickly and asked to sit in the chair placed centrally in the room.

The members sat along two walls with the chair, the director and personnel people seated across the head of the room, back to the window. So there I sat, at the end of a U-shape formation.

The chair was a fellow called Nick Snow, a brother of the famous TV journalists and broadcasting brothers, Jon and Peter

Snow. The interview had been arranged with the usual introduction by the chair, then followed with pre-primed questions put by each member in turn. It went quite well and I had no difficulty in responding fully to any of their questions. After a general exchange at the end, I was asked to wait outside. There were two others waiting outside, one was Alex Schweitzer, the architect I knew from Islington. The other person I didn't know. We talked about the interview and the questions, and then the interview door opened and out came a clerk, asking me to come in again.

I knew then, of course, this was it and sat down again in the central chair. Nick Snow then said the panel had selected me, would I accept the offer of the position of Head of Technical services. With pleasure, I said, thanking them for selecting me. I left the room and was in the lobby when the members started coming out. The leader of the Council, a large cheerful fellow personally congratulated me, shaking my hand and wishing me well.

Outside on the steps in front of the Town Hall, I came across most of the other applicants. They didn't look too happy, particularly Alex Schweitzer, but I felt fine and drove home in high spirits, eager to tell Jean.

It was a big job, as Head of Technical Services in the Housing Department, I was at assistant director level and would be responsible for and manage a staff of 150 professionals, architects, surveyors, engineers, admin etc., together with the Council's direct labour organisation, employing 1,000 operatives. At this time, the Council managed 62,000 dwellings and the approximate annual budget, including maintenance and capital works, was some 60 million, a lot of money at the time, although I had enjoyed my time at Islington, very much more than I ever thought I would, I looked forward to this new challenge enormously.

Also at the end of my time with Islington, I had been taken off the Post 48 Estate programme and put in charge of the commercial sector, liaising with the appointed consultants. I was never given a reason, except I think they wanted to place a politically active architect already in the Housing Department, to the position. It was Margaret Hodge who told me of the change of my duties, thanking me for my contribution to the Housing Programme, which was later confirmed in a Housing Committee meeting.

The London Borough of Southwark 1984 to 1986

Just one month later, I set off from my home to go to my first day at Southwark. It seemed further from home than I realised but I would soon sort out the best route. It meant an early start from St Albans to Peckham before 8 pm and miss the morning traffic.

After an initial introduction from housing personnel, I went along to my first meeting with the director, John O'Brian. He sat at the head of his meeting table together with my counterpart in Housing Management a chap named John Synnuck. He was younger than me, about 35 years old and in appearance, he was not too dissimilar to John O'Brian, about the same height, sparse light brown hair and was large to fat in size. If I recall correctly, there were two others at the meeting, one, a chap responsible for housing development and policy, and the office manager, a tall military-looking person, both in appearance and manner. Tea came around regularly via a lady who came in with a large teapot and simply topped up our mugs whenever they appeared empty.

Introductions were made and I was formally welcomed to the department. John O'Brian described how the meetings were held regularly with senior managers. By the time the meeting had ended, I had detected a slight change of atmosphere, quite different to the friendly exchange found in the first initial meeting, prior to the member panel. The warm sincerity of approach was gone and I didn't feel as welcome as I would have expected on my first day. So I went away from the meeting feeling unsettled and strangely apprehensive.

I walked from the meeting in Rye Lane to Peckham Road, to my new office on the first floor in "Pelican House", placed opposite a large housing estate, named the North Peckham Estate, well-known in housing circles, not only in Southwark but also around London, for its social problems.

Peckham House was later to be renamed "Winnie Mandela House", but when she fell out of favour, for a murder charge, it was renamed again. Not so long ago when I drove past, it had been boarded up, presumably for demolition.

My secretary was called Ilene, I have forgotten her surname. She was a very pleasant, mature woman and must have found me a complete change after John Wade. She was based in a small office directly outside my door and nobody ever reached me except with her approval. On one occasion, I had been out of the office and returned to find one of the women councillors sat in Ilene's office, waiting for me. She came into my room and we chatted about various things.

I got the feeling that there had been some sort of predetermined routine in John Wade's time and that she had come in vain. What it was I never found out and ended up deciding that I had, in some way failed her.

John Wade had gone to Camden, as director of architecture and it seemed an unusual coincidence that we should have exchanged Boroughs in this way. It wasn't many months after my arrival in Southwark that Ilene left to join John Wade in Camden. I know she missed him and his way of working, holding the highest regard for him personally. After she had given me notice, she made an unusual request, which was that I shouldn't consider appointing, in her place a girl called Rosie Ratcliffe, who at that time was the secretary to Bill Box, the chief building surveyor, placed in my department. I asked Ilene why not, but she wasn't specific, just said she considered her entirely unsuitable.

I never found out the real fact behind her comment. Eventually, I did interview a number of women for Ilene's post, finally deciding that Rosie was, in fact, by far the best applicant. Bill Box, a thoroughly reliable surveyor recommended her highly.

So Rosie became my new secretary. That meant I had by far the most beautiful secretary in Southwark's employment. She was, in fact, an Iraqi, was born in Baghdad and was married to an Englishman.

She was very good at her work, if not a little sensitive, some mornings coming in and dissolving in tears over some tiff she had had with her husband. It never lasted more than half an hour and she would recover and get on with her work.

North Peckham Estate, opposite the office contained some 1,600 dwellings and had featured in discussions during my initial interview with the director and my predecessor John Wade, who had asked, explaining that as he was an architect he had spent an enormous amount of time personally thinking of ways to revamp this estate, in an attempt to reduce the social problems there

Did I have any views on the best way forward? I had replied that in his position his time would be too valuable and that he should have instructed a consultant or an appropriate in-house person. Later on, in this narrative, I shall explain how I dealt with this problem.

My average working week in Southwark was very demanding. I had to get into my office by 8 am to miss the traffic, leaving home at about 6:30 am. There would be at least one, if not two committee meetings each week, or if not an evening meeting of some sort. This meant I would not get home until 11 pm, or even later. The day would involve meetings with my staff, or any form of meeting, from progress meetings to new staff appointments, to Trade Union matters.

At this time the Trade Unions were very influential in the Council, working for a hand in love with the members. The situation was particularly sensitive regarding the direct labour section, part of my department. The meetings were held with Nick Snow, the then chair of housing, myself and the director. I liked Nick Snow, he was always friendly and honest towards me, a man of obvious integrity, a cut above the other members.

At my level there was invariably much contact with the members who phoned, came in or wrote regarding pressing problems in their patch. Unlike some of the other senior officers at my level, I felt unable to ingratiate myself too much in their favour. I was quite unable to fawn over them and over respond to their every whim. It was just not my style. Perhaps I should have, it did me no good in the long run not to have done so. Nevertheless, I always responded thoroughly, in my own friendly way to sincere enquiries, often quite enthusiastically.

The Peckham Estate, opposite my office, was an ongoing problem regarding bad social issues, to a point that even the Department of the Environment became aware. The Council had pressure from tenants groups to do something, so like my predecessor, I was obliged to give priority in finding a way forward.

Once I started getting involved, it quickly became apparent that the tenants at large were very hostile to the Council and its officers, in whom they had lost all hope.

An intermediary body seemed, therefore, essential if we were to make any progress.

Then one day I had a brainwave following a suggestion from Rolf Rothermel and decided to appoint Alice Coleman, a Sociologist from London University, to do a study of the estate and then report back. I should mention that the estate was largely served off first floor pathways, called "pedways", a feature of certain estates of that design period. Anybody with bad intent had easy access and escape to all dwellings so as a result there were muggings, many break-ins and extensive vandal damage, plus as well a large number of voids. The estate had such a bad reputation that even the insurance companies wouldn't give cover. Alice Coleman's eventual answer was to extensively redesign the estate back to a "street-scene environment", entirely doing away with the pedways. Each dwelling would then have defensible space around, i.e., front gardens, etc. But this wasn't the end of the problem for I had then to find somebody very competent to prepare the scheme and supervise the eventual project. I knew there was nobody in-house remotely suitable, but this didn't stop requests from certain members of my staff to do the project.

In the end, I appointed an architect and planner I knew from my Camden days, Rolf Rothermel. He was an extremely capable person and I knew he could handle this project safely.

To pacify my in-house staff, I arranged for two of them to assist and monitor the scheme on behalf of the department. It was really an exciting project, around the 30 million mark and with the full interest of the Department of the Environment. Some 12 years later, I revisited the estate. Some blocks had been successfully remodelled, but there was still a lot to do. I know that had I remained with Southwark then I would have finished the project a long time ago.

There was an extremely nicely designed new development, to one side, fitting precisely the design and social criteria laid down by Alice Coleman, who incidentally later became a Professor, for which I am sure her involvement at Southwark played a big part.

This is just a brief summary for there were countless meetings with the tenant's representatives, their Ward Councillors, the design team, the project Committee and myself etc. I wonder what views my predecessor, John Wade felt when later visiting the estate.

So this was just one of my major involvements in Southwark, quite apart from my daily duties, which were extreme and always pressing. In my engineering section, I had a chief engineer, Reg Corbridge, considered to be a difficult fellow to control and work with. From the beginning, I went out of my way to establish a good working relationship with him, taking a personal interest in his responsibilities and concerns. This paid off and he was, in return always helpful and supportive towards me.

Southwark is rather unique in that it has some exceptionally large housing estates, the heating for which was mainly large central boiler plants, rather than the usual way of having individual boilers to each dwelling. Reg had a particular interest, almost an obsession in finding an alternative type of fuel for these boilers, one that would be environmentally friendly and was exploring the possibility of using household waste, processed into fuel pellets, then adapting the boilers to burn them. It struck me as an exciting possibility and together we looked at successful conversions already made in East Sussex. As time went by we became more and more convinced that this was a real possibility. The potential was enormous, just right in environmental term and would put Southwark really on the map in district heating terms. Sadly the entire idea lost was eventually when Council decided to follow some idea to tie in with another nearby authority, in a burning disposal process. "Green House Gases" were not such an issue then, unfortunately.

On one occasion, I went back to Camden and met with John Wade, my predecessor. Ilene was still my secretary then. He was very pleasant and we chatted for quite a while, with him telling me about how he had slipped on a newly sanded and varnished hall floor, badly putting out his back. It was bad enough for it to develop into a serious problem.

I told him about how I had been getting on, my range of problems and he offered opinions and advice. It was, overall a very pleasant meeting.

Later I learnt he had reported back to John O'Brian, telling him of all my problems and concerns. It was disappointing, he was not the person I thought him to be, so much for a confidential chat.

Not long after I arrived in Southwark a new chief executive was appointed. She turned out to be a comparatively young woman, in her early forties. Up to then, the post had been vacant and the duties covered by the deputy chief executive, a particularly nice, cultivated and helpful man. The new appointment was blatantly political. She had a Social Services background and I wondered how they managed to get away with it.

In the past, all chief executive officers were noticeably impartial, politically, and nearly always solicitors. Her appointment disrupted the senior officer level of the authority, over a very short period of time, and quite dramatically. Up to then, John O'Brian was the strongest chief officer, with the others giving way to him. He was articulate, forceful and particularly good at committee. Within two weeks of the arrival of the new chief executive, he was gone! Prematurely retired, in just two weeks! Not long afterwards the deputy chief executive also went, presumably by some agreement. This, of course, changed the character and style of events, with many jockeying for position.

The director of finance, a young man of about 40 went out of his way to be at her side, at every beck and call. As he was bright and capable she must have found it a great help in her new challenging position.

But of course, in helping her he managed to enhance his own position in power and influence. All this became very apparent to me for once John O'Brian had been pushed out, myself and John Synnuck were instructed to attend all chief officer meetings, previously represented by housing. Some of these were a complete pain, they went on for hours! In reality, half of the time would have been enough. I had more important things to do.

It wasn't long before I realised that my colleague, John Synnuck had put himself in a similar position to be that adopted by the finance chief, going to see her often, staying after meetings and even calling on her first thing in the morning.

I got the impression that she, being new, was rather depending on the continual advice they were giving her, which probably ranged from pure work issues to personal advice and opinions. This state of affairs went on for some months, getting progressively worse, with the direction of our duties becoming more complex and bizarre.

Then, John eventually became acting director of housing.

One day I had been invited to a charity luncheon at the "Mansion House", given in the city by the "Guinness Beer Company", then a lunch consisting of oysters and Guinness. Late morning, just before I was about to leave to go, my secretary Rosie said that when I had been out of the office, just before, she had received a call for me from one of the women secretaries at the Town Hall, asking specifically to speak to me. Being told I wasn't in she then passed on a message, asking me to be sure I received it. It went along the following lines.

She said that although she didn't particularly like me (an odd thing to say in the circumstances as I had no idea who she was or what she looked like) she felt she had to say something, as it was on her conscience. She said that the members were actually plotting to stitch me up! To use me as a "fall guy", and I should be aware and look out for myself! I was, of course, deeply disturbed to learn this.

Sometime later, I got my secretary to write down her version of the conversation and even to this day, I can hardly believe it. To think council members purposely "planning" to do me a mischief, me a senior serving officer of their council. Looking back I can only think that at the time the council was in dire trouble over its rent deficit and other problems and sought to divert attention away. This suited those officers lobbying for better positions, who used their knowledge of my prior misfortunes to their considerable advantage, giving credibility to whatever accusations were being made against me. In addition, it was possible that John Synnuck had been commenting to members, to my disfavour.

Arriving at the dinner reception, my host immediately noticed something was up and I explained it all to him. He was quite shocked. For days afterwards, or should I say years, it has dwelt on my mind.

Of course, it is so easy to look back with the benefit of hindsight, knowing I should have taken the statement my Secretary made to a solicitor, to act in my best interest. If only I had then my life would have taken an entirely different course.

I can't remember precisely when, but it was about this time when I had a minor difference with the new chief executive.

I can hardly recall the precise details now, except that it was a correction I had made to her interpretation of some issue. My corrections were, of course, tactfully made, having in mind our relative placing. As it hadn't been resolved I arranged to meet with her prior to one of her many meetings, we both attended.

We met as planned and sat alongside the meeting room table. I immediately could tell something was very wrong. She could hardly converse, and was almost white with pent-up anger, with hostile vibes radiating from her, like something from "Star Trek".

So I said, 'Anna, what on earth is the matter, why can't you tell me what troubles you, and then I can at least give you my honest view and perhaps, clear the air.' But it was of no use, our meeting went absolutely nowhere and I remained even more uncertain and disturbed.

There was no doubt, she had really been got at and really wound up against me. Now I had the Council's members and the chief executive joined together to destroy me. "Oh, if only then I had sought legal help".

The Trade Unions had a considerable say in Southwark at this time, with their representative always in close liaison with the members and the new chief executive. But not quite so strongly placed, when compared with my previous service, with both Camden and Islington, but strong enough.

At my level and as part of my duties, I had almost daily involvement in regard to the sizable direct labour force under my control, usually regarding staff issues or problems. My department had its own union representative who would walk into my office whenever he felt inclined. He was quite friendly with the chair of housing and ward members and I was aware of the need to be careful.

Sometime around then the union rep., came into my room, sat down as usual and started making small talk.

Somehow the conversation went around to Alan Crane, the chair of housing who apparently had been making comments about me.

'Do you know that Alan Crane said, if he doesn't get rid of you soon, he will resign himself!'

Years on, many years on I am reminded of Alan Crane, for his picture appears periodically in the journal of the institute, of which I am a member.

The article reports on him regarding his latest success, in accepting whatever new prestigious post he had been appointed to. It always showed a picture of him sucking a cigarette, surrounded by smoke, as though he thought that the image gave him maturity or status.

About this time there was a bit of a witch hunt directed against the works manager of the DSO, a fellow named Ben Farmer, he reported directly to me. As a result, I had to openly support or defend him at committee. Also, at this time the Council's audit section were doing a few purges on the DSO, but had, up to then, reported nothing of their findings, or reasons to me.

Then suddenly the works manager decided to take early retirement. I believe it was on health grounds and left the Council service quite quickly. I thought this a bit odd at the time but I knew he was quite friendly with the director of personnel services and assumed he had been given the best advice.

He didn't know just how lucky he was to leave just then or did I, and I am pretty sure the director of personnel realised!

One morning, I sat in my office at the usual early hour of about 8 am, having avoided the commuter rush, when in bowled the Union rep. As usual, he sat down uninvited and said, 'Have you seen the local papers yet?'

'No,' I said, 'why? Should I?' Thinking something had happened to Council housing property, when a report would become necessary, and that I might be expecting a call from the ward councillor.

So at 8:30 am, when the newspaper stall, just outside the office opened, I went down and got a copy of the local rag. Sitting at my desk I opened it. The headlines screamed out at me! "Corruption in Southwark's Housing Department", and went on to describe how alleged meetings were being held in Council flats between officers and contractor, with money changing hands.

It would have been enough of a shock if I hadn't got the Camden case behind me, but with that and all the ghastly descriptions, I knew how events would now progress, feeling really shaken. I had never had or been advised of any likely problem in this regard beforehand, by any officer of the Council. I telephoned John Synnuck, then acting as the housing director, but he didn't answer, or even ever come back to me, in spite of my messages.

Then Rosie came into her office. Five minutes later, she came into mine and told me personnel had called, would I go down to Rye Lane offices, to a meeting. I guessed it would be about the newspaper story.

I arrived at the offices and was shown in. There was the deputy chief executive, John Synnuck, the Trade Union rep. and the DSO, acting as manager, also the chief services engineer, Reg Corbridge.

We were asked to sit down and John Synnuck read out a statement which in effect said that corruption was alleged to have occurred in the department as so as responsible lead officer he was advising us that we would be automatically suspended. That is myself, Reg and the acting DSO officer. The deputy chief executive then said we would be on full pay and that it wasn't a matter of choice, but standard procedure.

The office manager would go back with me to my office and I would be allowed to empty my drawers and remove my personal effects. Before I could say anything, the Union rep. caught my eye indicating that I should not respond.

The same old feeling of persecution and insecurity arose up in me again and I felt exactly as I had all that time ago, back in Camden. I didn't take long for me to remove my effects and I left a few odds and ends, naively thinking that I'd be back in a few days to carry on my duties, just as before. I had arrived at my office before 8 am that morning and I arrived back home about 11:30 am.

Arrived back home and sitting down in my kitchen with a cup of tea I told Jean what had happened. I still felt numb and she was obviously shocked to be faced all over again with a similar situation. In the afternoon a Trade Union rep. telephoned and told me to be prepared for a very long wait.

'How long?' I asked. 'Well,' she said, 'a similar situation in Lambeth Council has been going on for nearly two years!'

'Two years,' I said, 'how long can it take?'

'Oh,' she said, 'it just grinds on and on, so I suggest you find ways to make yourself occupied, but come in tomorrow and we'll go through it all.'

The next day, I went into the Union offices, not far from my own and met again two reps. a further senior rep. was there to take the lead on my behalf. Copious notes were made with him promising to do all the Union could.

Also, that he would telephone me soon with names of a private solicitor, who would be employed by the Union to run alongside and protect my interests. *Thank God I'm a Union member*, I thought. Soon after I was told that a Paul Stanley, a Principle of the Legal firm OH Parsons would telephone me in a few days' time to arrange to meet and go over the same ground, as the Union had. After that we had to wait as facts emerged from the Union and Paul Stanley, to evaluate and act upon. It was a slow process indeed.

The Union had already offered me either the services of a senior union person, one I had met and one I was impressed with, or I could choose to have an outside solicitor. I chose the union rep. thinking he would be better placed and advised to look after me.

An easy mistake in the circumstances but possibly one of the biggest mistakes I have ever made. I had omitted to take into account the close relationship between the trade union and council members.

That evening I sat down in front of my TV, just watching the news but not paying too much attention when suddenly I heard the name Southwark Council mentioned. Then on the screen was Alan Crane, chair of the housing committee, talking about corruption. I could hardly believe the things he was saying, like, 'We will take strong measures against any officer found guilty!' Then somehow my name was mentioned, nicely tying me into the guilty allegation. Now the whole world will know and think the worst, I thought.

The next day, I telephoned Paul Stanley and told him about the TV programme and how alarming and damaging I had found the programme's content.

'Right,' he said, 'I'll get a transcript of the programme and we will see how we are placed.' True to his word he did so, found it very damaging and agreed with me to issue a writ against the BBC. In October 1989, I received a check, in the sum of £6,500 and an apology.

This type of damaging event was to be repeated a further two times. The second time when soon after it all started the local Southwark newspaper published an article, similar to the BBC broadcast. Paul Stanley again issued a writ, with a further £8,000 compensation paid.

Then, amazingly enough, a senior officer of Southwark Council published an article in a council journal, also damaging me. By this time, Paul Stanley was becoming quite practised in issuing writs on my behalf. He did so with the seemingly standard damage fee of £8,000 being paid again. I could imagine both the chief executive and the chair of housing seething with rage at the financial gain I had made over their lack of care.

Luckily I am not the sort of person who is unable to occupy himself. I did some cabinet making, jobs to the home and those of friends but was in a state of mental limbo, waiting for something positive to happen. Although my standard pay came as before, the extras, like car mileage and overtime did not and so we were a little short of funds.

Then out of the blue, I received a telephone call from a friend, somebody I had worked with in Islington during my time there, it was Rodney Woods, the deputy works manager. We had spoken there on a number of occasions and gone to a number of meetings together, getting on well.

I liked his bright capable style and apparently, he liked me, had seen the plight I was in and then proceeded to offer me a job as a senior project's manager in "Russia"! I was to do better than he did when he applied for the works manager job in Southwark.

'Let's meet at my club for lunch, if you like and I'll tell you everything', he said.

So quite amazingly, in a way another chapter in my life opened up, with the previous one held in suspense, waiting for Southwark to play their hand and affect my future.

Disturbing as it was, it was so pleasant to be away from the not so hidden perils of working in Southwark. Prior to Southwark, my career in local government had been very fulfilling, satisfying and a pleasant time (the Camden incident had not spoilt my regard for Camden Council). All my work had a purpose and gave me a sense of achievement, and I had made many friends along the way.

Of course, there were some very nice people in Southwark, just as in the other Boroughs. But the person, who had alerted Southwark to my misfortune in Camden, had most effectively turned the senior controlling officers against me, as well as the members themselves. Even the then deputy chief finance officer, a Bob Coomber, who was a very nice chap (I believe he is now chief executive) joined the pack, howling for my blood and making the occasional unpleasant remark.

Possibly and most likely it started after my successful committee interview and appointment, perhaps with one of the other unsuccessful applicants reacting in a fit of sour grapes, telling the council about me and my past. It could have been somebody checking up on me before my arrival and finding out (what had happened to me in Camden, and it would have been with some glee!) I do know that somebody went right out of their way to destroy me, with the new chief executive and the members.

But who knows, maybe they were jealous of me, perhaps didn't like my appearance or accent, being in contrast to a number of them, as "Bermondsey boys"!

What should I have done when I started first of all in Southwark, all that time ago? Well many, I think, many things. I should have put myself about, very much more, avoiding the isolation of my position, and got to know all my staff and their problems and success

But of course, it would still have gone wrong, set off by whoever it was.

Then, Oh it was such a big mistake, to accept the services of the Trade Union rep., to look after my interests, when I should have chosen Paul Stanley, the solicitor of OH Parsons, but I will comment on that later in the time period I later returned back to Southwark, to face my persecutors.

To Russia with Love
1988 to 1991

We had arranged to meet before lunch in a bar at Rodney's Club in Park Street, which was right behind the Ritz in St James's. He was there before me looking bright and perky, slightly florid in the face and well-overweight. A bit in appearance like a well-matured schoolboy. There the similarity ended for he was a very articulate, bright fellow who communicates well, with a considerable degree of intelligence and ability. I have to say I liked him, we had a lot in common, the same things in life. We were never bored in each other's company and tended to stimulate ideas in each other's company, to the benefit of whatever was at hand. After a few drinks in the bar, we went into the dining room where, over the meal, he explained his proposal.

Rodney was a very ambitious character indeed, with a strong awareness of his own competence, visualising himself as head of a range of International companies, spread worldwide. When an architect friend of his told him of a project he was involved in, to design a large factory in Russia, and that the project controller was seeking to have the entire scheme well managed, he quickly put forward his own name and received a very nice commission, as the company providing "project management" services.

Then, fortuitously, or otherwise problems occurred and he thought of me, as the senior project manager on site.

'It's right up your street, old bean,' he said, 'Particularly as I know you to be well-experienced in the building process and above all most diplomatic in approach.'

'You flatter me', I said, 'or maybe you wish to hold down whatever salary you have in mind.'

'No, no,' he said, 'I have seen you in action in front of halls full of difficult housing tenants, many times and how well you coped. Diplomacy is almost more important than technical ability. The USSR is a most sensitive place and this is a big contract, possibly worth £30 million.' He then went on to describe the scheme, which was the brainchild of a specialist company based in Cambridge.

It was to manufacture Optical Glass Fibre, made in their specialist plant. This plant, all the building materials and the supervision of the erection of the buildings and plant, would all come from England, the onsite labour would be provided by the Russians. The foundations, which are to be piled will be done also by the Russians. I, as senior project manager, would lead a team of six English specialists, mostly engineers, to supervise the erection of the building and services. Another team from head office in England would then go out to install their specialist plant. The factory was to be built in a town in the North East of Moscow, called "Gus Krustalney", which in English means glass crystal.

The new factory is to be built on the grounds of a well-established glass manufacturing factory, employing over 3,000 people. The region is famous for a certain type of sand from which the glass is made, hence the choice of the town for this purpose. We would be housed in either a new block of flats, or a hotel and would be run about by our own chaffered transport, which would take us to Moscow, or the country for the weekends, and we would have our own personal interpreter. Our salaries would be paid "offshore" that is from a source in another country, of our choice. Tax would only be payable if we returned for more than 65 days of any one year.

'What if I am required to return at any time to Southwark, for a hearing?' I asked.

'No problem,' he replied, 'the contract has a generous number of business class return tickets and you would simply return when required, attend the hearing and then go back. In any case, you would all return home for leave, possibly at less than three-month intervals, so you won't be stuck there, in some Russian wilderness.'

We agreed on the salary, which wasn't bad, then shook hands on the deal.

The next step was for me to meet the client at Melbourne, near to Cambridge, then appoint two Engineers to serve with me on site. The remainder of the team was coming from a large steel fabricating company in England, called "Condor", who were providing all the material fabrication for the main building.

It was an exciting venture and would nicely take my mind off my present problems

I had strong Doctor Zhivago visions of walking in the Russian snow at below freezing temperatures, dressed up in furs and struggling through blizzards, except in reality I had little idea of what it would be like, even though I read a number of books on Russia, which gave me ideas, some of which did not match actual reality when there. It was a most unusual venture, full of a range of possibilities. Not long after this meeting, Rodney and I went to Melbourne to meet the client.

The company had their factory and office in an industrial park in a small village near to Cambridge. I was to go there many times to these meetings. The meeting room was full of people interested in, and in some way, connected with the project. The owner of the company, the client to the project, was a Dr Geoffrey Sturgess, a gas specialist in gas engineering. He was a large impressive character, positive in his manner, extremely capable and quickly brought the meeting together. The others were the architect and engineers to the project, financial people from the gas factory and the person we would liaise with, when on site. There were also two engineers from the steel factory providers, "Condor". It was a useful meeting with the project programmed, defined and set, subject to the Russian client's agreeing a start date. Basically, the project consisted of a very large modern steel framed building with a mezzanine floor carrying some plant and subdivided into offices and utilities, in part.

The main area of the factory was set aside for the manufacturing plant, which extended to some items being placed directly outside. The piled foundations were to be carried out by the Russians and when finished we would begin the steel building. Even the concrete floor slabs were to be provided from the UK.

The erection was to be carried out entirely by the Russians, supervised by six English Engineers, with me leading, as the senior project manager.

A new office building was to be erected next to the factory, but this was to be entirely the responsibility of the Russians.

The preliminary visit to Gus Krustalney, to visit the site was eventually organised for May 1987, including me as one of the chosen party members. The others in this party included Dr Sturgess, one engineer and one architect, and of course, Rodney.

We met at Heathrow airport for our British Airways business flight to Moscow and it took about three and a half hours to get there, arriving quite jolly at the thought of a visit and the attention we had received on the way from the flight stewards and the drinks during the flight.

Moscow's Solyetsin airport was then a large, modern, but a gloomy place with very few lights switched on. The ceiling seemed to be made up of millions of cake tins, the type you can push out the bottoms, all linked together. It was extremely busy with crowds milling about and the occasional Russian soldier, watching and observing.

We had to wait literally for hours at the luggage carousel. It would grind and clunk into action, raising our hopes that there, at last, our luggage had arrived, to suddenly stop, perhaps for 15 minutes. It was nearly two hours later that we passed eventually through the luggage check to the main hall. A party of four Russians, one a woman came forward identifying themselves as our reception party.

'I am Eana, I am your interpreter,' said the one woman member, and then introduced the others. One was a stocky bull like Russian as the driver, then a tall bright looking fellow, named Volyda, from the plant, later to be my personal KGB minder! We were taken outside to a small transport vehicle, like a small bus, called a "Rafik". Somebody asked how long it would take to get to Gus Krustalney.

'About five hours,' said Eana.

'Five hours, my God,' someone muttered, 'we'll be dead on arrival!'

It was early evening and already getting dark so we didn't see too much of Moscow that first time before getting on the main road out to the country.

After Moscow, we continued along a virtual straight road, with silver birch trees either side, going on and on.

The road surfaces were poor, large potholes and bumps. The traffic lanes badly defined and all the traffic baulked by whatever lorry was in front.

One soon began to realise that most of the other traffic was commercial, Lorries, buses, vans, huge lorries trailing timber behind. A few Russian cars, of a clearly antiquated origin, like old Fiat derivatives, which had long gone off the scene in their native country.

Some stretches of the road were boarded by typical Russian detached single-storey timber houses. They were painted in bright colours with ornate fret surrounding the windows, picked out in contrasting colours. Nearly all had a small dormer window, nearly always wide open, in spite of the extreme cold. In the main they were very attractive, having the merit of a design of their own. Most had a "lean too" conservatory to one side. It was clear from our professional building eyes that the workmanship left everything to be desired. The foundations were inadequate and had settled. In some cases, quite remarkably so. The quality of all timber work was exceptionally poor, ignoring even the most basic carpentry rules. The roofs varied from being covered with corrugated asbestos, to flat painted metal, with 15 mm ridges, running from the eaves to the ridge. There was no guttering and the water just ran down the sides.

Almost every house had a little picket fence running around and groups of these houses appeared to be served from a single water standpipe, or even a well. Every now and then, the houses would fade out into flat barren fields, or fairly dense birch forests, in which the trees all seemed quite young.

Almost halfway we stopped and were given mineral water and biscuits. Eana our interpreter was a charming woman who spoke extremely good English, she was an Engineer when she wasn't interpreting. About 200 kilometres from Moscow, we arrived at the historic town of Vladimir, which was about 850 years old and was at one time the capital city of Russia. By English standards, it is a large town of about 800,000 inhabitants, and now it was quite dark when we entered the wide streets, each side boarded with large official looking buildings and built on a grand scale, with classic influence.

The Russians pointed out the first special sight, the "Golden Gates of Vladimir", with its shining gold domes, catching the beams of floodlights, looking quite wonderful. Apparently, it is the last surviving part of the town's defence ring, but actually, the gates were not there.

Eana told us that it was said the gates were made of solid gold and were in the Klyazma River and that so far, in spite of endless searching, they had never been found. We drove around the side of the gateway, did a circle, ending up under a bridge, then on to our road, to our destination, "Gus Krustalney".

Going out of the town we could see another magnificent sight. The floodlit "Cathedral of the Assumption", perfectly placed on high ground, overlooking the river. After leaving town we were then to go a further 70 kilometres to our destination, but it seemed forever.

Then at last, for the first time, we entered the outskirts of the town named Gus Krustalney, which housed some 80,000 people. As in the country silver birch trees lined each side of the streets.

Our hotel, the only one in the town, appeared on the left and we drew up outside. It didn't look the slightest bit attractive to me and when we struggled in with our luggage, my very worst fears were confirmed, broken front steps, an air of bland neglect and bleakness greeted us. The reception had no reception desk or anything! Directed to upper floors, we were each shown into individual rooms, the doors closing like prison cells at each entry. The rooms were ghastly, fitted out with the cheapest, most basic furniture. An old-fashioned TV that didn't work, everything dilapidated and bodged up, quite beyond belief. But the bathroom was about the worst I have ever seen. The plumbing was incredible, really unbelievable. It looked as though the plumber must have been demented. The pipes went everywhere, no hot water, broken uneven tiles, a dark and dingy atmosphere. The only saving factor was that the bedlinen looked clean, but the bed was extremely short. Wondering how the others had found their rooms I stuck my head out of the doorway to see them looking equally incredulous. Then Eana and another woman came down the corridor, giving us each a cup of tea, which was very welcome.

I didn't sleep at all well as I was plagued by mosquitoes that hummed in my ears all night, leaving me to wake up feeling a little jaded, especially so after that tedious journey. We met in the dining room, for breakfast and were just about to face whatever they had brought us when in came our coordinator, telling us through Eana, that breakfast had been laid on at the factory.

So we were back into the Rafik again and then a drive through the town, including the centre, which looked quite grand and interesting, down a tree-lined road and up and into the factory. We went up some broken marble steps, along a rather dark corridor and we were at our meeting place, the director's office. With the client leading, we went into the office, it was a large room with tables running parallel to the window and we were introduced to 19 Russians, shaking hands with each in turn, the leader of their delegation, a big bear of a man called, Victor Nickolaevich Kalinin, who was a deputy minister of the Ministry of Promstoymaterial. He had the most ferocious handshake. I had hurt my hand some weeks before and it was taking a long time to get better, but he soon put paid to that, cracking my fingers like dry twigs. Each time I met him afresh, I dreaded that handshake.

We sat down the six of us, opposite Kalinin and the names and titles were given from both sides.

Their titles seemed extremely grand, many chief engineers for example, and brigadiers. We were there to tie up the contractual details for the project, to build a factory that would manufacture "Optical Glass Fibre". It was quite a venture, with the entire project worth about £30 million, including the equipment.

This rather tedious meeting went on for three days, broken by breaks for tea, supplied in an adjoining room where a large table had buns, biscuits and sweets and tea glasses, set in their ornate metal holders. The first time we entered the tea room we were rather surprised, only expecting tea or coffee, then to find a small feast. One of the Russians showed me how to drink tea through a sugar lump clamped between my teeth, Russian style. Then he asked in halting English, 'How do you like us, as people, are we OK to you?'

It was a touching question and immediately humanised the relationship. Eventually, I realised that even at top director level, the Russians were not so concerned about how long the project might take, or how well it was going. Rather, did we like it there, and above all, did we like them!

The main meals were provided in the factory canteen and were not very good, even though they tried to do their best.

We had our own dining room, off the main dining room, but had to walk through theirs and endure the very off-putting canteen smells. The entrance to the canteen was dirty and next to rather smelly toilets. The canteen itself, I feel certain to say would automatically be condemned by any English environmental health officer. The careless control over hygiene was obvious by dirt collecting around the feet of each item of cooking equipment. Broken service ducks ran across the kitchen floor, giving a clapped out feeling. Added to all this was the very unpleasant canteen smell, which I am sure everybody dislikes, including the Russians. They made a special effort for the first meals, which were interesting, and then it became a bit of an ordeal, starting off with a vegetable salad, the dressing of which, in my taste, had an off flavour, soup, quite passable, except for partly cooked lumps of meat, or chicken. The main course, usually, meat of some kind and chips, was always suspected.

The chips were terrible, cut from small, to nothing in size, some burnt, some quite raw and with far too much fat, which floated in the bottom of the plate, quite cold. The meat might have been good had it been served on hot plates.

I tended to pick ay it, eating as much as I could, but never all. Sometimes filing up with bread and cheese, except that the bread was rather flat and tasteless, as was the butter and cheese. I forgot to mention the glass of "soc", which is a grape juice, watered down. It was a sticky and sickly type of drink and extremely sweet. The Russians like sweet things, tea always followed.

At one period, when I was sat opposite Eana I noticed a conversation going on at the bottom of the table, between the senior Russians, who seemed to be having a good exchange of opinions. I had been saying to Eana about my long-standing desire to visit Georgia, hoping I could get there while working in Russia.

Apparently, the other Russians had caught the gist of my hopes and were suggesting ways how I could go there, with an interpreter. They were like that, always trying to find ways to especially please us.

After two and a half days of close negotiations, everything that could be done was done, except one thing. We were, at last, going to see the actual building site which was about ten minutes' walk through the factory grounds. Our initial impression of the factory was one of general dilapidation, untidiness and there being no sense of an overall plan, or aim.

On the way was a huge factory building on which work had been stopped, about halfway through. Four storeys high and very long, it stood there with its steelwork and windows red with rust. A number of railway lines crossed the road throughout the factory grounds, and trains were always hooting at the crossings, shunting to and fro. The older factory buildings were in a terrible state of disrepair, almost unsafe to walk by, in case something dropped off.

The quality of workmanship, in every trade, was at rock bottom, especially the brickwork, the standard of which was almost beyond belief.

We reached the site, which was fairly large and about two-thirds of it had already been piled with square piles, presumably driven in readiness for the cross foundation beams. Our contractual obligation would start off at zero level, which is the finished floor level. But of course, it would be necessary for us to check the foundations first for dimensional accuracy, level and square. So having seen the site we were more or less finished, except that visit to the local glass museum was planned.

The museum was housed in a church building that had long been adopted and very skilfully, to display all sorts of glass, both historic and modern. One end of the main area had a religious mural and the other end a beautiful mosaic, it was all very impressive. Eana acted as the interpreter for the very attractive Russian girl who was guiding us around the showcases. She seemed to take a delight in making eye contact with each of us in turn, making the tour all the more interesting; perhaps it was because we were the first foreigners she had ever seen.

There was just one more thing to be done and that was to show us, me, in particular, our future Gus Khrustalney accommodation. We were taken there by Volyda, my future KGB minder, a very pleasant young man, good looking and strongly built. He was always very helpful and tactfully around, he knew his place. We arrived at a fairly large old house, not so far from the factory main gate, the house was probably built about a hundred years before, and it was a little dilapidated, but in good order by Russian standards, our accommodation was placed on the first floor.

There were a number of bedrooms off the main central lounge. The kitchen was very small with an old cooker and a single floor cupboard unit, rather sparse for the number to be staying there. Just off the kitchen was a single shower, showing rusty marks from the dripping taps and a yellow plastic shower curtain. The flat had a single toilet entered from the small lobby between the lounge and Kitchen. It was most unattractive, slightly smelly and had one of those ghastly Russian toilets in which all one does is deposited on an intermediate shelf, left steaming to be inspected, before being flushed away. I never did become comfortable or adjusted to sitting in there. The kitchen window looked out onto the backyard, a tarmac surfaced area with clotheslines running over most of its rear. At the beginning, we had been met in the flat by a middle-aged Russian woman, and I was sure she had recognised the expression of disapproval showing clearly on my face. I was later to learn that she was Volyda's mother, who was keen to see if we would like the flat.

After seeing the flat we all had a stroll around the lake in the centre of the town. It was quite a large beautiful lake and is possibly the most attractive feature of the town.

We were now finished in Gus and it was time to go back to Moscow that was to be straight, after breakfast the following day.

I was pleased to learn that we were going to have a sight of Moscow in the afternoon, before returning to the UK. Handshakes all around, then off, the five hour car journey, although long it didn't seem quite as tedious as the first time.

Our hotel was in the Mezdunarodnaya Hotel, the most modern hotel at the time in Moscow, it had been built for the Russians by the Americans to promote international trading (it has now been renamed as "The Crowne Plaza Moscow").

It was quite a large spectacular modern hotel with glass-clad lifts rising up in the internal landscaped centre area. In the centre was a clock tower and at the head sat a huge metal cockerel. It crowed at each hour, with its neck stretching forward as it did so, quite spectacular. It was a treat to be housed in decent rooms, an absolute luxury.

I bought some vodka, a few presents in the hotels Beriozka shops and sent off some cards, just for the novelty of posting them from Russia.

We went around Red Square in the afternoon, watching the changing of the guard outside Lenin's tomb, looked at St Basil's Cathedral, but couldn't get in because of the crowds, and then back to the hotel for a farewell dinner in the Japanese restaurant.

It was some months later, November, in fact, before Moscow gave the OK to start, and this time I went alone, flying to Moscow airport in the usual Business-class British Airways, arriving there late in the afternoon, recognising again the gloomy airport surroundings and the soldiers standing around, watching. Eventually, I spotted my bags and dragged them off, stacked them on a trolley I had bought for that purpose in England and went out to the customs area. Another long tedious wait, it seemed that unless we were deliberately held up then they were not doing their job properly.

Finally, I struggled through the crowded barrier to be met by a rather excited Russian who clearly recognised me. He and his colleagues took hold of my baggage and we went outside to meet a fairly young pleasant looking Russian women. She introduced herself as Olga and was to be my interpreter from now on. She was lively and very pleased to see me.

'We've been waiting for nearly two hours', she said.

'Oh, I am sorry,' I said, 'the plane was delayed for half an hour, then on top of that was the delay in getting my luggage.'

The car came alongside, a large black Volvo and the luggage was put into the trunk. Volyda was also in the meeting party and looked pleased as well to see me finally arrive.

It was a different driver, again a bull of a man, real solid Russian stock. Both men wore Russian fur hats, called "shapka" and as I was getting a bit cold, I fished out of my bag my own fur trappers hat that I had bought in London.

'You look a real Russian now,' Olga said, much later on, when we got to know each other better, she referred to 'that' hat, as one suitable for a drunkard! By then I had purchased a proper Russian one. Outside the car, it looked very grey, exceptionally cold and the thought of five hours in this gloom was a depressing thought.

'Do you know, Brian, you are my first Englishman!' said Olga. Although, her English was very good I thought she could have phrased the comment better. 'I am really very pleased to be your interpreter,' she said.

'That's good, Olga,' I said, 'but I must tell you I have a very bad fault, I talk much too fast, so in fact being here will be a good thing, because I will simply have to talk more slowly and more distinctly. Do tell me, Olga, without hesitation, if I speak too fast.'

'And you must tell me if I get the interpretation wrong.'

'Your English is really very good, Olga,' I said, thinking we would get on extremely well. We chatted virtually non-stop the entire way and the next day she had acquired a headache. Not surprising, I thought it really is such a long and tedious journey, especially in the dark.

The roads were just a mess and slush from half-frozen snow and mud splashed up from the traffic in front, mostly Lorries, which also emitted particularly foul exhaust fumes. The sides of the road showing a few lights from the little timber houses alongside parts of the road and the occasional small town we passed through. About three and a half hours later, we reached Vladimir and I remembered the floodlit gold domes of the Golden Gates and the two Cathedrals, up there on the hill, which we had seen when we first came in August. A further one and a half hours along quite deserted dark country roads and then the welcome lights of Gus Khrustalney. The wide tree-lined streets, the repeated five-storey blocks of flats, with the ground floor made into shops. Then the town square, well lit up at night, looking majestic, in its wide low classic style. The usual statue of Lenin, hand held out, preaching to an imaginary audience.

Near to the lake, on the right-hand side, past the glass museum and over the railway crossing, up towards the factory gates. Turn left and there on the right, about 200 metres was the block of flats. The car drove alongside, over the hard packed snow around to the back and we got out, stretching our stiff limbs. Near to the block on another building was one of those large digital clocks showing both the time and temperature, which was just minus 22 degrees, precisely the temperature maintained in my fridge's deep freezer, back home.

Up with the luggage and Volyda opened the door. It was exactly as I remembered it, "unfortunately".

The flat was fairly large and utterly soulless. Somebody had gone to a lot of trouble to leave food on the table, bread, butter, roast beef, cheese, cucumber etc., all neatly prepared and laid out on a nice white tablecloth. Olga, Volyda and the driver had a cup of tea.

'Brian, said Olga, we will see you tomorrow, at 9 am and show you where breakfast will be, have a good night's sleep.'

We all shook hands, I thanked them and then they were gone, leaving me suddenly to my solitude.

They must have been so tired for they had done double the journey, all in one day! The flat wasn't very warm, in fact, quite cold and I was tired. But in spite of that my thoughts buzzed around my head. By the time I had washed, cleaned my teeth I was getting very cold and decided to go to bed in my tracksuit, with the hood up and a pair of thick socks on. The bed was a little short and my feet pressed against the bottom but I didn't sleep too badly, considering, waking up at about 8 am. I showered, did my exercise and looked at my teeth in the mirror. Umm looked good so far and I felt OK too (I will tell you about that a bit later!) It looked very cold out here and I could see fur-clad people hurrying along the sidewalk. It all looked very Russian with the snow and frost on the birch trees, a bit like a "Lowry" painting. Olga came punctually at 9.

'How are you this morning Brian?' she asked. 'Is everything all right?'

'Yes, thanks, Olga,' I said.

The canteen wasn't too far away, just down the road, a little way. The front of the factory also had a huge temperature gauge, in the shape of a clock dial, some two metres in diameter.

It was still 22 degrees Celsius, below freezing, the coldest I had ever been so far. The way into the factory was through two large swing glass doors, one in and one out, and the same for the nearby short corridor. Two women, sometimes a man sat there watching the door swing to and fro, day and night. It seems to be the custom in Russia if it's a public or commercial building, the door is always guarded and watched.

The canteen hadn't changed, just as awful as I remembered. One aspect of the canteen scene always stays with me, that is the posture of the diners, for they sat there, leaning forward on their forearms, their heads bent low over their plates, shoulders rounded, in a sort of demoralised pose, as if saying, the foods horrible and such a posture displays my feeling for it and everything in my life. Every mouthful was obtained by dipping their head down to the plate. Everybody, man and women sat there that way, bending their heads down to take a mouthful, while their elbows still remained on the table. It was an odd scene, looking across the canteen, seeing the head go up and down, almost like watching a lot of birds in a cage.

Later, I was to see the same style of eating in Romania and it seems to be an East European habit, but not displayed in those better placed, socially.

We, English experts, as we were called, had been allocated a special room of our own, next to the one we had back in August. Today, the long table was prepared just for two. Breakfast came in, tea in glasses, in metal stands, bread, butter and the inevitable strawberry jam. Then an omelette, it would have been OK except it was completely cold, as were the plates. So, I filled myself up with bread and jam.

'Where do we go from here, Olga?' I said.

'Your office won't be ready yet so we go with the sub-director of building for a few days, then an office next door, until the site offices are ready.'

It was about ten minutes' walk to the main factory, past the flats. It was strange that morning, walking along in the intense cold, well wrapped up in my thermal underwear and my fur hat. Couldn't help noticing again how attractive the birch trees looked, covered in snow and frost, and how much it all looked so much like a "Lowry" painting. Now, every time I see a Lowry painting my mind goes back to Gus. The main factory building front had a large political mural painted on the side, facing down the street.

At the top of the building, above the entrance steps was a huge digital clock that changed periodically into a temperature readout, and then back to the date. The glass factory was called, "The Glass Factory named after Dzerzhinsky".

One's first steps into any Russian building is, in a small way, an adventure. This is because the heights of most of the steps are never, ever the same. You have to literally watch each step you take and these steps varied enormously in height.

This fault occurred, to my astonishment in the modern Mezhdunarodnaya hotel.

Back at the factory, we went into the director's reception room and I was introduced to his secretary, Tania and then shown into his room. I had seen him at the big meeting last August. Olga made the introductions and we shook hands, his name was Boris Vladimirovich Zhbanov. I immediately liked him; he had a twinkle in his eye, a good sense of humour, and struck me as a thoroughly cultivated pleasant person. He looked Russian, having wide jowls, quite exceptionally wide and had an air of distinction about him. It was the expected welcome, the hope that all would go well and that they would do their best to make us comfortable. If I needed anything he would always be pleased to help me. I said in return how pleased I was to be there and would do my very best to foster good working relationships etc.

Then next door to meet the deputy director of construction, Boris Veniaminovich Stavrov. He was the man I would be liaising with most of the time. He was every Englishman's idea of a Russian, Slavonic features, grey swept-back hair, and heavy jowls, stocky and again, a man with a twinkle in his eye. He was also, in his way, quite good looking. I knew I would also like him and enjoy working with him. His assistant was a much younger version of himself and he explained that they were tidying up the office next door for my later use, and in a few weeks' time I would have an international telephone. So I settled into his office with Olga and spread out my large carrier bag of drawings, I had brought with me and started work. All of the drawings had to be translated into Russian, laboriously by people like Olga, as were all written minutes of meetings, important letters etc. But some had already been done before my arrival.

The morning went quickly and it was dinner time, dinner was always at 1 pm and supper at 5. Always, Olga and Volyda kept me company, a kind gesture I thought. Both meals were fairly similar. The usual bread, butter, soup, meat and undercooked chicken which always clung to the bone with those little pink bits showing the undercooked parts. I always managed to drink most of the soup, it was the other courses I had a problem with.

Dishes like cold rissoles, resting on cold, oily, fried macaroni, or so-called chips. The sweet might be a large bun with a sour cream-filled centre, there might be an omelette, which was always cold.

I learnt later that it was normal to have it cold, so-called hot meals in Russia, odd in such a cold country.

The days jogged on uneventfully and Olga suggested that she should show me the shops, particularly the main food store, which was near to the factory, on the other side of the road, from the factory. The store was quite unbelievable. I know it was Soviet Union times and things were hard, but it was so bad it will stay in my mind virtually forever. It was the most awful and depressing shop I have ever entered. Like most shops in town, it was on the ground floor of a five-storey housing block and ran most of the length of the block. The glass front projected from the face of the building by about one metre and the short roof was covered in asbestos, but without a gutter, so when it rained the water splashed all over the glass windows. Then we come to the doorway. Whereas in every other country in the world, the doorway is arranged to "entice" customers into the shop, there in Gus it was the opposite. Double doors, one always locked so all the customers had to push past each other, through a dirty dark lobby and through another door. The outer door was kept too, either by a piece of elastic, or a long steel spring. As a result, the door crashed too, behind one, always it seemed when not expected, shattering one's nerves. Right in front of the first door, in the lobby was a roughly made wooden-frame clad in wire netting in which people placed their waste dry bread crusts, presumably for the pigs. The steps up to the doorway were unequal in height, badly broken, with missing paves, and the floor to the lobby was badly worn with hollow areas filled with snow or slush.

Once inside one's nostrils are assaulted by the stale smell of fish, rotten potatoes or some other unmentionable odour, all extremely unpleasant.

We walked from one end to the other and there was fruit juice, the local "soc" on sale next to Russian cigarettes. Next to it, the vegetable store, with no vegetables, no potatoes, carrots, nothing! Once in a while, some onions might appear. Oh, I forgot the jars of pickled green tomatoes on the shelves.

Past the check out and where the customers were required to put their own shopping bags when going in, just in case they actually found something to steal, and this was always manned by a member of staff. Next, the meat counter, but no meat. There was some fish, of sorts, looking like old dried mackerel.

Later on, I was to see chickens on sale, looking rather odd in that, instead of being neatly tied, with legs together etc, these hung over the counter in a most haphazard fashion, looking as though they had been beaten to death with clubs, because of the way their limbs poked out at such odd angles. Later but rarely, I did see meat for sale, and then, accompanied by the usual long line of expectant shoppers. It would be a very strange sight, huge lumps of meat would be on the floor behind the counter in the middle of the shop floor, where on a metre high lump of tree trunk, they would hack the meat into smaller pieces, using what can only be described as the sort of axe that has been used for beheading in the Tower of London.

The lucky customer would be seen hurrying off with their piece wrapped up in a bit of polythene, tied up with string. But in all a very rare sight, for many townspeople were obliged to go all the way to Moscow, to buy meat, cheese and even sugar, and that meant a five-hour bus journey, each way, perhaps, every weekend. The bread was often really hard and stale, always tasteless and quite often there was no milk, even for days. The entire length of the shop window had crude metal stands on which stood glass jars containing pickles, vegetables of a sort, tinned fish. They did sell Cuban orange juice, which was good but cost roughly one rouble, 40 kopecks, being about £1.40, and just for a three-quarter litre bottle. There was a limited range of kitchen items, a couple of toys, odds and ends and that was about that. But it was the general atmosphere, the dilapidation of the building itself, the cracked windows, the smell, the sour-faced assistants, that made the place so very unpleasant. I was glad to get out, back into the fresh air.

That evening, back in the flat, I sorted out my luggage and put it away. The main Lounge area had two long tables, surrounded by chairs, two armchairs and a number of rexine-covered easy chairs. There was also a cocktail cabinet and a large old-fashioned TV, an old radio and record player, which packed up after two nights of wasted effort to make it work.

Off the lounge were three bedrooms, two doubles and one single. I chose the single, which opened off from one of the doubles. The curtains throughout the flat were cheap thin and unmoveable, they simply could not be pulled open. As a result, the flat had a dark, dingy appearance.

That night, I was too cold again and slept in my tracksuit. When I woke up the next morning, I felt decidedly "off colour", very much out of sorts. Looking in the mirror, I was alarmed to see that my tongue was quite black, so black, in fact, my toothbrush became stained black.

Oh my God, I thought, *I have got the plague!*

Precisely one week after my arrival my colleague, Andrew Stuart was to arrive. I had interviewed him some months earlier with Rodney Woods in London. He would be welcome company, being alone is not really my style at all.

Our car driver preferred always to travel on weekdays as he wasn't paid for weekends. So it was arranged that I would be dropped off at the Mezh. Hotel on Friday night and stay there until Monday midday, when they would pick me up, that is both of us. But as the week progressed I felt more and more off-colour and decided to go a day earlier to see the Embassy doctor, to have the stitches out from my prior gum operation.

The three days before passed quickly in the office and I soon found out that communication was to be the big problem when working in Russia. Even telephoning Moscow was a problem. I would get eventually through to the Mezh, only to find out I could hear the receptionist but she couldn't hear me, or the other way round, and as for telephoning, or telexing that office, for onwards transmission to England, or telexing that office, it was virtually impossible, for I had to shout each letter down the phone.

We had been told that for some technical reason a telex would be impossible from the site. If so I thought, then we are really in for some problems. During the three days, I discovered, regretfully, one of the worst features of living in Russia, that is apart from the food, is the toilets!

The one I used at the office which served the director and his top colleagues, "was foul". No other description can be used. The two urinals were never flushed and were coated in slime and God knows what else, smelling to the high heavens.

The toilets, apart from being filthy had no seat covers and a staggering fact emerged, they put their soiled toilet paper in a basket alongside! You can imagine the effect, but later I was to see much worse, very much worse.

Olga was a wonderful person who was totally supportive of me. Literally, my happiness was her happiness, maybe she was Oriental in her previous life. When I joked or felt particularly happy, her eyes would sparkle with pleasure, which gave me pleasure.

Thursday came and off we went to Moscow, the five hours seeming as long as ever. Moscow is very interesting, as a place to drive through with enormously wide streets, trams, trolley buses and the "M" for Metro here and there. The traffic was always very heavy and it took about 35 minutes to get from the outskirts to the Mezh.

'Goodbye Brian,' said Olga, 'do have a good weekend and we'll see you here soon Monday, at about 1 pm, all right?'

The very minute I entered the luxury of the hotel I felt different, civilised, more alive and in communication. It was the most luxurious of the new Hotels in Moscow and had been designed with the business centre for commerce. It also had about four main restaurants, numerous bars, shops and nightclubs, a post office and information centre, as well as the usual "Beriozka" shop. I went up to the offices on the ninth floor, finding Natasha there and discovered. I had been given a different suite this time, just along the corridor. The hotel was luxurious by any standard and for Moscow, it enjoyed worldwide recognition. I put on the TV, which for a start had one more channel than the one at Gus. I had a shower and then decided to walk around the Hotel. I admired again the clock in the centre area, with its cockerel, watching the neck stretch out at each hour, for the beginning of the chimes. Then the Swiss-style movement below in which the figures dance around the clock, also as each hour was reached.

After a while, I decided to go back to my room and sort out what I was going to do in the evening. Some months before somebody told me that all the Embassies in Moscow had bars and that they were a good meeting place.

So that's it, I thought, *I'll go to the British Embassy bar, as it was their open night, anyway what else could I do*.

About 8 o'clock I got a taxi and was driven there. It was really a very cold evening, about minus 20 degrees, thank God I had bought the felt hat and the fur coat. The taxi stopped outside the Embassy club where two soldiers stood guard. I paid the taxi and went up to them.

'Embassy bar,' I said.

A deep Russian voice asked, 'Your passport, please.'

Luckily, I had it on me, he looked hard at it, handed it back to me and said something to the other guard, and they then startled me by doing a full military presentation of arms. *A good start,* I thought, then found myself next to the entrance and went in. It was much smaller than I imagined it would be and was, in fact, a little way from the actual Embassy. A few people sat about, some gathered at the bar. After speaking to the barman, I discovered that one had to enrol and get a credit card, paying for it in sterling. I did this and sat down with a lager, chatting with a couple of people but feeling a bit out of things, half deciding that I might go when a fellow came in. He seemed to know everybody and chatted to all, in a breezy, pleasant, English sort of way. I soon got involved in some of their comments and discovered that he was the Commercial Consul for the Embassy, quite a high position. Oh, I thought, he is just the person Rodney and I would wish to meet. He asked me what I was doing in Russia and I told him. He sounded quite intrigued.

'Surely nobody was mad enough to actually attempt to build something by Russian labour,' he said. Others near to the bar joined in and I felt a little like some sort of pioneer. The rather quiet start had turned out to be a rather pleasant evening.

'How far is the Mezh from here?' I asked him.

'Oh, it's about half an hour,' he replied. So saying goodbye, I left. I'd just got my hat and coat on when Stuart, the Consul chap came out and up to me.

'I'll give you a lift,' he said. When we got there, I asked him to come up to my suite for a drink.

Up in the room, I could see that he was very impressed with the quality of the suite, obviously assuming that I must be very well placed in the company to warrant such accommodation. After a few drinks and some general chatting he said, 'Look here, we are having a party at the Embassy in December, would you like to come?'

'Very much,' I said thinking what an evening, meeting the very person I wanted to and now being invited to an Embassy do, things were certainly looking up. He left not long afterwards to see other friends in the Hotel and I decided to telephone Rodney. He was thrilled to hear the news and we chatted for nearly 30 minutes, before closing. Before going to bed I looked out of the window, across Moscow and it looked spectacular from the ninth floor, with the lights twinkling across the river.

How I wished my job was in Moscow itself, rather than in Gus. Life would be completely different. Going to Gus, in comparison, was like going back to the Middle Ages.

The next day was mostly taken up by going to the Embassy to see the doctor. His practise was around the back and while I was there, I told him I was feeling decidedly off colour and that my mouth had turned black! He had a look at it and said, 'Oh, it's the change in water. I can't see anything else wrong, but I'll give you something for the diarrhoea.' Then, with the aid of his nurse, he took out the stitches from my gums. It was quite late and I had a great problem in getting a taxi back to the hotel.

Back at the Mezh offices were a couple of fellows from another company, which, in fact, owned the offices. One was a brother of the vice president, who seeing me at a bit of a loose end, invited me along to a restaurant they were going to, called. "The New Delhi". Although still a bit off colour the idea cheered me up and off we went in their car. It turned out to be a very good with a very good band, a most incredible looking singer, and the food wasn't bad either. It was interesting looking around the place, seeing the other people dining there, a lot of Indians, of course, and quite a few very attractive, wealthy-looking women, delightfully dressed, the whole atmosphere seemed a bit incompatible, to the idea of a Soviet State.

'One of the fellows,' Steve said, 'now let's go onto the boat,' which turned out to be a floating extension of the Mezh Hotel. It was reputed to have a very high-class restaurant and disco. We arrived there about 11:00 pm and the disco was just getting warmed up.

Never had I seen, in one place, so many spectacularly attractive women, many really quite exotic. The prices, by Russian standards, were very high, so I suppose it was able to be selective, hence, the quality of its clientele. The evening had turned out to be vastly more unusual than I had ever expected possible, giving great promise for the future.

Sunday arrived and Andrew Stuart was due to arrive. I got to the airport quite early and waited, and waited. "Where in the hell is he?" I asked myself, something must have gone wrong. I checked with British Airways, yes, he was on the flight, so I then telephoned the Mezh. Low and behold, he was already there.

'Do you realise I've been waiting here, sodding about for nearly two hours?' I said.

'Why didn't I see you?' he said.

'Surely, you can't have missed seeing me!'

'I didn't see anyone, even though I hung about, so I came by taxi,' he said.

'Well, never mind,' I said, 'I'm glad that you are there, and I'll be with you in about half an hour.'

Our trip to Gus on Monday surprised Andrew for the time it took and he did most of the talking to Olga. The drive is possibly the slowest I had ever encountered, almost coming to a halt, or so it seemed. I could have done the entire trip in my own car in about two and a half hours.

We eventually arrived at the flat and I showed him around. I'd already apologised for the poor accommodation, but he said, to my great surprise, that it wasn't as bad as he had imagined it to be. Food was laid on the table, as before and we sat down to eat. Andrew's immediate comment was that his friends said he ate "like a pig" and then set about proving them right. But I liked him a lot, a cheerful chap, attentive and caring to me, in a friendly way, nearly always good humoured. He was also a good Engineer and was quite hard working. What more could one wish for, except better social manners, but he was young.

There was one thing that slightly irritated me, he would leave his lower jaw hanging down, and it quite got to me. He was tall, about my height, blond hair and slim. He was a conspicuous figure, seen walking around Gus by the local inhabitants.

By the end of that week, we had got our temporary office, next door to Stavrov's, with an international telephone, but it was small and narrow and only just housed us. Also, it was cold and so we complained, almost within hours in came two office-girls who set about draft proofing the room. They had a bowl, with wallpaper like paste, a huge roll of cotton wool and set about filling up all the spaces and gaps to the windows, then taping over each joint, *a permanent job*, I thought, *and how will we breathe!*

We were then a bit stuck, in terms of work progress, the basic foundations had been checked, and we now awaited the two further English engineers, from the steel company, who were to guide the Russian erection team. The whole process was going to be a difficult job with the temperatures around minus 22 degrees and at least, 18 inches of hard-packed snow and with ice everywhere.

We learnt that the two Engineers were due out on the 7th of December, that Monday night. They came quite late, at almost 11 o'clock. I knew I would like Derrick Burgess, the steel work supervisor, as I had met him in England, sometime before. He had done his army national service in Hong Kong, just like me and was about the same age, we, therefore, had a lot in common.

He and Andrew also had a lot in common, their fanatical interest in mountain climbing and they were often seen hanging around the flat from the head of the door frames, by their fingertips! I understood that this was an essential part of their exercise. Pat, an Irishman, to be the site charge hand was a lot older, but a solid dependable sort of chap, in fact, one of the hardest working people I had ever met.

Life in the flat, although crowded, picked up. So nice to chat in the evenings, play cards, or go for a walk together. Three of us, not Pat, doing quite strenuous exercises, jogging around the room and countless other things, which Derrick had set for us. The three of them were mostly site based, with myself spending most of the time in the office.

Pat was always up very early, about a quarter to 7 and off to the site. The Russian workers were, of course, never there that early, so he just stood about getting cold. So I said one morning, 'For God's sake, Pat, it's below 20 degrees out there and there is no need to get there so early and freeze to death!' But he wanted to go and so he went, just in case they might turn up.

The steelwork that was required on site was stacked elsewhere and Pat had to identify each and every piece, to be taken on site in the right sequence. Simple enough, you would think, but not when the men either didn't turn up or had messed up the lorry arrangements.

Derrick and Andrew checked out the column bases and the Russian team commenced work, terribly slowly, to cast in the column holding down bolts, but not without the most incredible collective meetings held on the site.

They would shout at each other, expressing personal opinions, as to the best way to do the work and it was like bedlam. In the beginning, I suffered the same problems at my office meetings, but more on that later.

I learnt, to my pleasure, that we were to have a leave at Christmas time, a bit surprising, considering how short a time Derrick and Pat had been there, but very welcome, nevertheless. Then problems arose as to who should pay for it. The Russians said they only covered the return flights back to the UK at the finish of each contract. The firm in England said, not true, they pay every time. So the discussions went on for some time which rather concerned us all and we grew anxious as to whether between them they would mess it up. In the end, it was OK and I went to Moscow with Olga and Volyda whilst they actually purchased the tickets from Aeroflot. That, in itself, was an experience for the assistant, exceptionally unhelpful in every aspect of her so-called service.

My Embassy "do" was on the 18th of December and as I couldn't get into the Mezh, one of the Embassy officials kindly put me up in his palatial flat. I say palatial because I could hardly find my way back to my bedroom having been to the loo in the night because of the size and complexity of the place. It was not only palatial but also luxurious and fitted out with micro ovens, cookers and washing machines, etc., all the things we didn't have.

I got a lift to the Embassy with two girls who worked in the travel company that served our firm and we all set off in their car arriving nicely on time.

The Embassy was at one time the home of a Ukrainian Sugar Merchant, and was magnificent, possibly the best stately home I have ever been in, anywhere. Quite exceptional, especially the room in which the reception was being held. I only knew a few people so Stuart, the First Secretary I had met before, introduced me to many others. I spotted the doctor, who had treated me, and we chatted to him for quite a while, then a very attractive Russian girl introduced herself to me, she had a slight Irish accent obtained from her Irish husband. I have forgotten what position she held, it didn't matter, and just being near her was a pleasure. Stuart then introduced me to the British Ambassador who had the charisma and charm and dignity one would expect from somebody holding such an important post. He was easy to talk to, a very nice person and was very interested in what I was doing in Russia. Like Stuart especially surprised that we were going to supervise Russian labour, out there in the country.

I can't remember how it started but somehow we got onto the awful subject of Russian toilets, and he told me of his experiences, and I told him of mine.

One event in particular. I told him how I visited the site quite early on. It was a very cold day but with a bright blue sky. Sat there right in the middle of the site, resting on quite deep snow, was a galvanised steel clad toilet. I went up to it and opened the door to an unbelievable sight, for there on the floor was a pyramid of brown stools about a metre high, rising up to almost a point. It was such a sight, there with the background of snow and the bright blue sky above, that I took a photo.

It made us laugh so loudly that others turned to see what had made us enjoy ourselves so much.

Later, Stuart asked me what I had been talking about with the Ambassador since I had held his attention for by far the longest period of anyone during that evening. It was a very special event in the circumstances and nicely finished off my time before returning to England.

I don't know what the Russians thought, about me suddenly going off to the British Embassy, only just after I had arrived in the Soviet Union, it must have really raised their curiosity.

Especially, when very much later, I learnt that during our entire time whilst in Russia, we were watched by the KGB. Volyda being my special one.

A bit like so many incidents in my life, when a simple innocent action on my part, raises the greatest suspicions in the minds of others.

I returned to Gus after my leave and it hadn't changed, still very cold, in the lower twenties. The streets looking even more like a Lowry painting. Nothing much had changed on the job either, in fact about half of what they had promised. Talking of promises, the flats were supposed to be ready in January and when I checked with Stavrov, I learnt, "not for a while yet, but soon we will have a look!" One thing I learnt rather quickly about the Russians was that they have endless patience, quite endless, it's called "Vsegda Savtra" which means, always tomorrow, and they mean just that. Going back to the canteen, the smell of its environment and not forgetting the food, "the cold food".

I picked at it, usually filling myself up with raspberry jam on bread, taking vitamin pills and hoping I wouldn't suffer, as a result. But it wasn't long afterwards that both Derrick and Andrew suffered from mouth ulcers, presumably from dietary deficiencies.

Pat was still doing his thing, which is getting on site very early, and then waiting about in the cold for the site labour to eventually turn up, so he could direct the various parts to the right positions. Some of the steel frames were, at last, being erected, even in that cold and it looked quite impressive, the yellow painted steelwork against the white to the grey of the snow and with everybody stood about in their fur hats and felt boots. It was so cold that the concrete around the basis of the steel stanchions had to be cured with the aid of electric anodes, a series of fine steel rods pocked unto the grout or concrete and wired up like a child's crystal set. The whole approach to electricity on the site was quite alarming. All the cranes were electrically driven, even the largest power crane with the heavy power cabled draped across the site, tied here and there, and sticks propped off the ground.

Talk about a dangerous potential, the ends of the wires were wound together and left there naked in the air, for anyone to stumble upon.

Another real hazard on the site was a number of deep holes in the foundation slab, which were unseen, because of the thick covering of snow. At any time one could walk into a pocket, or fall into a service duct.

Luckily, it never seemed windy, if it had been then, at minus 25 degrees, even the Russians would have had to call it a day, it would have been impossible then, and the slightest breeze would give an impossible chill factor.

One day, Andrew and I were out walking, we had to walk everywhere in Gus, to the local shops and the only Hotel in town. We went to the Hotel mainly for the food and possibly the entertainment, for it had a small band of sorts, who knew only about four tunes. These they played, amplified to vastly high volume. It was painful to the ears. It was an actual physical pain to sit there and suffer. At the end of each piece, they spent about half an hour tuning up for the next piece. Then crash, boom, bang and back to that incredible din.

The Russians have quite a good custom in their restaurants where they have dancing. For whenever asked, a Russian girl will always say yes, well always it seemed to an Englishman. Andrew and I decided to have a try and we went up to a table where some attractive girls were sitting, asking two of them to dance. Mine was quite exceptionally pretty.

'*Kak vas Zavat*,' I said which means, what is your name.

'Tania,' she replied, their name is always Tania, Olga, Natasha or Lena, so it seems.

'*Menja Zavut Brian*,' I said, which means, my name is Brian.

She immediately chatted on, completely leaving me in the dark.

Eventually, she had the good grace to bow out, so I said, '*Spazeebah*,' which is thank you.

I suppose we were a bit of an oddity, the only Englishmen in Gus, in particular, Andrew, at six-feet five-inches tall, blond, and myself just three-inches shorter than him, red-haired, we were such a contrast to the average Russian.

The whole town seemed to be informed of our movements, for example, during one week we had been seen walking along the other side of town.

But of course, we were in Soviet Russia, working as foreigners in a semi-closed town and certainly we were being watched day and night, at whatever we might be doing, indeed I had my own KGB minder, Volyda, nice as he was.

I also knew that Olga would have to tell her superiors absolutely everything about me, what I did for every minute of the day, what I said and even what I might even be thinking. I never had a problem with that for there was absolutely nothing about me that would worry them, and clearly, I was pro Russian, as one human being to another, also I had that romantic view on life, something the Russians liked and understood, being so themselves.

Back to the restaurant, as it didn't sell either beer or spirits we would take our own, bought at the Beriozka shop. Then one day the manager telephoned the factory asking that we didn't, the Town was a dry area! How ridiculous, we thought, when in Moscow, the capital, you could get anything, from vodka to wine, even champagne.

Walking back to the flat it was so cold that our moustaches completely froze over, when I got inside I looked in the mirror above the kitchen sink.

Christ, I thought, my face was very gaunt with the cold and my moustache was a solid band of ice. It took me half an hour to unfreeze it, painfully breaking off the pieces, bit by bit.

Another day we decided to go down to the local market, quite a long walk, past the town centre. The market building was just as one would expect it to be. A large covered hall with permanent tiled-counters set out in rows. But like the town's main shop, there was virtually nothing there, one counter had some sort of black seeds, which people bought in little bags, and then cracked them between their teeth. A few withered apples, at very expensive prices, onion, always onions, the smaller ones, in particular, cabbages and a few withered, strange looking carrots, and one or two other things of no consequence. Oh, there were some homemade bars of what looked like popcorn.

'There is nothing here at all,' said Andrew, but it was interesting to see the Georgians peasants, very dark and very brown, some quite good looking, a strong positive looking race. There was one stool selling handmade scarves, woollens, hats etc.

The poor living conditions didn't help our relationships in the flat, although generally, we got on quite well. But it wasn't always sweetness and light. Pat and Andrew often flared up at each other, over the silliest things, for example, Andrew might say, 'Who left all that dirty crockery in the kitchen sink?' whilst looking at Pat.

Pat would then be immediately deeply offended and say, 'I always clear away my own stuff,' and to prove his point he kept his knife and folk in his room.

Andrew was a guitar enthusiast, I remember discussing this when I interviewed him, thinking, I hope he's good, or it will be hell. He both tried and was at times trying. Fortunately, I liked his choice of music, which softened things a lot. Sometimes he came in an evening and strummed away for half an hour, that would satisfy him and he would put it away.

So we would sit there during a typical evening, the TV on, just in case for a change there wouldn't be a long-winded political programme, each of us with a drink, me possibly drinking whisky. Andrew or Derrick playing chess, or something else and Pat playing patience. The room was always too cold, in spite of all the windows being taped up, alter it got so cold that I complained and they gave us an electric fire. Then "bang", the extra load on the circuit fused the lights, so for an hour we sat there in the dark, whilst the more experienced neighbours had repaired it. This happened time and time, but by then we had our candles ready.

Every now and then, I would see the factory director, accompanied, of course, by Olga, he didn't speak any English. Boris Zhbanov, was a charming cultivated man, a perfect man, with perfect manners. The meetings were a bit like a "Chinese Tea Party", the very last thing we discussed was the work.

I remember on one occasion we sat there and I expected a question on the programme, instead, he said he was concerned about our "cultural programme", would I work out in advance where we would like to go weekends, so they could arrange the transport and the hotel bookings etc. Then he said were we comfortable, no, I would reply, it is too cold so he said he would provide another heater, of course, it was hopeless, the extra one we already had had blew the fuse so what good would another one be.

'And the food,' he asked.

'Not good or acceptable,' I said, 'It is not to our taste, the plates and the food is always cold, we don't like completely fatty pork, or cold uncooked chips etc., etc.'

He would make a note, then, almost as an afterthought, 'Oh, how is the job getting on?' I would explain and the meeting would end with handshakes all around.

Eventually, our site office was ready. Two long huts with electric heaters and with the toilets being sited in the adjoining factory that had been specially adapted for us, at my insistence, and locked up, of course, between uses. We had two telephones, one factory and one international on which Olga would place our firm's call back to Moscow or England. She would even book our private calls back home, via the telephone in our flat.

We had at last organised our weekends, Moscow was the best, as there was more scope there. It would usually go like this. In a Rafik or car on the five-hour journey to Moscow, on a Friday night and then picked up again on noon Monday. We normally stayed at the Mezh Hotel but sometimes at another, like the National, opposite the Kremlin, the four of us usually in two rooms. On one occasion, I went down to the Mezh by myself, Olga and Volyda came along, as usual. Since it was such a long way, I said to them, 'Come on in and have lunch with me,' it was the very least I could do, and I also said, 'Do not falter at the hotel door or the "doorman"', I emphasised doorman, 'will pounce on you and demand passes, etc.' They never stopped foreigners. I understood later that nearly all the doormen in Moscow were ex Gulag Guards, chosen for their positive approach.

I could see that Olga and Volyda were nervous, for being Russian they expected the bureaucratic treatment, as a matter of course, but they managed it.

Unfortunately, all the restaurants were closed, so after trying several bars we settled for an ice cream parlour. I could see that they were quite amazed at the flamboyance of the place, the lights, the crowing cockerel clock and all the red carpet, what an eye opener after Gus, I thought. I didn't expect that they have ever seen anything like it before.

At the bar, I said, 'Well, what will you have, whisky, gin or anything else?'

They seemed stuck and followed my lead with a gin and tonic, and some ice cream and a pack of cigarettes for Volyda. It was clear that Olga and never had a gin and tonic before and found the taste rather strange. But they enjoyed it and I enjoyed their surprise and pleasure.

When the four of us were there in Moscow we went onto the Inn tourist hotel and asked to be booked into a suitable restaurant, with dancing but able to pay in rubbles. The extremely helpful assistant got us a place called "The Fairy Tales". It sounded odd, but we hoped for the best. The all in cost each was 20 roubles, not bad since it included drinks. When we arrived there by taxi it didn't look too good outside, but inside it was quite spectacular, a large open space, with a high ceiling. There was a band at one end and round tables in all the remaining spaces. We were shown to a table, not far from the band.

The table was beautifully laid out, with caviar, smoked sturgeon, salad, champagne, vodka and wine and a number of beautiful wine glasses, of various sizes, it was very attractive. The food matched the table and was very good, indeed. Looking around, the other tables had a mixture of people and the one next to us had four attractive Russian girls, two, in fact, quite beautiful.

'Right,' I said, after the starters, 'I'm on the floor.'

'You mean we are,' said Andrew.

After the bleakness of Gus, it was so good to relax in such pleasant surroundings, the band was playing and I went up to the table, choosing one of the most attractive of the four girls. She got up immediately and we danced, I tried my Russian and she responded, in her faltering English, saying that I was a good dancer. Then I noticed that she was married and asked her what a lovely girl like her was doing here, without her husband, and what does he do for work?

'My husband he works in the Kremlin, he is a "political captain"'. I thought she meant the KGB, then, should I be dancing with her?

Andrew was also on the floor, but Pat and Derrick were still sat there at the table. The evening became quite lively and in the end, we got Pat and Derrick to join us all at the girl's table, where we chatted or attempted to with the aid of a Biarritz Russian phrase book.

A few more dances then the band packed up at 12 sharp. Being gallant Englishmen we agreed to walk them to their bus stop, but what was really agreed was that they would walk us to a taxi stand so we wouldn't be lost! The restaurant was at the back of the "Gum Store", which meant that we had to walk to the front, across Red Square, past St Basil's Cathedral and down to the Rossia Hotel, where the taxi rank was. The walk was quite delightful, the four of us with a girl on each arm, linked together, all happily chatting away and the moon shining brightly across the square, catching the cobbles and the gold domes in its silvery glimmer. The square is always spectacular, at any time, but that night it was really quite something.

Now, many years on, whenever I see Red Square on the TV, I always think back to that magical evening.

On other occasions, we had been in the Gum Store, which is absolutely huge, facing across the square, directly opposite the Kremlin, but inside, and to me, it was a disappointment. It's rather like a huge market area in looks and feel, but in building terms, it is very impressive, a large glazed barrel-vaulted roof, balconies that run around at each floor level, leading off to open-fronted shops. The balconies link across with little bridges and it's all a bit of a maze, a building to see thoroughly, once.

The place of all places to see in Moscow was the "Armoury", within the Kremlin, which exceeded all our expectations, it was spectacular, beautifully displayed exhibits, with items you would never see anywhere else in the world.

The icons and their jewelled frames were my favourites, there were also the jewelled dresses of the Tsars and their crown dresses, one with an incredibly small waist, reputed to have belonged to Catherine the Great, as well as their gilt coached. "The Fabergé" collection was something in itself, with eggs that had belonged to all members of the Royal family, but I still returned to the Icons and their frames, a favourite of mine.

We had three cultural places to visit, which were reasonably near to us, they were Moscow, Suzdal and Vladimir. Suzdal was especially good for us, it was only one and a half hours by car and we were able to stay at Russian rates in roubles in a modern Intourist hotel.

The food there was just passable, but the town itself was well worth a visit. It was quite small for one thing and it was possible to see everything on foot. It is a wonderful historic place, full of historic buildings, monasteries and churches, even period timber houses. One church was almost entirely covered in the most incredible frescos, every space, either wall or ceiling had a painting covering it. Suzdal was the place where the film, "Peter the Great", was filmed and we were especially lucky because Olga had a friend who lived there. Her husband was a senior official for the Vladimir region, which was marvellous, as we had an expert tour guide, visiting places where the public does not normally reach. I even had my photo taken in the "Troika" that was used in the film.

On one of our visits to Suzdal, when it was particularly cold, I think down to minus 32 degrees, Pat was warned by some local people that his nose was getting "frostbite" and for him to rub it. When he came back, I said jokingly, 'For God's sake, Pat, you had better be careful or it will drop off!'

He didn't venture out again that day. The view from the hotel, across the frozen snow-covered river, over the trees and the gold-domed churches, was spectacular, the sun catching the hard crisp frost, and giving everything a bright silvery shine and sparkle. But for me, the most exciting and memorable event was when we stayed at Vladimir.

Pat had finished period and had gone back to the UK, being replaced by George Langham, the building work cladding supervisor. We were staying in another Intourist hotel, an easy walk distance from both the Uspenskiy and Dmitrievsky Cathedrals. All one could see of the Dmitrievsky Cathedral was the wonderful carved limestone exterior and the imposing symmetrical shape of the building, but we couldn't get inside. However, it was possible to go inside the Uspenskiy, or Assumption Cathedral, we had been before, admiring the fabulous interior, all its gilt and paintings, the "Andrei Rublev" frescos and the breathtaking icons. The Cathedral is older than the one of the same name inside the Kremlin, in Moscow.

The sun was shining that Sunday morning, as George and I walked across to the Cathedral, the gold domes looking brilliant against the white walls and the blue of the sky, and then, as good fortune would have it, there was a very special service going on. It was full of people, 50 percent of whom seemed to be the classic Russian peasants, mostly old women.

A special event was taking place right in the middle of the Cathedral, which appeared to be the crowning of a local Bishop. It was clearly a very significant event, with so many dignitaries attending the changes in routine, and the way the jewelled crown was placed on his head. Quite apart from this breathtaking spectacle, was the intense religious atmosphere given by the magnificent deep based singing of the principal priest. It made the small hairs on the back of my neck tingle, a sensation I hadn't had for decades. I have never heard anything so beautiful, or so atmospheric. If all this wasn't enough to fill one's senses, it was accompanied by the singing of a choir, which soared up and around the Cathedral, in unison with the deep bass voice of the priest lead singer. Every now and then, the Bishop would chant something and all the old peasant women would respond, crossing themselves and bowing. Tiers of candles were burning all around, placed in front of particular Icons, where again, peasant women would gather, sometimes with tears in their eyes, prostrating themselves on the floor, kissing the flagstones, or the Icon frame itself.

How really wonderful, I thought, *to have such an absolute faith, such belief and doesn't it help to simplify and justify everything in life.*

The service went on for a long time, I felt I could stay there forever. I couldn't imagine any scene, wherever it could be, to be more impressive, or spectacular, that this service, which we had seen entirely by chance! Then something else was happening, all the priests proceeded towards an open door at the back of the altar, where we could see inside to a large room, a table and a throne. The bishop was going to take his rightful place. *This is going to be too good to be true*, I thought and in spite of the no photography sign, I lifted my camera and took a shot, getting shouted at and pushed by an irate peasant behind me. The picture did come out but never did justice to the atmosphere of the event, but it didn't matter, the entire event is held in my memory, just as though it was yesterday.

The other rather special visit was to "Leningrad", now St Petersburg, unfortunately, it was taken at the wrong time of the year and was very cold and very wet, but it was still a special event. How we came to be going there is another story which I will relate later. The party consisted of myself, George, Derrick and Olga, who of course, was thrilled to go. We had a contact in the Leningrad Institute who was going to assist during our stay. Olga had had her work cut out organising the hotel. It was difficult to get one, even during that time of year, in fact, without the help of our Leningrad friends, we would never have found one. The trains were not any easier, either, for crazy reasons. Olga couldn't book a return ticket, apparently, it's just not done. I didn't really believe it, it was just their bureaucratic nonsense. Anyway, we were off, on a sleeper between Vladimir and Leningrad, a convenient four-day berth cabin. Tea was served, a glass of tea that is, and we brought along some sandwiches. It was a terribly slow train, but it was an enjoyable journey, bowling along and we had vodka, to keep our spirits up. The scenery from the train window was flat and totally uninteresting, as was the approach into Leningrad. We were booked into a hotel called, "The Karelia", nothing special, but it served our purpose. But there was a problem when we arrived, we had booked in roubles and they demanded hard currency, we had no choice but to accept.

Our contact guide was called Mark, a kind very considerate person. He had arranged a small minibus and driver, which was very handy in taking us around.

So, we went off on a long tour around Leningrad and were shown all the wonderful churches, the war memorials, the Peter and Paul fortress and not least, "The Heritage", which was marvellous, so huge and impressive, one could spend an entire week there and still miss something.

Yet, it was difficult to get around without missing out. It should have had a clear route, marked up, for each section, perhaps colour-coded. Also, the lighting for which many paintings it was very poor, too bad.

Every exhibit had, of course, a Russian title, but why not, as well an English, French, German ones, etc. It was a worldwide very famous museum, such an oversight, perhaps, now that fault has been rectified. I had found the British Embassy, in Moscow to be lust that bit more spectacular, as a building, but of course, the setting of the Hermitage, fronting onto the river Niva, with the huge square behind is quite unique, and better weather would have helped. During one of the evenings, we were taken to a restaurant in the Peter and Paul fortress, it was OK, in fact quite good, but by far the best evening we had while in Leningrad, in fact during my entire time in Russia, was when we were taken to the "Troika" restaurant. It had been very difficult to book up and get in, but we managed and arrived, passing over out hats and coats. Just behind us were four Russian girls who passed over their hats and coats and changed their shoes into something more appropriate. They were stunners, in spite of the shortages in the Soviet Union, and couldn't have looked more healthy and lovely. We got to our table, which was well seated, the girls were placed fairly nearby, within easy sight. The food was excellent, much like the "Fairy Tales", in Moscow, and the show, it was the best show of its kind I have ever seen, anywhere, in all my worldly travels. It started off, after a lull in the proceedings, when the lights were dimmed right down. Then a spotlight lit up a spiral staircase, set in a deep red recess.

Set at the top, coming down the stairs was the lead male tenor and he was singing "Kalinka, Kalinka", in a fine operatic voice, which carried around the restaurant, filling every possible space in or receptive minds. It was so good, that the particular moment always comes flooding back to me whenever I think of Russia. A truly magical moment.

When the cabaret part of the show finally ended, then the dancing started, on the same stage, with the floor glass panels lit from below, in changing coloured lights. Andrew and I looked at each other, put up our thumbs and we headed for the table with the four girls. Smiling, they readily agreed and we danced with them for the rest of the evening, eventually, going off in their taxi, while we returned back to our hotel in our minibus. Oh, they didn't speak any English, but that didn't matter one bit.

So our most enjoyable visit to Leningrad came to an end and we returned to Gus. It was like leaving Paris for Auschwitz, but that's a little cruel.

Just going back to how we managed to go to Leningrad in the first place, it happened at one of my meetings with the Director Zhbanov, I had asked him would it be possible for us to visit Leningrad, perhaps for a weekend.

'A weekend,' he said, 'you can't go there just for a weekend, it's a wonderful place. When I was a young man I was at the University there, you must go for four days.' We didn't argue, and it was a typical example of how cultural events were more important to them than the job at hand.

Throughout my stay in Russia, I had felt unwell, slowly and surely I just deteriorated, losing a great deal of weight. Of course, I was aware of how unwell I was becoming, but not so aware of the weight loss, except every now and then I would tighten my belt until my pants hung on me like a drawn curtains. For one leave period I had gone home when Jean's sister came down to see us, and on seeing me, she said, 'Oh my God, what's happened?' She told Jean separately that she thought I had a terminal illness, and the same thing on one occasion when Derrick returned from leave, with the same reaction. The very worst indicator, that something was seriously wrong, was when we had gone to Suzdal for one of our weekends. I had been out for a walk with the lads and had been feeling quite terrible, so much so in fact that I thought to myself, I simply must get back to my room and lie down, even thinking I must be dying!

Then one day, I sat at my desk facing Olga, she had been a little quiet then she told me I didn't look well and ought to see a doctor, could she fix up an appointment to see the town's doctor. So very soon we paid her a visit, she was a pleasant quite attractive woman (you can see that I am not quite dead yet!), perhaps in her early forties and very personable, but she didn't speak any English. Through Olga, she examined me, pounding my chest and feeling my stomach. Oh, I forgot to say that my stomach was now the main cause of my concern, giving me continuous discomfort.

'Would you be prepared to go to Hospital and have a test?' Olga asked on behalf of the doctor.

'Of course,' I said, 'anything if it will help identify the problem.'

So a telephone call was made and quite early the next day I went with Olga. It was the town's central hospital, slightly ramshackle, in building terms, with people milling about all over the place. Most of the staff appeared to be stout, typically Russian-looking women, in white coats with their hair tied back in buns. We went up to the first floor, found our room and went in. There was a doctor and women assistant clearly waiting for us. Quite a long conversation followed between Olga and the doctor, then Olga said, 'He would like to see inside your stomach, are you agreeable?'

'Yes, of course,' so I laid down, as directed, on the bed, on my side, facing into the room. Olga had sat down on a chair nearby, watching. A pink plastic funnel was put between my lips, with the doctor, gently pressing my jaws shut to receive it. Then he took off from a nail on the wall, what initially appeared to be a length of car speedometer cable, about the same diameter of ten millimetres, and just as stiff. Without even sterilising it, and to my great alarm, he proceeded to feed it through the centre of the mouthpiece, down my throat, to my stomach. Everything in me repelled the intrusion, I gagged, my eyes rolled, my feet twitched and a sense of panic overcame me. During all this time, the doctor's assistant was holding me down.

After what seemed a lifetime, the tube had reached its destination, presumably the base of my stomach. He then attached an optical viewing apparatus to the end and peered in, turning the cable to see different parts of my stomach.

The entire process, I suppose, took about ten minutes before the cable was withdrawn and the mouthpiece removed, he gestured for me to sit up, which I did gratefully, feeling quite shaky, my throat ached and did so for the following two days. Olga had turned quite white and didn't look much better than me. She said we are to go back for the results in two days' time.

The next two days quickly passed and we were back in front of the town's doctor, but there at the hospital, Olga said, 'She says that you "could have" three serious problems, one cancer of the stomach, you do not have,' *Thank God for that*, I thought.

'Two, you could have a bad ulcer, but no, not there,' *Good*, I thought, so what is it.

'Three you have chronic gastritis, a severe inflammation of part of your stomach, and more tests are needed,' *Christ*, I thought, *I hope they are better than the last one!*

'Now two doctors come to examine you, OK?'

'Of course,' I replied, and then two distinguished-looking men came into the room and got me to remove my top clothes, then to lie on the couch, on my back. They then pressed and poked me, talking all the time. One pulled up the loose skin to the front of my stomach, as high as it would go, which was high, amazingly it stayed up there, just like the back of a lizard! *Good heavens*, I thought, *is that really me*?

'Now you have X rays of the stomach, in the same hospital.'

'Now?' I asked.

'Da, Da,'

'Well,' I said to Olga, 'there is one thing for sure, they are certainly taking my problem seriously.'

'Why not?' she said, 'for you to die would be very difficult.'

'Die, die,' I said, 'I'm not that ill.'

'You have a very serious problem, Brian, you must do all they say.'

It was the usual X-ray machinery. I had to stand up against it, but this time he gave me a glass of a milk-like substance and indicated that I should drink it. This I did, in one gulp, thinking it may taste awful, it didn't, but he wanted me to sip the liquid and see it trickle down into my stomach.

Nevertheless, he continued, pressing my side and squeezing my stomach, pushing the contents on the screen into weird shapes, a bit like a child's game, eventually, he finished.

'He says, tomorrow we get the final answer and remedy, then we see,'

It was the third time to see the doctor and gesturing me to sit she started off immediately to Olga. After a while, Olga looked at me and said, 'Brian, you are to go immediately to hospital, they expect you, are you ready?'

'To do what and for how long?' I asked.

'They will restore your health, but you will be there for about three weeks!' *Three weeks*, I thought, however, the decision was easily made as I felt particularly off-colour gain that day.

'We go now, the doctor at the other hospital expects you, what you need I will fetch for you.'

Considering how I felt it was quite a long walk, this time to the other hospital, which was a low rise group of buildings, set back amongst the trees, with a gated main entrance. The doctor allocated to me was a charming, handsome, dark-haired man. He reminded me a little of Doctor Zhvargo! I was shown into the room I was to occupy, set aside for important guests, and then introduced to the two nurses who were to look after me, they were very nice, one quite beautiful. I have a picture of her somewhere, standing beside my bed.

'They will look after you for everyday needs,' said Olga, *not in my health*, I mused to myself. Unfortunately, neither of them spoke English, which was a pity and the doctor who started to examine me as they had in the hospital, repeating the lizard skin effect, and tut-tutting, shaking his head slightly until I began to think it was an undertaker I needed.

'Now please, get into bed,' said Olga, 'I will go to your apartment and bring whatever you need OK, I will soon be back.'

So I did that, lying on the bed and thinking that three weeks will be a long time. The door opened and in came my two nurses, giggling and one wheeling a device with some sort of bottle suspended on a bracket. The other one brought in a tray with two injection syringes, laid on a cloth.

Gesturing me to move across the bed a little, Anna, the taller, dark-haired one sat next to me, pushing up my sleeve and then inserted a needle into my arm which was attached to the drip tube from the bottle. She got up and Olga, the beautiful one sat down on my other side. She pushed up my sleeve and inserted the other hypodermic syringe into my vein. It was a good thing that "Aids" was not a concern at the time because I was to receive this treatment twice a day for three and a half weeks, plus more until I felt like a pin cushion. The other treatment, which was much worse I will describe later.

Each day Olga came along to bring whatever I needed, paper to write, because I was in the middle of writing a book, she also brought some food, as I couldn't stomach the hospital food which generally consisted of a strange brown like rice, with sausage-like meat, but it had an off flavour.

She also brought some books for me to read, like "The Forsyte Saga", and a few books by "Jack London", and others.

Next to my room was an on suite bathroom, if it can be called that, being extremely basic. Unfortunately, during the entire period I was in hospital there was only cold water because they had dug up the mains outside to do repairs. So each day Olga came with the driver and took me back to my apartment to have a shower. The process exhausted me and it took hours of rest afterwards, laid on the bed, to recover. For one thing, I felt unwell and secondly, I was very weak. I tried a cold shower on one of the first mornings and quickly decided against it. Each day, my nice doctor would come in and examine me, with the nurses standing by, giggling like a couple of Japanese schoolgirls, but they were very nice, very efficient and obviously caring, What more could I expect, beautiful nurses to wait on my every whim and a personal attentive doctor.

Apart from reading, and there is a limit to how much one can read, sleeping on and off, during the day and receiving visitors, mainly Olga, and the chaps from the site, who called now and then, I occupied a good deal of my time writing and gradually a large pile of sheets developed, which, thanks to my terrible handwriting only I could decipher. This activity was of great interest to my two room cleaners, who came in on alternate days, to mop the floor, while I sat on the bed writing and lifting my feet as the mop swished across the floor, under me, to dusting and generally, tidying up.

Each was fascinated by seeing me writing, looking over my shoulder and going, Oh, Ah, opening their eyes wide in astonishment and probably thinking, what a crazy Englishman.

I wasn't entirely alone in my room, for each day, after the respective cleaner had done her chores and left I got back into bed and resumed writing, in comfort. Then, when all was quiet, out popped my pet "mouse", near to the bathroom door, it sat on its hind legs and proceeded to wash its whiskers, watching me intently. After ten minutes of this, he, I assumed it was a he, he craned his neck forward, then ran around the skirting and then disappeared. This happened every day unless it coincided with a visit if so he would appear again when all was quiet and then do his act. Had I believed in reincarnation, and I do to a degree, then one could assume that he was the reincarnation of a previous occupant, who perhaps died and now was revisiting the very room he had occupied, when alive.

He was a sort of comfort to me and after a while, I developed a form of conversation with him. The first time he shot off as though under threat so slowly I started speaking softly, then a fraction louder and longer until I swear he seemed to squeak in response, certainly when I used to say, 'Hello there, mouse, you have come to visit me, Da!' Of course, it would be a Russian speaking mouse, who wouldn't understand English and therefore wouldn't talk a lot. I started by putting down a little crumbled cheese, as he did like that, much better than that awful brown rice.

I told Olga about him and she tried waiting quietly but he never turned up for her. I'm sure Olga thought I was slowly going mad.

Next to my room was another room full of middle-aged women, about six of them. When I passed their glass door, going into my room, they would look up and wave and I waved back. What a pity, I didn't speak Russian, by now Andrew, who had a natural gift for languages, was progressing extremely well.

As the days passed by I got a little stronger and used to sit on a wooden bench under the trees outside. I sat there amongst the other patients who were receiving visitors. We were all dressed in our hospital-issued stripped pyjamas and I used to think that any foreign looking on would think we were an extension of "Auschwitz", except we looked reasonably normal.

One morning, Olga said the two nurses wanted to do a small test, did I mind, of course, I said no, so the next day Olga and the other nurse came in and taking me by the arm led me into a room, where Anna was waiting. They had laid out on the nearby table a number of small jars with screwed caps and managed to convey to me that they wanted to take a number of samples "from my stomach!"

OK, I thought, then Anna produced a metre long red, rubber tube, about seven millimetres in diameter, pointing to my nose and tracing her finger down to my stomach, to let me know I was to have it passed up my nose and down into the contents. *Christ*, I thought, recalling the ghastly experience I had had with the speedometer cable.

'*Problema*,' I said and gave a good demonstration of retching.

'*Nyeht problema*,' then they repeated the chorus, '*Nyeht problema*.'

No problem, what could I do but submit. It was as I anticipated, a ghastly repeat performance of the speedometer cable. We stood with my back to the wall, next to the window while Olga held my arms and Anna started gently pushing the tube up my nose. She got about halfway when I violently and in a panic, pulled out the tube. This didn't put them off and they became more persistent, after about four more attempts and considerable self-control, on my part, they succeeded in getting it down my stomach. Olga then attached a large syringe to the end and started drawing off samples, emptying a bit into each of the jars, in turn. What a relief when eventually the tube was withdrawn and about seven days later the results came back, of no special interest!

About three weeks into the stay, I was told that a crisis in the project had developed over the floor screed and I was to go with the director to a Ministry meeting, in Moscow, where Kalinin was to be, even though I was supposed to be critically ill.

The floor screed I had previously questioned had now been laid in large floor bays and was cracking up, surprise, surprise. A meeting in Moscow was hardly necessary, but off we went, to go there and back, all in one day. I felt extremely weak when walking into the meeting and noticed that Kalinin looked a little shocked, although trying not to show it. *I'd better look in the mirror when I get back*, I thought.

At the meeting in Moscow with Kalinin, I simply told him, and the others, that they would have to ensure that the precise site instructions were followed, and not to carry out their own interpretations. If they did then I would not accept any responsibility for the consequences. Kalinin repeated this back to the director in no uncertain terms and that was really the substance of the meeting.

Going back to my hospital stay, I was sure my doctor thought Olga and I were having an affair, perhaps by her habit of fondly holding my hand, at every opportunity and stroking my forehead etc. Anyway, one day he gave me a key which fitted the outside door of the bathroom, presumably so she could enter at night, unnoticed! The key was never used but it was a kind thought, typical of the romantic thought process that went on in the mind of every Russian.

In fact, through Olga, doing her duty and reporting back, on me as a person, in Soviet Russia, what I did, my thoughts and what my writings expressed, clearly identifying me as an extreme romantic.

This factor, above all else, endeared me to them. I was one of them, a romantic, never mind the job, this was far the most important thing about me.

Three and a half weeks came to an end and I was finally examined and found fit enough to resume light duties back on the project. Certainly, I felt better, but nothing near to one hundred percent. My stomach still continually ached, on and off and does, and did for a long time afterwards. So life resumed as usual for me in the Town, and on the project, which had made reasonable progress, getting near to the completion of the building itself.

There was one person I haven't remarked upon who came into the picture when the engineering part of the project started. It was Emil Molner, a Hungarian Engineer who lived in Ware, near Hertford with his Turkish wife and baby. Emil was a delightful character, and a very good Engineer, and a friend of Rodney. His task was to oversee the installation of all the engineering plant, carrying on where I left off. He was a very fit person, though not large in stature and he had one eye, the other one he had lost in a motorcycle accident, many years before.

One weekend, we all decided to have a day alongside the lake in Gus, have a picnic, swim a little and generally enjoy ourselves. Emil , who did a lot of deep sea diving went out to explore the bottom of the lake, and we had almost forgotten about him when he appeared coming up the beach to where we lay, and he laid down.

'Emil,' I said, 'where is your glass eye?' It had dropped out in the lake and he hadn't noticed.

He clasped his right hand to his face and said, 'Oh my God, it cost me a fortune!'

'Quick,' I said, 'go back in, it may be looking for you!' a cruel joke, but he thought it funny.

In the winter time, when the lake was frozen over, local fishermen would cut a hole in the thick ice to drop a line in, fishing there in the freezing cold for hours. What they caught if any were tiny little fish, hardly worth the bother.

Eventually, the building side of the factory was complete and there was no real need for me to be there. So I agreed with Rodney to return to the UK. I had been in Gus Khrustalney from November 1987, until the September of the following year. It was sad saying goodbye to Olga and all the others who had been absolutely marvellous, and I knew her lifestyle would, in the near future, change back to something less interesting for her. Over the years, we have remained in touch, first by letter and now fairly frequently, by email. It is my intention and a great wish to return to Gus one day and visit Olga and her family, walk around the old familiar haunts of the town, alongside the lake. Maybe Stavrov and Zhbarnov may still be about and I can see them also. Perhaps a visit to the glass museum and see if the same girls are there, but of course, they won't be.

As part of his many interests, Rodney had acquired a so-called full-time job for a large Building Development Company, based in Weybridge, Surrey.

'Come down and see me, we'll have lunch and will see what's next,' he said.

Over lunch he proposed that I remained with him whilst he formed a new international company, specifically set up to provide a 'project management service,' to the many joint venture developments, shaping up in the USSR.

He explained that a firm called "Condor", the large steel fabrication company that did such a good job in Gus would be happy to join us on a stand, in the forthcoming Soviet/British Industrial International Fair, soon to be held in Moscow. It was an exciting prospect, with seemingly enormous potential and I readily accepted and agreed to join.

As Rodney lived in East Essex and his new job was in Weybridge, Surrey, he bought a luxurious flat in Weybridge, partly to stay there whilst at work, and also to turn part into a new office for our Russian venture. This was fine for him but I still lived in St Albans, Herts, so I arranged my hours to the best advantage, by coming in at 10:00 am and leaving about 6 pm. It was also clear that for the potential future Russian jobs we would need, a Russian speaking person, who could also double up as an office manager. It was left to me to find a suitable person.

It was around this time that Rodney with his wife, and with Jean and, went to a small theatre of Upper Street, in Islington. If I recall correctly it was to see a "Chekhov" play. When it finished we all came out and there, just outside the theatre was a Katie Dolici, who was a famous Georgian film producer, and who Rodney and I had met in Georgia. We met her originally when we were having a short holiday in Tbilisi. We were staying in one of the few acceptable hotels in Tbilisi and had made friends with an American Journalist, called Jo, who worked for the Wall Street Journal. She was intrigued to learn that I, in particular, was "working" in Russia, building a plant with Russian labour. In fact, we arranged to meet when I was back in Moscow when she would tape my story for the Journal. It was great stuff for Rodney's company. Seeing that we were a bit of a loose end she invited us to meet a friend of hers, Katie Dolici. Katie and her family couldn't have been kinder, a real display of Georgian hospitality, a meal around their family table with everybody there, grandmother to many uncles. In fact, we went there two times and thoroughly enjoyed ourselves. So it was a great pleasure to meet her, so suddenly, outside the theatre. We chatted, introducing each other when all the time I quite expected Rodney to say, 'Lets go and have a meal together,' or arrange something consequential, just to show our appreciation of their hospitality beforehand.

I waited and waited and all he said was, 'nice to see you,' and excused himself! *How could he*, I thought, how embarrassing, when clearly, they were waiting to be asked. It was, in fact, a typical display of just how mean he could be.

For me, I shall always remember the event, perhaps one day I'll see Katie again and shall be able to respond appropriately.

It wasn't long afterwards that Jo called me and we arranged to meet at the National Hotel, in Moscow, and then she would tape my story. It was an exciting thought so I arrived as planned and waited, then all of a sudden she came running in, saying, 'Oh, there you are, Brian, so glad you waited, I am terribly sorry, we can't have dinner, as planned, my editor suddenly telephoned me and said I must interview "Robert Redford" who happens to be at this hotel.'

So there I was, turned down for Robert Redford!

Back to the new way forward, by chance I had a Russian friend, who knew a lot of people in the overseas Services Section of the BBC, based at Bush House, Holborn, at the bottom of Kingsway, where it meets Aldwych, so I asked her to ask around in the Russian section. Not long after, she telephoned me to say she had somebody in mind, could I go to her flat to see if she suited. My Romanian friend was named Doina and she and her beautiful sister, named Anca, lived there. Doina was married to an Englishman, who I saw on few occasions, but he never seemed to be about.

They lived in a flat in Abbey Road, not far from St John's Wood, an expensive area on the West side of London. I went into their block, up then in a metal caged lift, to the second floor, where I was introduced to a Ludmila Blakeley.

'Please call me Luda or Lucy,' she said, I settled on Luda. She was an interesting, bright woman. I guess in her late forties and she had been working at Bush House. Her English accent was rather strange and had developed into a rather grand middle-class sound, but not quite. It would be difficult to tell she was Russian.

She had been married to a Denis Blakeley, the one-time BBC's English Correspondents to Moscow, but he had died not so long ago. I liked her immediately, her sense of humour and sense of fun. She explained that she had also lived in France where her husband had had a good managerial banking job. Clearly, she was a positive person and a strong character, with a university education, quite ideal for the job, and so I booked her on the spot, subject to Rodney's approval.

Later, I found that her typing skills were worse than my own, which were not up to much, but it didn't really matter, her other attributes for the job were.

Apart from finding Luda, I had also met a similarly bright, educated, younger woman, on a previous flight from Moscow, who had done the same sort of work as Luda, her name was Irena Waterhouse. Well-educated, a positive personality and very attractive, she had a marked Russian accent, in spite of having been married to an Englishman, and she had already agreed to assist us on our stand at the Moscow exhibition. So already we were very well set up for the off.

The show wasn't far off and we all met up to plan the event. That is myself, Rodney and Condor, represented by their manager, a David Evans and his representative, Peter Titus, both capable, assured people and I knew David from the Gus days. It was to be a joint stand between Condor and our firm, with us selling our Joint Management Services, and Condor, their Steel Fabrication Service. The exhibition was to be held in March and set up in a large hall, which was part of the Mezhdunarodnaya Hotel complex, we all decided that it would be convenient to stay at the same hotel, for the week of the exhibition.

It was an exciting time, setting off from Heathrow, in readiness for the show. Quite a little jolly party. The hall was a hive of activity hardly anything in life more exciting than flying off to a special event in a foreign country. Nicely settled in the Mezh hotel we made our way to our stand early the next morning to be ready for the 10:00 am kick off.

The hall was a hive of activity, somebody connected to Condor had nicely set up the stand beforehand and Rodney and I pinned up various items of explanatory information regarding the company and also set out some "freebies" like plastic rulers with our company name and some pens etc. This, later, turned out to be a big mistake as we were surrounded by Russians grabbing handfuls, and within one hour, they had all gone.

It was surprising just how much interest our stand attracted, we could hardly move on it, but of course, we were very green to the whole arrangement. The Russians thinking that with the new climate of "Perestroika", the West was open for grabs and all they had to do was to put forward a feasible scheme for the West to inject vast funding and then away would go a new Joint Venture, making millions for all. They literally queued up to have a chance to put forward their ideas. We in our part understanding that any viable project put forward by the Russians would have to have their Governments support, and part funding, so in simple terms there seemed endless exciting possibilities.

Some of the Russians had come from far afield, believing the same. Two distinct and exciting possibilities came to the stand quite early on, and only after a couple of days into the show.

The first was a visit by some Government Officials, who explained that a large electrical manufacturing company in Ukraine were seeking to manufacture their product, an item called "Vacuum Interrupters", being heavy electrical switchgear, and to sell them worldwide. They wanted to get into a Joint Venture with a worldwide market name, say in the USA, or Japan, where the technology was available, via possibly a "franchise". They gave us the name of the company and sure enough, three fellows called a day later, the managing director, an impressive character named Drobot, and two co-directors. Yes, they wanted a suitable foreign company found, who would be willing to participate in a JV and give their marketable name to the product. More exciting was their wish to build a plant in Rovno, a town in Ukraine, something like the factory built at Gus, but of course, to their specific requirements. Our company and Condor agreed to go to Rovno directly after the show to get the ball rolling.

The second request was quite different but nevertheless, equally exciting. Two men introduced themselves as coming from a hospital complex in "Odessa". The leader, a very charming man, named Valeri Nikolayevich Zaporazhan was, in fact, the youngest professor in the entire USSR, at this time. His colleague was the hospital's finance director. They appeared quite desperate to get involved, wanting to improve their existing buildings and also, to build a Health Spa on the coast of the Black Sea, and to western standards. Could we go immediately, whilst here in Russia?

Immediately, it was too good an opportunity to miss and it was agreed that I should go, with Luda, the next day! Things were certainly picking up, the potential seemed vast and the show had hardly begun.

So we flew to Odessa the next day and were put up in a nice hotel in the centre of town, then after breakfast, we were ferried by car to their hospital. Their requirements were carefully explained to us, both the present hospital refurbishment and the project for the new health spa clinic, by the Black Sea.

We were even taken to the beach site, on the black sea. Clearly, this scheme would be a winner and would fill a great need in the Soviet Union, especially as the future prospects for the country were now opening up.

But they badly needed to update to Weston standards and we promised to find a solution, and then invite them over to the UK to develop the ideas.

Apart from being highly involved in their scheme proposals, whilst there in Odessa, they were extremely friendly and hospitable. We were there two nights and on the second night, taken to the "ballet" within a wonderful complex of buildings designed as a large round building and in classic style. We were placed in a box in a most advantageous position and enjoyed a thoroughly superb performance.

Our last meeting was held in an old property in Odessa town where it was explained to us that the meeting was being held in "Count Tolstoy's bedroom" that certainly gave me a bit of a buzz. Much later on, when back in the UK, I took Irena Waterhouse and a friend of hers out to dinner in London, to a restaurant in the Chinese Area. When we met up, Irena introduced her friend as the present day "Countess of Tolstoy", an attractive and charming woman of about 35 years.

Apparently, she had a flat near Marble Arch and was staying there with her husband and two children. After parking the car, we walked down the road with me arm in arm with both of them, through to the West End. As an avid reader of classic Russian novels, could I ever have dreamt of doing just that, who would believe me!

Our time in Odessa came to an end on a very positive note, and when we told Rodney, he was beside himself with excitement, it showed in his walk. When happy, and things were going well it always showed, he would strut along, twitching with personal satisfaction, doing his walk of achievement. Like a Cock Robin, on a fence.

Later on, the Odessa team came to England and we took them to see a very upmarket private hospital group, located in Stoke Podges, in Buckinghamshire. They were greatly excited by what they were shown, which indicated the potential for their proposed Spa and improved hospital amenities.

There were many other interesting enquiries but as the situation was so green to all, on both sides, nobody realised at the time, that it would be extremely difficult to produce truly viable schemes, schemes that would be suitable to all, especially to the British Banks, backing the financial provisions on the UK side, not forgetting the Russian Ministries, as each scheme would need all sorts of approvals and comparative Russian financial backing, a most complex and complicated process, taking a great deal of time. Also, there were political overtones for any large UK/Russian venture, later to be realised to all our costs. Naivety is a wonderful thing, enthusiasm flows unchecked until abruptly brought to a halt by practical reality. The show ended with us having a large portfolio of potential schemes.

Back in England, Rodney immediately commissioned a firm of architects he knew, to design the project and do a feasibility study, with costings, to present to the Russians, at Rovno.

Unfortunately, at the same time, two things were going badly for him. One was that the company who had hired him for the Gus job had become dissatisfied with their return and had cancelled his commission. This meant an immediate major reduction in his cash flow.

Secondly, his Spanish ventures, always sited to us as having enormous potential, with multi-million pounds returns, went sour, as he seemed to have fallen out with his co-partner.

'Not to worry, it will be sorted,' he said when we expressed concern over the company's future, but our worst fears were realised when our monthly checks stopped coming in. This went on for several months with Luda and myself struggling on to pay our own mortgages and other commitments. It reached a point where either it all had to come to an end, or that Rodney would give us written confirmation of the money owed to us. This, he declined to do and after several attempts on our part to persuade him, we had had enough and resigned.

What's next, by then Luda and I became quite involved in the process of setting up the initial liaisons that occur, prior to the more formal set up meetings, that usually progress into declared "protocols", that is contracts of intent. Luda had a very good Russian contact, a senior person named Vladimir S Khavronsky, who was a retired high ranking banking official to the Russian International Bank of Commerce. She contacted him asking that he found, on a commission basis, future potential leads for Joint Venture projects. This type of work had been his main task whilst at the bank, so he seemed perfectly placed to act.

We met up with him quite quickly as he had phoned back already with three leads followed-on as he made contacts, being well-motivated by thoughts of his likely commission.

The first three went something like this, we would meet up with him on a previously agreed schedule, then go off and talk to the companies, Somehow the first three were the most exciting, the first was an internationally respected brain surgeon, who had a hospital in Moscow but, like the Odessa scheme wanted to establish his own private clinic, charging dollars, of course. Going to his hospital was quite an event and he described how people were referred to him, from all over the world. We were walking along a corridor when we met a girl who had had back surgery and to my amazement, the wound appeared open to the air, right there in the middle of her back.

But she seemed well enough, in good spirits, walking there along the corridor, carrying a drip bottle. Another Australian guy had been given up as beyond repair but had somehow made a good recovery, it was all very impressive.

The second meeting was unusual as we were whisked off in a closed-curtained car, like the Kremlin higher ranks, into a closed town and then into an electronics plant. They wanted to manufacture electronic gadgets and toys, via a JV with the West.

The third was an engineering plant who made a variety of things, including ironmongery items, mainly for the building industry. To this day I have in my home a sample they gave me, a rebated mortise lock.

Not long after our return from this visit we had a telephone call from Drobot, the director from the Rovno plant, in Ukraine, asking how things were progressing, as they hadn't heard from us. When Luda had finished explaining to him that we no longer worked for the same company, I could hear his excited response from across the room, the gist of which was that he "must" work with "us", he was used to us, liked and respected us, we must go and see him immediately!

'Tell him', I said, 'we can't because it is Rodney's job.'

His response was that they were starting again from the beginning and were totally redesigning the scheme, 'Do come down and see us, please.'

We set off two days later with Peter Titus, from 'Condor', who were delighted to be included in this new venture. We boarded the train at Moscow for Ukraine, a journey taking long enough to warrant a night on the train. It wasn't so much the distance, but how slowly the train went that required this, but as it turned out it was a most enjoyable trip, as were the many trips later. There we were jogging along, watching the countryside, eating our prepared meals, drinking wine, reading and chatting. Occasionally, a tea lady brought in tea and on one occasion, an old peasant lady came on the train selling freshly boiled potatoes, nicely decorated in chopped mint, they were simply delicious.

At Rovno, we were warmly welcomed to our hotel, welcomed at the station by Drobot and two of his co-directors and were taken immediately to our hotel, told to take our time, enjoy our lunch in the hotel, and then a car would take us to the first meeting.

It was held at the plant which was a large heavy engineering workshop, on the main block, in Drobot's office. Apart from Drobot himself, there were three others, introduced as co-directors, one a fierce looking individual, we nicknamed the fierce man, actually, he was quite nice. An amusing fellow, who was the finance director and always smiling, and another technical fellow.

These meetings were quite formal, only mineral water to drink, no alcohol and lasted a long day. Again I explained our ethical position, in that our first introduction was via Rodney's company, but they quickly assured us we were there for an entirely new project, on a fresh brief and nothing of the old scheme was salvageable.

'Ok,' I said and we started. There were several days of meetings and on the last day, at the end, we all ushered into a Rafik and taken off into the forest, with absolutely no idea at all as to the arrangements. I had a crazy idea that we were being taken there to be shot! This fantasy probably entered my head because they had already shown us some of the terrible things the Nazis had done, and some of the monuments depicting the suffering of the people, when at the time, over 70,000 local people died.

Eventually, we came into a clearing in the middle of which was a small lake. There in the centre was a tiny island linked to the shore by a short wooden bridge. In the centre of the island was a timber lodge with a couple of attached buildings. We all went across the bridge and into the lodge, and to our surprise the inner room has been set out with a long banqueting table covered in every type of meat, from roast pork to salamis, fresh bread, jams and dozens of what appeared to be decanters of water, identified as "vodka". There were also bottles of Russian brandy. The kitchen area opened off, via a hatchway, into the dining area, behind which there were three smiling ladies waiting to serve us.

'First, we have a sauna, men first,' said Drobot, leading the way into the adjoining hut. We stripped off and were soon sweating profusely. Then we were ushered out, with me at first being required to lay down on a bench. Up came the finance director who started to rigorously soap me down. It was really quite pleasant and I turned my head to one side, thinking I could almost nod off, what with the heat and the length of the day. Then "whoosh", a huge bucket of icy cold water was thrown over me.

I let out a shriek of alarm, at which the Russians fell about in hysterics. I was still lying there recovering when he picked up a birch-switch and started flicking me all over, gradually increasing the tempo until I was literally being birch whipped. It wasn't bad really, in fact, quite pleasant and I began to glow nicely all over. Eventually, we all received this treatment and went back to the dining room, glowing pink, ready for the mosquitoes to feed off us.

Luda and the serving women went next and then we all sat down to eat, only to have to stand up immediately as Drobot proposed a toast, welcoming us as old friends and wishing a long profitable partnership, all this Luda, of course, translated. Of course, I had to stand up and responded by saying how pleased we were to be there and how optimistic we felt about the scheme.

The meal went on for over three hours and all the time toasts were being proposed and responded to. This meant, of course, that we were consuming vast amounts of vodka, each tot followed by a brandy, which was poured out by the laughing director. Luda said to me, 'Eat plenty of fatty meat and drink plenty of water, it will help.'

But it was too late, slowly at first, then more obviously both I and Peter became quite drunk. I had even forgotten my sensitive stomach.

The rest I do not remember, but Luda told me later, that at the end both Peter and I walked down the bridge from the island, singing "Rule Britannia", then fell flat on our faces on the other side. All this, pleased the Russians because unless their guests had become utterly drunk, then they wouldn't have enjoyed themselves, and Russian hospitality had not been seen to be done.

On our return to the UK, we met up again with Peter and David Evans of Condor and planned the programme for the project. The estimated rough value of which was about £30/40 million, but a little early then to be precise. Of course, it all depended upon Ministry and Russian government's approval and finding a suitable western company, with a world name, willing to become a partner in a Joint Venture.

Then disaster struck, we hadn't heard anything from Rodney, which was not surprising since he owed us money, and then out of the blue, we received notice of a High Court injunction, to prevent us working on the Rovno scheme, placed by Rodney and based upon his belief that we had stolen his scheme. I could write another book on the sag that followed but will keep it brief.

Luda and I appeared at the High Court with our legal support team and we went into a fairly small personal court to appear in front of Mr Justice Kennedy, a good-looking, distinguished man of about 50. Rodney's legal team presented their case with little intervention from the judge, except a comment he made which I thought rather telling, he said, 'Where is the complainant (Rodney), why isn't he here in this court?'

Rodney's barrister gave a feeble reply; in fact, Rodney was skulking around the lobby, just outside, almost hiding away.

Then his barrister made some comment which I thought outrageous, in fact, untrue. I told my barrister, giving him a letter I'd sent to Rodney a long time ago, in respect of our deteriorating relationship. It was passed to the judge who read it with great interest, muttering as he did so, and then he looked up across the court at both barristers and said, 'I am dismissing this application for an Injunction in favour of the defendants, Mr Brian Edwards and Mrs Ludmila Blakeley, and my reasons are a "non-disclosure" of evidence by Mr Woods. Costs are also awarded to Mr Edwards and Mrs Blakeley.'

Luda and I were more than delighted, for it had cost us a small fortune. Good, we thought, we'll now get it back. That proved rather naive as a High Court ruling only opens up the way for further legal action.

That will spoil his swagger, I thought.

About this time David Evans, of Condors, who had just become aware of the High Court injunction, telephoned me to say what shall we do, it will spoil everything, is there no way you can retaliate. I thought hard, then it came to me, although Rodney was so-called fully employed by some upmarket firm of developers, he continued to run about six other subsidiary companies on the side.

Although it went a bit against the grain, I telephoned the company and spoke to the managing director, explaining the situation.

'Come in and give me the details please,' was his response.

So I did and went to their very up market offices, near to Victoria Station, meeting two directors and giving them chapter and verse about Rodney's various enterprises. The result was that Rodney got the sack and all he deserved, but in some ways it also backfired, for thereafter, even years after, he went to the trouble of finding out wherever I was working, then sending them newspaper cuttings of the Camden case, in the early stages when the accusations were being made against me, never mentioning of course, that I had been completely acquitted. Mud sticks and one can easily imagine the reactions of prospective or present employers even, when receiving the newspaper cuttings. They would check, find out I had been complexly cleared, but the thought would always remain, there at the back of their minds, and on record. We live in a culture where once an accusation has been made by a public body, such as the police, or the Crown Prosecution Service, then we all assume there must be something in it. I find myself doing it now, in spite of my experiences.

We were now back on track with the Rovno project, I had managed to get a huge, well know American Company, named "Westinghouse", to be very interested in the project.

Luda and I met up with their UK representative, a Peter Collins, who had an office in the High Street in Marlow, Bucks. Peter was a true English gent, well educated, full of charm and very supportive throughout. I always enjoyed his company and we spent many hours together, either at meetings, here, in America, Russia, or on the train, or plane, travelling to one of them. His English Secretary amused me once when she remarked that Peter had the perfect legs she had ever seen on a man, she was right, he could have advertised for men's tennis-wear any day.

During one long journey on the train to Rovno, we had been chatting for hours and he told me of an affair he had had years ago, with a French girl, finally deciding to pack it up and remain faithful to his wife, and how long it took him to come to terms with it. Ten long years before he was fully over it. How many men, I wonder, have had such a magnificent obsession!

It was not long after Westinghouse had expressed an interest, and at their suggestion, we invited the Russians to meet us all in America, with Westinghouse, to progress the venture. If I recall correctly Drobot came, and two of his co-directors. The whole visit was about Westinghouse providing a license for their product, and Drobot's company manufacturing, what is called 'Vacuum Interrupters,' which is large industrial switchgear, and forming a Joint Venture between them.

The company Luda and I had formed was 'East European Products and Marketing Ltd,' which would act as the facilitating company, between all the parties. The Russian's market was huge, for it covered all of the USSR and India, where they had already established a market, then with the Westinghouse good name, to market the product anywhere else in the world. Westinghouse had expressed an interest to me, not only to manufacture the Interrupters, that would just be a lead in but to manufacture and sell in this market, all their other switchgear products. The potential was mind-boggling.

Before the Russians had met with Westinghouse, Luda and I had travelled to an associated company of Westinghouse named "Coors" in Denver, Colorado, they already made the ceramic insulators for Westinghouse's own interrupters. I remember telephoning their representative in Denver who apologised for the delay in coming to the phone, as he had just been chasing a "mountain lion" off his roof! The visit was very enjoyable and they showed us around their beer-making plant, where one man quite amazed me. He would stand next to a high-speed conveyor belt, containing beer cans flashing around at an incredible speed, and then suddenly pluck one out, to check. He just stuck his hand into the blur and grabbed one.

The other meetings were held in Pennsylvania, which was quite something, very high ranking officials attending and weighing up the potential.

We made a presentation, as did Westinghouse and the Russians. Westinghouse expressed an interest in the project offering to contribute, I think it was £1.4 million, to be matched by the Russian Government, as a start. Actually this was by no means sufficient and I could see Drobot's face fall when he heard, so after everybody had left for lunch I stayed behind and spoke to the Chairman of Westinghouse, explaining that, at least they would have to contribute 2.5 million, for the Russian Bank to match, thus rendering the project viable. He agreed almost immediately, thanking me for my advice. Drobot was over the moon.

There were meetings with us and the Russians in London and the supporting professional team I had assembled, namely the architect, Roger Pollard, Charles Harris, the structural engineer and the firm of quantity surveyors.

Everything progressed towards a project, when eventually the blanket was pulled from right from under us, by the American government, for after the fall of the USSR in December of 1991,

15 Russian Republics were formed, Ukraine being one of them, and because initially, they refused to disband their nuclear armaments, the Americans lost interest in any trading possibilities at the time, as a result, our scheme became dead on the shelf!

Around this time, also the excitement of the potential in Joint Ventures between Russia and the West, to a great extent fizzled out. Very few schemes ever got off the ground, mainly because of the lack of organisation on the Russian part, and perhaps mainly because of the complexities of financing by the Russian state, not forgetting the cost to the participants in financing themselves during the waiting game.

There are many other stories and events I am able to relate around this time and I could go on forever, but just as an example Luda and I met with a Theatre Company desperate to achieve a JV with an English counterpart, so we invited one of their directors over to discuss the potential. We had already seen their vast wooden theatre somewhere outside of Moscow, I still think about the fire risks! The chap who came was very nice, rather a positive type and Luda thought he was a member of some military special service.

We put him up at my house in St Albans and wined and dined him, showing him around, he really enjoyed himself. But at night he would creep down from his room and have a very long, deadly serious telephone calls, back to the USSR, almost as if he was in some form of trance, or dream, very odd.

Sadly, the Russian ventures flagged, then came to an end, nothing had been realised, except some incredible experiences. As they say, it is better to have lived and lost, than never to have lived at all.

Back to Southwark

After all this time things started happening at Southwark, and I received a letter regarding a hearing I was to attend, one of a limited number. This was an exploratory meeting, prior to the eventual meeting at which my fate was to be decided. At this time, I was still suffering from my stomach disorder and didn't feel too good. The meeting was held in the office of the director of planning and was led by the director, a Robert Maxwell, who had been instructed so by the chief executive. I always liked him, he had always been friendly towards me. He looked a little shocked at my appearance but proceeded, it was routine stuff and hardly needed me there. Just before the end, he said, 'I want you to know that the Council are not accusing "you" personally of fraud or anything like that, you are suspended, as a procedural matter, there being an investigation into the department for which you are responsible.' I thanked him but forgot to ask him to confirm what he had said in a letter, a big mistake.

Some months later, I can't recall the precise date, but remember the event very well, I was called to attend the main personnel panel investigating the event in my department and the part, if any I played. After all these months, years, it was finally coming to a conclusion.

I was there early and wandered around the waiting room, when I found, absolutely by chance, a union disciplinary booklet, and started to read it. I found a part applicable to my situation where it stated that if found guilty, I couldn't be sacked, only demoted, and showed it to my Union rep when he turned up. "That was such a big mistake on my part".

So the meeting started, chairing it was the director of personnel, not too bad a chap, but totally under the control of the chief executive. My prosecutor was to be John Synnuck, now the acting director of housing. There and then I should have objected violently, as he was highly prejudiced against me. A council member and a couple of admin personnel and of course, my Union representative looking after my interests. Again, they were a little shaken by my appearance, but not put off, especially John Synnuck who was clearly intent on enjoying himself.

All sorts of questions were asked of me and I could see they were trying hard to question my technical decisions, at a question from John Synnuck, I said, 'Are you questioning my technical judgement, can you offer a precise alternative?'

Of course, he backed down immediately, to avoid making a fool of himself.

Then, a Dick Mortimer was called to support their case. He had been my financial assistant and was very good at his job.

I always considered him supportive of me, just before the hearing started, I said to him, 'How many pieces of silver are they paying you?' He shuffled uncomfortably. The case he was making, clearly put by Synnuck, fell apart when I questioned it in detail, and he withdrew his opinions. Part way through, I became very irritated by the obvious sniggering of John Synnuck and said to the Chair, 'Do I have to put up with John Synnuck's sniggering like an excited schoolgirl?'

My union rep. tried to hush me but I wasn't having any of it.

Eventually, the hearing ground to an inconclusive finish and they retired to consider their verdict. It wasn't long before they came back in again and then the Chairman read out their verdict, which was, I had been found guilty of mismanagement and would be demoted to the grade PO3, vastly below my present grade.

What a tactical mistake I had made in trusting my union rep. who had just before the hearing been talking to the Chair, no doubt telling him of the handbook restrictions. If he hadn't then I would have been sacked, and then could have appealed to an Industrial Tribunal, where, without question, I would have won my case and substantial damages. Such a mistake on my part.

Again, what a shame I hadn't chosen a solicitor instead of a union rep. Had I done so then the entire outcome would have been so different. Before they could get a letter off to me, demoting me. I resigned my position as head of technical services, as had Reg Corbridge, the chief engineer. If I hadn't felt so terribly off-colour then perhaps I would have been sharper in my tactics, but that was that, I thought my local government service was at an end.

Still feeling unwell, I paid a visit to my doctor who referred me to a specialist at Hemel Hempstead hospital, a consultant named Mr Barrison, we chatted and I told him what I had been doing and how I felt etc.

'Ah,' he said, 'you have been to Leningrad, you have Leningrad tummy, it's from their water you know. I'll soon put you right.' And he prescribed a range of tablets. I took them over the following week and felt a lot worse, so I made another appointment to see him. He had already carried out the "lizard process" and then decided he should carry out an "endoscope" examination of my stomach. *Oh*, I thought and told him how they dealt with it in Russia. He laughed and said it wouldn't be the same. So I lay there again, on my side, a plastic guide in my mouth, but also I had been given an injection, to minimise the effect. It was OK and there were not the same problems a before, not at all. A week later, I met him again when he said I had "Crohn's" disease and he would put me on a course of steroids. It did the trick, greatly reducing my discomfort, however, even now, as I write this, I still have a twinge. Luda had a friend visit here from New York, a surgeon who had actually met with Dr Crohn, the very person who found and identified this disease, giving it his name.

Romanian Interlude and After

Just after the completion of the job at Gus I decided to have a look at Romania, for a number of friends had aroused my curiosity, after all at the time it was a Communist state, like Russia. The revolution of Romania, against communism was in December of 1989, and the Russian one followed on at 1990, but I'll go to the time just before then. I liked the Russians and I immediately liked the Romanians, another romantic people, a much better looking people, on average than the Russians, between whom there was little liking, thanks to the Russian occupation of Romania beforehand.

My contact with the Romanian intelligence at Bush House and outside, were most helpful. For example, through a contact, I became very friendly with an elderly Romanian lady, who had retired from being a secretary at Bush House. We were spiritually completely compatible, like soul mates and became very good friends. Her name was Simona de Roma and she was the "Countess of Rome" having married Manuel, the Count, a man I was later to meet. Through Simona, I met a number of rather special, rather unusual people, some by carrying food parcels to them, from the UK. One was an elderly lady living in the centre of Bucharest, her name was Renee Bratianna and she was the one-time wife of the Liberal Prime Minister. Simona and Renee went to school together in Switzerland and had remained good friends ever since.

Renee lived in a small side building that had previously housed the servants to the large adjoining mansion; the communists had put her there, out of the mansion, when all bourgeoisies were either locked up or put out of harm's way. I found the older educated Romanians to be very interesting, their liveliness of spirit, their curiosity and humour. What a wonderful place Bucharest must have been, all those years ago, when it was called "Little Paris".

I tried to help her, for she was clearly impoverished, by taking a few of her husband's "icons" to London, selling them in a shop in Burlington Arcade, and giving her the proceeds. I continued to do this until the customs people at the airport became difficult.

I took a food parcel to another elderly women friend of Simona's, again in Bucharest. She lived in one of those dark, dilapidated, old-worldly homes, in a side street, still with an aura of charm, and was met at the door by an elderly man. He spoke English and explained that she didn't, so he was there to help.

'Your English is very good,' I said to him.

'Thank you, you think so, I do not have much opportunity to practise it now days,' and explained that he learnt his English by going frequently to see English films. Remarkable, I could go and see a thousand Romanian films, and learn only a few words. The friend I went to see, Annie, was a most lively soul, literally dancing around the flat, then suddenly sitting down at the piano, playing the most wonderful music; well she ought to be able to, for she had been a "concert pianist" before the communists locked them both up for being of the bourgeoisie class. Thinking I should bring her something next time I said to him, what shall I bring when I come again, thinking of, perhaps some cloth, or a bottle of wine.

'Oh, what she really wants is a good man!' he said.

The first food parcel I took there, was, of course, for Simona's husband Manuel. Actually, she had divorced him when she escaped to England, and he was remarried to "Vicki", nevertheless, they still loved each other and were in constant touch. He even came to the UK to see her and came by train, on a couple of occasions. I went to Bucharest and got a taxi outside the Bucharesti Hotel, where I was staying, to Manuel's home. When we got there, he was standing outside the front entranceway, right next to the rubbish containers, ready to receive his English guest, with his old-worldly good manners. I have retained that vision in my mind and can easily see him now, slightly bowing to me, and greeting me, in his halting English. He was a man of rare qualities, speaking English, German, and French and of course, Romanian, as did Simona.

When the communists took over they were, of course, aware of his title and as he wouldn't comply with their political wishes, they made him work in an unheated basement cellar, making toilet pans! He remained unaffected to the end. His father had apparently carried out some great service for the Pope many years ago, who at that time, said to him, 'You have served me well, what favour I may bestow upon you in return,' and his father chose the title of the "Count of Rome", could there be a better title. Simona came from special stock too; her father had been the head of the "Romanian Securitate", (police, for the entire country) and he had also been a diplomat.

Sadly, Manuel died a couple of years later, both Vicki and Simona were distraught.

During my many visits to Romania, I made a number of younger friends. I always found that young Russians and Romanians were very curious about the English and very pleased to make contact. One was a young doctor named Bogdan Andreescu, a friend of a cousin of a friend. He was a great help, for prior to going there on a visit, when we met, I had to make contact with a large English/American company in London, called Allied Lyons, thinking, why not do a repeat of Russia and see if I can do some business. They said why not speak to an Associated Company called "Baskin-Robbins", who are famous for ice cream and dessert cakes, there must be an opening in Romania now. With this in mind, I mentioned my hope to Bogdan and he said, 'I'll speak to my father, he's a Government Minister and can arrange some useful contacts.'

So I met his father and he put me in touch with the leading Mayor of Bucharest, a large friendly character who even identified suitable shop premises, in very good locations, saying all of Romania is open for joint ventures of this sort, and now is a good time. To cut a long story short all went well, I even had a meeting with the Romanian Secretary of State, a "Napoleon Pope", a most helpful fellow. Baskin-Robbins were keen to meet all who mattered and get the ball rolling. Through Bogdan, I arranged for the manager of Baskin-Robbins to meet, in about two weeks' time, with five Romanian Ministers, quite an achievement.

At this time my mother, who had been very unwell, sadly died on the 7th of November, 1990. My meeting with the Ministers was for the next day! What could I do, the meeting was a one-off and couldn't be repeated, the family agreed and my Mother's funeral would be postponed until my return. I was in no condition to even go, let alone participate in such complicated arrangement, but I went. Bogdan was most sympathetic, very helpful and kind. That evening Bogdan and I were to go to the airport and collect the Baskin-Robbins manager and take him to a special hotel top meet with the Ministers.

We went to the airport and waited and waited, no manager. It was a disaster and did I have egg on my face! Bogdan told his father who told the Ministers, no free dinner tonight, perhaps another time.

Later, I learnt that he didn't come because the Americans said it was a bad time to do trade with the Romanians, they weren't stable, what with the Miners strike (much on the news at the time). So it never happened and possibly the best opportunity I had, went out of the window. Not long after this sad turn of events, Bogdan's aunt was tragically killed in the High Street and he asked me to come to the funeral to take pictures with my camera. It was an odd experience, taking photos of the body laid there in her coffin, her poor face bruised and scared, but that's what they wanted. At the wake, I met with one of the Ministers who was so pleased I had helped that all was forgiven over the dinner cancellation, but it was too late to revive the project. Many other events occurred and are the subject of another book.

After this and on my return to the UK, I had many short-term periods of employment, listing them briefly as follows. As a surveyor carrying out assessments for a large company of Loss Adjustors, mainly on subsidence work, then as a surveyor for Bucks County Council, carrying out surveys for improvements to Educational premises, it was quite enjoyable going around the various village schools, rather a repeat of my Bristol days.

One particular job I had lasted for 6 months and was found for me by Paul Wenham, one of my Redbridge colleagues, who had by then considerably risen in the ranks, working for large housing Associations. It was for the St Martins Community Partnership, an offshoot of the same Association. I was a senior surveyor carrying out surveys for repairs, voids, and troubleshooting over technical issues. I enjoyed meeting the tenants, making their lives better for them, by quickly organising their repairs, or by resolving disputes.

Not long after, I saw a job advertised for some maintenance surveying work, for the London Borough of Redbridge, and thought, that will be OK for a few months, so I applied and was called for interview for 1 pm on the 9 August 1992. It was quite a pleasant drive from St Albans, along the M1 and M25, then off and through Epping Forest to Chigwell and down into Ilford, some 40 miles.

The London Borough of Redbridge 1992 to 1999

The interview was held in Lynton House, at the top end of the High Street, on floor 7. I entered the room and met Roger Smith who was the manager of the technical building section and who was chairing the interview. He introduced me to Phil Nunn, The chief quantity surveyor, and an A F Harrison, a senior admin person and then Roger's deputy, altogether a friendly-looking bunch.

They asked me the usual questions, about my experience and career, and were particularly interested in the "Schedule of Rates" contracts, especially when I said I had introduced this contract format, whilst at Camden.

It came to an end and I was told they would let me know, and they did shortly afterwards, offering me a much better job than the one I had initially applied for. It was titled, "Maintenance Officer", controlling a maintenance surveying group of seven youngish men and one female admin, support person. Our function was to monitor the Schedule of Works contract placed with the Council's direct labour building department. I won't go into too much detail, or I shall go on forever, except to say this so-called short-term job, in fact, lasted from 1992 until I was aged 65 years. These seven years were the longest period I had ever worked for anyone. Redbridge were very good to me and I enjoyed my work, especially the companionship of my younger colleagues, "young Essex, Jack the Lads", but all quite sharp and bright, we developed a very good working relationship with humour and respect, and it wasn't long before the department heads were letting me know how much they appreciated having me there.

Roger was a good manager, fair and respected, but he could be a little touchy. Not long after I had arrived, I was having a little difficulty in adjusting to that sort of job again, I sometimes amused myself by writing short funny poems, or ditties, and did one about our role with Building Works. I pinned a copy on the wall for all to enjoy and gave one to Roger's deputy who thought it amusing.

The next thing I knew was that Roger called me in and complained bitterly about the poem, saying that he ran a professional department, and letting me know in no uncertain terms that "he" was not amused. I was very put out, feeling rather embarrassed and annoyed that such a fuss was being made over so small an incident. I was not far off from resigning but needed the job. Even to this day, I feel annoyed.

After quite a long period in that section, I was transferred to the Housing Department, with a title I chose myself, as "Manager, Housing Technical Services", and all my lads came along too. We were then under a new manager, John Baxter, I believe he had been an environmental health officer before, within the same Council. He was OK, in fact, a nice sort of person and we got on well. He was tall, slim, with premature grey hair, a good fit physique, but he had one trait, when he was obliged to tell small lies, his eyelids would blink, completely giving him away. The person over Roger during this time was Allan Smith, who was an assistant director to the consultancy services division. Throughout my time with Roger, Allan would go out of his way to show appreciation for my services, either by letter or by a friendly chat, more than one would expect. I was grateful for that, as it helped to dispel my old fear of being made redundant.

So at last when I retired from Redbridge that really was the end of my full-time employment. I messed about for some time afterwards, then discovered that I could train up and do what were called "English house condition surveys", for the central government, who were seeking the information to obtain an appreciation for the countries housing stock. It was part-time work, for a few months each year, but it was consistent and helped out in supplementing my income. It also got me around the local countryside, into peoples homes and gave me quite a pleasurable purpose in life. Then all that came to an end for me, I had carried out roughly 500 surveys, from Suffolk to Bedford, and that, overall is a great deal of work, requiring many hours of travelling, report preparation, not forgetting training each year.

At the end of this time I learnt of a new pending government legislation, requiring all house owners seeking to sell their homes, from June 2007, to comply with a "home information pack", containing a property survey, to a specific requirement, which can only be carried out by a government licensed inspector, irrespective of any other qualifications a person may have which may supplement, but not replace the license.

Just right for me, I thought and enrolled for an intensive three-month course, with one of the accepted institutes. I passed the course, and government-set exams and awaited my diploma in home inspection.

I actually carried out three of these surveys in 2006/7, earning £235 each, when out of the blue the Government abandoned the scheme!

Then, at the beginning of 2007, the Government required a compulsory EPC (Energy Performance Certificate) for any existing home that is "either sold or let". Knowing that this was about to happen, I had completed a training course and was then able to carry out my first one on the 4th of April, 2007.

At the time of writing this account, which is July 2017, I have completed 2,170. The numbers per month and location have varied over this period of time, as have the fees paid, but it has helped with the finances, gets me out and about and able to meet some very nice people along the way.

Between all the forgoing employments, where ever they were, and there were "many" more not listed here, I have always continued with my hobby of cabinet/joinery making, making anything from bookshelves to new doors, fitting out kitchens, totally redecorating house etc. Virtually anything that came up.

Now, at age 83, I am still doing the Energy Surveys, always pleased to hear that most of my customers think that I am around 65! But as they say one is as old as one feels!

So that is where I am, at the end of this saga, am I a lot wiser. I am a lot more experienced, in both life and work.

Would I change things, if I had my time again, of course, many things, but then, almost certainly, I would have missed out on all those rich experiences, missed meeting so many interesting people and would have led a more mundane more predictable, normal life, no, that's not for me.

Isn't it said that it is the misfortunes of life and one's experiences, which shapes us, as people!